EUROPEAN ECONOMIC AND POLITICAL ISSUES, VOLUME 5

European Economic and Political Issues
Frank Columbus (Editor)

European Economic and Political Issues, Volume 5
2002. ISBN 1-59033-322-5.

European Economic and Political Issues, Volume 4
2002. ISBN 1-59033-137-0.

European Economic and Political Issues, Volume 3
2001. ISBN 1-56072-908-2.

European Economic and Political Issues, Volume 2
2000. ISBN 1-56072-793-4.

European Economic and Political Issues, Volume 1
1999. ISBN 1-5672-686-5.

EUROPEAN ECONOMIC AND POLITICAL ISSUES, VOLUME 5

FRANK COLUMBUS (EDITOR)

Nova Science Publishers, Inc.
New York

Senior Editors: Susan Boriotti and Donna Dennis
Coordinating Editor: Tatiana Shohovs
Office Manager: Annette Hellinger
Graphics: Wanda Serrano
Editorial Production: Jennifer Vogt, Matthew Kozlowski, Jonathan Rose and
　　　　　　　　　　　Maya Columbus
Circulation: Ave Maria Gonzalez, Vera Popovich, Luis Aviles, Raymond Davis,
　　　　　　　Melissa Diaz, Vladimir Klestov and Jeannie Pappas
Marketing: Cathy DeGregory

Library of Congress Cataloging-in-Publication Data
Available Upon Request

ISBN: 1-59033-322-5.

Copyright © 2002 by Nova Science Publishers, Inc.
　　　　400 Oser Ave, Suite 1600
　　　　Hauppauge, New York 11788-3619
　　　　Tele. 631-231-7269　　Fax 631-231-8175
　　　　e-mail: Novascience@earthlink.net
　　　　Web Site: http://www.novapublishers.com

Printed in the United States of America

CONTENTS

PREFACE

Vexing issues concerning internal and external change challenge Europe, as it tries hard to regroup, reform and refocus. This series is intended to present an ongoing forum to stimulate discussion of these issues.

In: European Economic and Political Issues, Volume 5   ISBN 1-59033-322-5
Editor: Frank Columbus. pp. 1-26   © Nova Science Publishers, Inc.

Chapter 1

THE BITTER CURE OF BUDGET CONSOLIDATION: RESTRICTIVE FISCAL POLICIES OF THE WEST EUROPEAN LEFT AND THEIR CONSEQUENCES FOR EMPLOYMENT[*]

Karsten Grabow

ABSTRACT

This paper deals with the relationship between fiscal policy and employment in five West European countries which are governed by social democratic parties. Based on empirical data from Germany, France, Great Britain, the Netherlands and Sweden I argue that countries whose governments followed strictly restrictive paths (Sweden, the Netherlands) or did not change the course of its conservative predecessors (Great Britain) enjoy today much better employment figures than countries whose governments adopted to the restrictive way later or less consequently (France, Germany). Though the well performing countries experienced a short term deterioration in employment figures that is due to cuts in public spending they had the capacity to improve private investment conditions by comprehensive tax reductions. Paralleled with labor market reforms the combination of budget consolidation and tax reductions proved to be a promising policy to reduce unemployment significantly.

INTRODUCTION

Confronted with huge budget deficits which reached in some countries scales of more than 60 per cent vice versa GDP (e.g. Sweden 1995: 76.6 per cent), enormously high burdens

---

[*] Acknowledgment: This paper was written in the context of a research project on labor market policies of the West European Left that is financially supported by the Fritz Thyssen Stiftung, Cologne, Germany. For his helpful comment on an earlier version of this paper I wish to thank Lothar Funk.

of interest payments which limited the states' strategic flexibility to deal with economic problems, the shyness of international investors against indebted economies, and not least within the context of ongoing European integration, West European governments decided in the 1990s independently of their political composition to consolidate their budgets. Obviously, the paradigm of deficit financed economic policies seems to be replaced meanwhile by more conservative approaches. During the 1990s all EU-membership countries tried to reduce inflation with restrictive monetary policies, paralleled with institutional reforms (grant of more independence to the central banks, see e.g. Sandholtz 1993). Moreover, all tried to fit the Maastricht criteria that forced governments not to exceed public deficits beyond 3 per cent vice versa GDP. However, these attempts varied in pace, their strictness and in the use of opportunities.

Restrictive fiscal policies offer the chance to improve private consumption and investment. On the other hand they include the danger of a temporary economic deterioration if the state cools down its activities. Cuts in public spending (i.e. public investment, lesser expenditures for public employment or welfare transfers) may lead to an increase of unemployment. The increase of unemployment is an economic as well as a social problem for all governments. But for social democrats it is the major evil since they were always committed by program and ideology to the maintenance of full employment. Until the late 1970s European social democrats tried to fight unemployment in principle with expansive fiscal and – if possible, i.e. were no independent central banks existed – monetary politics, even at the expense of "hard money" (e.g. Scharpf 1991, Iversen 1998 Notermans 2000). Background of these policies were Keynes' ideas of an anti-cyclical and, if necessary, deficit financed support of the domestic economy, especially dedicated for sectors as construction, transportation and the whole public sector (see Przeworski 1985, Rothstein 1996). Later, these approaches became cemented almost independently of what party governed. Public expenditures rose steadily in western Europe and contributed to the increase of budget deficits up to the mid 1990s (Tanzi and Schuknecht 2000: 61-9). Today major West European countries are governed by Social Democrats,[1] either as senior partners in coalitions, or alone. They either inherited from their predecessors binding restrictive pathways since it has been decided in the EU-treaty of Maastricht or they developed themselves to advocates of restrictive policies.

This chapter explores for five West European countries – France, Germany,[2] the Netherlands, Sweden and the United Kingdom – how consequently the present leftist governments pursue restrictive fiscal policies and which consequences these attempts have for employment. I argue that countries whose governments followed strictly restrictive paths (Sweden, the Netherlands) or did not change the course of its conservative predecessors (Great Britain) enjoy today – after a short term deterioration that is due to cuts in public spending – much better employment figures than countries whose governments adopted to the restrictive way later or less consequently (France, Germany) because the latter had not

---

[1] Under the umbrella of "Social Democrats" I cover all left parties which are included in the study, i.e. the Social Democrats in Germany (SPD), the Netherlands (PvdA), and Sweden (SAP), the French Socialists (PS), and British Labour.

[2] The policies in France and Germany only reflect impressions because the French PS and the German SPD are governing not a full legislation period yet. But we can clearly see first approaches and outcomes which should be compared with the experiences in the other cases.

enough capacity to improve investment conditions by comprehensive tax reductions for potential employers.[3]

This relationship shall be highlighted in more detail. Despite differing dates of taking office, we can observe different approaches chosen by the governments and varying outcomes to deal with the problem of reducing both public deficits and unemployment. The following section gives a more general overview about the development of public deficits (or surpluses) and unemployment ratios since Social Democrats took over governmental responsibility the last time. In the next section I will analyze in detail the fiscal ways that each government followed. The final part summarizes the findings and gives some explanations for the variances in the attempts to consolidate the budgets and fight unemployment.

FISCAL POLICY AND THE DEVELOPMENT OF UNEMPLOYMENT – GENERAL OVERVIEW

At the first glance both variables seem to go in the same direction. All governments have begun to reduce deficits and in all countries the unemployment figures have been falling since 1997 (see Figures 1 and 2). This parallel development could be read already as a confirmation of the hypothesis that restrictive fiscal policy contributes to a reduction of unemployment. But this conclusion lacks not only causal explanations but also mechanisms *how* consequent consolidation efforts contribute to a reduction of unemployment. What is discernible from the figures below is just a parallel development of the two variables with significant national differences in the beginning of budget consolidation as well as in the success of reducing unemployment.

---

[3] Of course, fiscal policy is only one variable that influences employment figures. More comprehensive research should include monetary policies of the national banks or the European Central Bank (ECB), the design of national labor market institutions and policies (e.g. organizational strength of tariff partners, their coordination in negotiations, working time regulations, employment protection and others, see e.g. Gual (1998), Nickell (1998), Visser and Hemerijck (1998). The focus of this paper is limited to fiscal policy because the above mentioned variables do not fall always into the governments' responsibility, i.e. they are negotiated usually by tariff partners and are not set by governments. Moreover, the governments handed out monetary responsibility to the ECB or lost sovereignty to international markets (see Scharpf 1991: Ch. 10). From the palette of labor market affecting policies governments control beside some legislation (e.g. working laws) and moderation (e.g. concerted action) especially fiscal policies and related fields like tax policies and labor market measures.

Figure 1. Financial Balances of General Governments

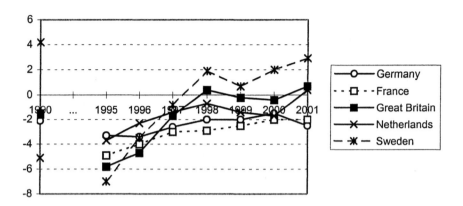

* in per cent compared to GDP.
Source: BMFi (1999): Finanzbericht 2000, Bonn: 397; OECD (various years): National Economic Surveys

Figure 2. Unemployment Rates

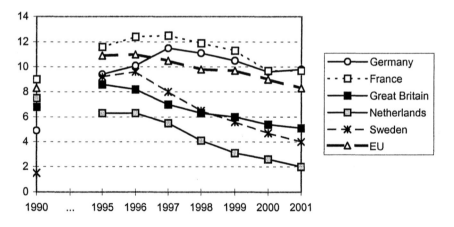

Source: OECD (2000a). *Main Economic Indicators*. Paris: December 2000; *The Economist*, November 3, 2001. Economic and financial indicators, 104.

Looking at the national unemployment figures we can see that especially France and Germany still suffer high unemployment. Both countries also have the highest deficits although the French as well as the German government tried to meet the Maastricht criteria. However, these data indicate that unemployment cannot kept low indispensably by higher deficits or more expansive policies as frequently have been argued with look at earlier politics of left governments (see Hall 1986: 198-9, Notermans 2000: 175). On the other hand, restrictive policies do not necessarily lead to a rise of unemployment, as the figures from the Netherlands, Sweden and the United Kingdom refer to. Cuts in public expenditures can even cure the evil of unemployment if they are paralleled by tax incentives for private investors and potential employers and comprehensive labor market reforms – even if it hurts for a while the core constituency of the (old) Left. In other words, if governments start to consolidate their budgets they have less to spend for constituency supporting policies, i.e. maintenance or even expansion of the public sector, expenditures for labor market programs or welfare politics like subsidies for old age pensions, health care or social relief. But they win capacity to improve investment conditions by lowering tax burdens for private investors. This marks a complete turnaround in social democratic budgetary as well as labor market policy. Given the current global and the domestic constraints it seems to be without an alternative. Moreover, it seems to work successfully as the following section will highlight.

BUDGETARY AND LABOR MARKET POLICIES OF SOCIAL DEMOCRATS – FIVE CASE STUDIES

In the middle of the 1960s the Keynesian Welfare State (KWS) was fully developed in most continental West European countries (see Esping-Andersen 1990). Whether it was labeled as "socially embedded market economy", as in Germany, or "social democratic welfare states", as in Scandinavia, welfare states were designed to link two socio-economic objectives. *Economically* it was committed to sustainable growth and full employment (e.g. Garrett and Lange 1985). Both ends were usually reached by high state activities, be it with public investment (especially construction), public ownership, state subsidies for domestic industries, the continuous expansion of the public sector and not least with high expenditures for labor market programs. To be sure, this has been pursed not only by Social Democrats but the enlargement of the public sector as employment field and expensive labor market programs are regarded as distinct left approaches (e.g. Rothstein 1996: Ch. 1). A large public sector absorbed masses of the workforce into the labor market whereas labor market programs either concealed unemployment or improved the employability of job seekers. Both the expansion of the public sector and labor market programs not only helped Social Democrats to reach high employment schemes in their economies. They were also convinced that – at least in the long term perspective – it is better to spend billions for public employment and labor market programs than to pay the costs of unemployment, including the absence of tax revenues. In terms of *social policy*, welfare states tried to guarantee at least a minimal living standard by transfer payments for low income groups or other needy people (e.g. poor, disabled) to ensure both a living standard above poverty line and a minimal purchasing power. Moreover, welfare politics were designed for comprehensive public health care (partially even without social security contributions from income) and old age pension subsidies. Necessary conditions of these politics were (i) high tax incomes that allowed for the socially driven re-distribution and (ii) stable societal institutions between employers and unions that made wage settings possible to anticipate and left enough profits for employers to accept this kind of "class compromise" (see Przeworski 1985, Kesselmann 1996).

Although welfare politics and state activities in the labor market contributed to a rather stable socio-economic development at the heyday of the KWS and high employment figures, they caused steady rising costs (see Offe 1984). The other side of welfare politics were high social security contributions for employers and tax burdens because the means had to be collected first before allocated. During the 1980s the former stable domestic institutions began to erode (e.g. Scharpf 1991: Ch. 6). Employers draw back not only from negotiations but also from domestic markets if they discovered worthier places to invest, i.e. with lower wages, social security contributions and taxes (e.g. Ferner 1998). Politicians, on the other hand, were bound to their own electoral promises to guarantee full scale social security. They could not cut back easily social insurance and health care standards, contributions or taxes to keep domestic capital at home because thousands of employees – usually the core electorate of the Social Democrats – were either employed in social services or lived on transfer payments (see Callaghan 2000: 204-5).

Faced with these pressures, i.e. re-locations, tax and wage competition on the one side, rising budget deficits because public employees or needy people had to be paid or supported, huge interest payments on the other, and finally in the context of European integration the governments begun to reduce deficits. One fiscal reason behind the new restrictive turn was to set free capacities for later tax reforms which improve both purchasing power and business confidence (e.g. Block 1977, Cameron 1984). Another reason was to send out signals for foreign investors since capital markets and potential investors honor consolidation (see Kreile 1999). Yet, for this purpose Social Democrats had to expect of their core constituency to accept a bitter cure. If they want to attract private investments by tax cuts, the governments have first to reduce expenditures. But in doing so, there is less to spend for welfare and labor market programs and public employment. Therefore it is to expect that, if governments turn to restrictive paths, unemployment will rise intermediately. Exactly this has happened in Sweden, and to a somewhat lesser extend in the Netherlands and in Great Britain.

When the *Swedish* Social Democrats took over office in 1994 they had to deal with poor economic data (see Notermans 2000: Ch. 5). Unemployment was high and the budget deficit alike (see Figures 1 and 2). However, within the first two years in government the SAP reduced the deficit from minus 7% to minus 0.8% as equivalent to GDP. This consolidation course was achieved by a general slowdown of expenditures[4] that hit employment figures. Unemployment rose from 9.2 per cent to 9.9 per cent, especially due to cuts in public employment and labor market expenditures (see Table 1 and 2).

---

[4] These cuts are reflected in lesser public investment and government consumption (i.e. wages for public employees, civil service and debt services). Public investment and government consumption together fell from 29 per cent equivalent to GDP in 1995 over 28.4 per cent in 1997 to 28 per cent in 2000 (OECD 1998: 36; 2001: 50). Moreover, the government reduced welfare transfers, e.g. old age pension subsidies, health expenditures or family support (see Trautwein 2000: 148). Also the state's quota, the part of GDP that is due to all economic state activities, fell from 65.5 per cent in 1995 over 60.8 per cent in 1998 to presently 58.5 per cent (BMFi 1999: 394). Although Sweden has still the highest state's quota, the relative drop during the first two Social Democratic terms (1994-6 and 1996-8: minus 4.7 per cent) marks most clearly the shift in the state's reserve in economic activity compared to the other four cases. Britain shows the lowest quota with presently 40.2 per cent (minus 1.8 since Labour took office in 1996), followed by the Netherlands, where the PvdA-led government reduced the state's quota in its first term from 51.3 per cent to 47.2. In France and Germany the quota was left unchanged when the Socialists or Social Democrats took over government (see BMFi 1999: 394, OECD 1999: 35, OECD 2000e).

Table 1. Public Employment as Percentage of Total Employment

	1995	1996	1997	1998	1999
Germany	13.3	12.9	12.7	12.4	12.2
France	24.9	25	24.9	24.8	24.7
Netherlands	10.3	9.9	9.7	9.4	9.2
Sweden	32	31.6	31.3	30	29.8
Great Britain	14.4	13.8	/	12.5	11

Source: OECD (1997): *Historical Statistics*, Paris 1997: 44, OECD (2000g): *Economic Surveys France*, Paris 2000: 63

Table 2. Expenditures for Labor Market Policies*

Year	1996			1997			1998			1999		
	a	*p*	*t*	*a*	*p*	*t*	*a*	*p*	*t*	*a*	*p*	*t*
Germany	1.43	2.49	3.92	1.23	2.52	3.75	1.26	2.28	3.54	1.3	2.12	3.42
France	1.34	1.79	3.13	1.35	1.83	3.19	1.33	1.8	3.13	1.33	1.8	3.13
Netherlands	1.51	3.98	5.49	1.6	3.53	5.13	1.74	2.97	4.72	1.8	2.81	4.61
Sweden	2.36	2.26	4.62	2.04	2.11	4.15	1.97	1.94	3.92	1.84	1.7	3.54
Great Britain	0.45	1.24	1.7	0.41	1.03	1.44	0.37	0.82	1.19	0.4	0.8	1.2

* as percentage of GDP.
a = expenditures for active measures; p = expenditures for passive measures; t = total expenditures.
Source: OECD (2000b) *Employment Outlook* 2000: 225-30, Eichhorst et al. (2001: 204).

Table 2 shows that the overall expenditures for labor market policies have been reduced steadily. These cuts affected especially passive payments, i.e. public subsidies for wage compensation in case of unemployment or the duration of unemployment payments. These policies stand in line with meanwhile widespread strategies to increase the pressure for unemployed people in order to force them to seek more intense for a return into the labor market (so-called *welfare to work-* or *workfare-*strategies).

Both a high employment quota in public service and high labor market expenditures were seen as typical for Swedish employment policies (Merkel 1993: Ch. 6, Rothstein 1996, Ch. 1 and 9, Trautwein 2000). The restrictive path that was gone by the Carlsson-administration (1994-6) and has been continued by the two Persson-cabinets since then, marks a clear watershed in Swedish labor market politics, however. The relationship between fiscal policy and the development of unemployment confirms the hypothesis that budget consolidation may cause an intermediate increase of unemployment because the state reduces employment in the public sector and, moreover, screws back the engagement in labor market support. On the other hand the Swedish government was able to improve the conditions for private investors and consumers significantly. It introduced a tax reform with a total of 40 bill. SKr. This reform relieves consumers up to 2001 on average 16 bill. SKr per year and contributed to an increase of private consumption of about 2 per cent per year since inauguration in 1998 (OECD 2001: 105-8). Although Sweden is usually still evaluated as tax intense economy (e.g. Wagschal 2001), what follows – in spite of all cuts in public spending – the still quite comprehensive welfare services, the Persson administration pursued consequently the path of budget consolidation and tax reliefs for business. Already inaugurated by Social Democrats in 1991, the present government let the tax reductions for corporation untouched. Corporation tax rate is only 28 per cent, compared to higher rates for example in France and up to summer 2000 in Germany (see below). The following table[5] reveals that not only the taxation for corporation but also for all other tax items the development points to an improvement of conditions for both investors and consumers. The table also displays reductions in the employer's shares to social security contributions.[6] These have been either deleted completely or reduced so that employees and workers have to carry the higher burden meanwhile.

Table 3. Development of Tax and Social Security Revenues* Since Social Democrat's Incumbency

	(1)	Δ	(2)	Δ	(3)	Δ	(4)	Δ
Germany[a]	4.1-4.4	+0.3	28.4-29.4	+1	3-2.4	-0.6	40.6-42.3	+1.7
France[b]	5.8-5.9	+0.1	18-24.3	+6.3	5.1-7.3	+2.2	43.1-36.4	-6.7
Netherlands[c]	7.5-10.6	+3.1	26.3-25.8	-0.5	4.1-4.9	+0.8	41.9-39.3	-2.6
Sweden[d]	6.1-5.7	-0.4	41.4-40.6	-0.8	3.8-3.7	-0.1	29.1-25.1	-4
Great Britain[e]	12.1-11	-1.1	36.6-37.4	+0.8	10.8-10.7	-0.1	18.7-18.1	-0.6

* as percentage of total taxation; (1) corporation tax; (2) taxes on income and profits; (3) property tax (including trade tax, inheritance and real estate taxes); (4) social security contributions
[a] 1998/99, except (1) and (3); 1997/98;
[b] 1997/99, except (1) and (3); 1997/98.
[c] 1995/99, except (1) and (3); 1995/98.
[d] 1995/99, except (1) and (3); 1996/98.
[e] 1997/99, except (1) and (3); 1997/98.
Source: OECD (2000c): *Revenue Statistics*, Paris 2000: 71-4; BMFi (1999): *Finanzbericht 2000*: 398, Eurostat: New Cronos, 'Wirtschaft und Finanzen', Berlin. May 2001.

This improvement of investment conditions has been really honored by private investors. Business fixed investment has been rising since 1995 on average by more then 9 per cent per year – what is the peak level of all countries included (see Figure 4). These high private investments more than just compensated the reductions of public employment. Moreover, Sweden is the only case under study whose industrial sector, which has experienced larger waves of privatization since the Social Democrats returned to power in 1994, suffered no decline in employment (see Figure 3). Even more important, employment in the private service sector developed extremely positive, with an increase of 3.6 per cent, especially driven by information technology and the finance sector (see Financial Times, Dec. 4, 2000).

---

[5] Tax policies are still complete domestic policies with all responsibility to national governments, e.g. what taxes are collected. Because of national variance, I used the OECD classification (see OECD 2000c) and looked at the generalized tax positions as percentage of total taxation in each country. The relative decline, as reported in Table 3, are in principle due to real tax reductions, for example the lowering of general income tax to meanwhile 20 per cent. Another factor that contributed to relative shifts is that new taxes were introduced, e.g. environmental levies, whereas other tax positions were left unchanged. Capital gains, for example, have been taxed since 1991 with 30 per cent, and corporation taxes have been also kept constantly at 28 per cent since then. Up to summer 2000, when the German *Bundestag* passed a new tax reform, Sweden had the lowest corporation tax rate within this sample (see below, notes 12 and 20).

[6] Employer's shares to health care have been reduced slightly from 7.9 per cent of gross income in 1995 to meanwhile 7.5 per cent. More significantly, their contributions to obligatory old age security of 6.8 per cent were deleted completely whereas those to additional old age pensions were halved to 6.4 per cent. These reductions were moved to employees whose contributions rose from 1 to 6.95 per cent (see Sweden 2001).

Figure 3. Employment quotas in industrial and private service sectors[*],[†]

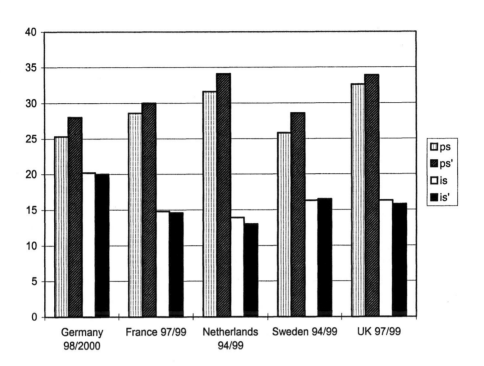

[*] percentage of total employment

[†] employment in service sectors: (i) wholesale and retail trade, restaurants and hotels; (ii) transport, storage, logistics, communication; (iii) financing, insurance, real estate, business service.

ps = employment quota in private service sectors at the beginning of social democrat's incumbency in each country

ps' = employment quota in private service sectors in 1999/2000

is = employment quota in the industrial sector at the beginning of social democrat's incumbency in each country

is' = employment quota in the industrial sector in 1999/2000

Source: OECD (2000d): *Labour Force Statistics*: 148-279

For the Swedish case we can state, that once the government turned to the restrictive path, it had to stand a short phase of an increase of unemployment that was due to cuts in public employment and labor market expenditures. On the other hand the government had the capacity to change its tax policies. The tax incentives for private investors really favored investment. These investments indeed contributed to job growth in private sectors that was larger than the losses in the public sector.[7] Insofar, Sweden's social democrats reduced their

---

[7] The Swedish government got support also from the Rijksbank that lowered interest rates since 1995. The short term interest rates fell from 8.7 per cent to only 2.9 per cent in 1999. This has not only fueled the whole economy constantly with cheaper money, it highlights also the favorable combination of restrictive fiscal policies of the government, tax reductions for potential investors and moderately expansive money policies of the national bank (see e.g. Notermans 2000: 224). Lowering of interest rates happened in the other countries as well, but with some significant variances. In the Netherlands the short term interest rates fell from 4.4 per cent when the PvdA entered offices in 1994 to meanwhile 2.7 per cent. The Bank of England supported the supply side course of Labour with a interest rate reduction of 1.9 per cent. In contrast, in France and Germany the interest rates fell

expenditures for an expensive state engineered economy, including high public employment, and performed a significant turn to private sector compensation in terms of jobs and overall economic growth.[8]

A similar pattern is visible for the *Netherlands*. However, the first PvdA-led government (Kok I, 1994-8), did not turn into a restrictive path. Instead it continued the course of the preceding government that the PvdA did belong to as junior partner. During the first legislative term the budget deficit could be reduced successfully to minus 0.7 in relation to GDP (see Figure 1). Affected by this consolidation effort was employment in the public sector. The employment quota fell from 10.3 per cent in 1995 to 9.4 per cent three years later (see Table 1). Moreover, the Dutch government spent less for general labor market policies, but clearly at the expense of passive support, whereas the share for active labor market programs rose in spite of the overall reductions (see Table 2). Although the unemployment rate did not rise, as in Sweden, the fall of unemployment stagnated in the first two years of the PvdA's incumbency, due to decreases in public employment and further cuts for general labor market programs. After this stagnation the figures recovered. The Netherlands enjoy quasi full employment although the state reduced its overall economic activity notably.[9]

The positive development since 1996 is explained by several factors. The Dutch labor market profits from high shares of atypical employment, e.g. part time work[10] and reductions of the weekly working time to 32 hours *without* full wage compensation. Moreover, wages increased only moderately[11] (see Cavallè 1998, Visser 1998, Funk 1999, van Paridon 2000, Hemerijck, Manow and van Keersbergen 2000). Finally, to recall the focus of this chapter, the fall of unemployment goes back to constant high private investment after the government reduced taxes and social security contributions for employers. Favored by falling unemployment – and consequently fewer people who were supported by unemployment schemes – the government reduced the overall contributions that employers have to pay for social security from 20 per cent of gross income to 10.1 per cent (see Table 4, Funk and Winkler 1997: 164). At the same time responsibility for old-age pension was delegated to

---

weaker (minus 0.9 per cent in France and minus 0.8 per cent in Germany), what has to do with the lesser rates before (France 1998: 3.6 per cent; Germany 1998: 3.5 per cent) and also with the shift of responsibility to the ECB. Nevertheless, because in economy signals often affect more than real data, the economies in Sweden, the Netherlands and Great Britain benefited more from the lowering of interest rates.

[8] That the private sector compensated the retreat of the state becomes also visible with a look at the growth rates. Though the government reduced its activities, GDP grew by 3.3 per cent on average during the first term of SAP government (OECD 2001: 24). This has been the most robust GDP growth within this sample (see below).

[9] The Dutch data resemble those of Sweden. Despite the state slowed down public investment from 26.4 per cent of GDP in 1995 to 25.2 per cent in 1998 (OECD 2000e) and reduced the state's quota (see note 4), the GDP growth was not negatively affected. On average it has grown by 3.26 per cent per year since the PvdA is in government. In this case again, private sectors compensated the state's retreat because they found attractive investment conditions.

[10] Part time work (less then 30 hours weekly) is attractive for both sides. Employers have to pay less for wages compared with full time jobs, and part-time employees enjoy full participation in unemployment protection, although they have to accept lower real incomes. Since 1995 the share of part-time employees has been growing constantly. Today approximately 33 per cent of the Dutch workforce is in part-time contracts – compared with 23 per cent in Britain, 17.1 per cent in Germany, 14.7 per cent in France and 14.5 per cent in Sweden (OECD 2000d: 150-277).

[11] Although the development of nominal wages has not been very high with an average increase of about 2 per cent per year, wage development alone can not explain variances in unemployment between the cases under study. In France and Germany the nominal wages developed similarly but unemployment is much higher. In contrast, wages increased in Sweden and Britain by roughly 4 per cent (OECD 1999: 79-82, 2000e 24-8, 2000f: 32-5, 2001: 40-4). So it seems that labor market regulations, side payments as social security contributions and especially taxes count more than nominal wages alone.

employees who carry the main burden of social security contributions meanwhile. These overall reduction are also reflected in Table 3 (column 4). Moreover, Table 3 shows that the share of income tax on overall taxation fell, due to significant cuts in both the top rate and the entrance rate of earned income. These two measures fell from 70 per cent in 1995 to 52 per cent for the top rate and from 14 per cent to 6.35 per cent for low incomes. Especially the latter translates in the longer run into real income gains for low-paid employees without increasing labor costs for employers. Though the share of corporation taxes on overall taxation increased[12] (column 1), the effects of income tax reductions, including the complete cut of capital gains taxation, stimulated private consumption and investment. Between 1995 and 1999 business investment grew on average 7 per cent per year (OECD 2000e: 18, 32, 47-8). After Sweden and Britain the Netherlands range with that comparatively high annual growth rate at third position (see Figure 4). As in Sweden, especially the private service sector benefited from these development. Although already highly developed before, the employment growth in the private service sector reached an increase of 2.5 per cent (see Figure 3) and contributed significantly to the fall of the unemployment rate.

In sum we can state that the Dutch government pursued paths that favored private sectors at the expense of traditional politics. It cut overall labor market expenditures and the enlargement of the public sector in the course of fiscal consolidation and had to stand an intermediate slowdown in the reduction of unemployment. But the cabinet, supported by consensus oriented tariff partners, flexible labor market regulations, and favorable interest rates (see note 7), lowered taxes and social security contributions and was rewarded with high private investments that led unemployment fall.

This holds true in a similar way for *Great Britain*. As the Dutch government, the Labour administration set forth the restrictive course of the preceding conservative cabinet and presented a balanced budget in 1998 (see Figure 1). Although this let not rise unemployment, the fall of the unemployment rate cooled down during the first two years of Labour's incumbency (see Figure 2). Today, however, Britain's unemployment rate is not only far under EU-average, the British economy enjoys the lowest unemployment rate of the last thirty years.

The state's austerity contradicted traditional employment policies of the left, as it did in Sweden and the Netherlands. Labour continued to reduce the employment in the public sector (see Table1), especially at the expense of public health services and public transportation.[13] Moreover the Blair-administration lessened its expenditures for labor market policies further (see Table 2) – despite a "New Deal" that is designed to integrate the younger work force into the first labor market (see Merkel 2000b: 285-6; OECD 2000f: 99-111; Eichhorst et al. 2001:

---

[12] This increase does not reflect higher corporation taxes, however. Tax rate for corporations were reduced from 35 per cent in 1998 to meanwhile 30 per cent. The increase relative to overall taxation rather reflects a nominal increase of corporations, higher profits and consequently higher overall tax incomes of the state, caused by a flourishing economy.

[13] For these figures we have to consider a slight statistical distortion. When the Tories privatized railway and public transport services not all work force has been laid off. According to the OECD *Labor Force Statistics*, employees in this sector are subsumed today under "private service sector, transportation, logistics, telecommunication". This sector really experienced a significant job growth that has also to do with the privatization. Also the cuts in public health services were introduced by the Tories. Between 1991 and 1996 the number of employees was reduced by about 1 million to 84,000. Since Labour's incumbency this development has slowed down somewhat, but was continued in principle. Presently 77,000 people work in the National Public Health Service (OECD 2000f: 93). If one speaks of a "bitter cure" in which cuts in public employment are compensated by private sectors , it is obvious that already under the Tories this course was introduced and Labour did not change it.

227-8). Equivalent to GDP, the British government spent the smallest share for labor market policies of all left governments in this sample (see Table 2).

Figure 4. Private Investment[*,†]

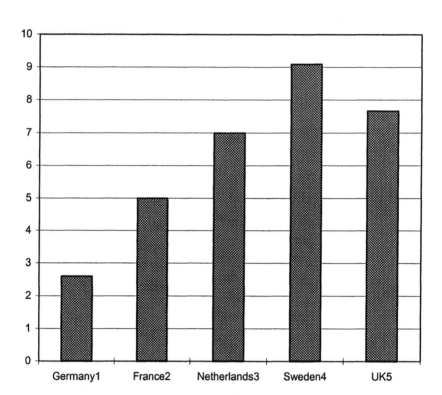

[*] business fixed investment.
[†] average year to year-growth for:
    1 Germany: 1998/1999; 1999/2000.
    2 France: 1997/1998; 1998/1999; 1999/2000.
    3 Netherlands: 1995/1996; ...; 1999/2000.
    4 Sweden: 1995/1996; ...; 1999/2000.
    5 Great Britain: 1997/1998; ...; 1999/2000.

Source:
    1 Statistisches Bundesamt; Volkswirtschaftliche Gesamtrechnung, www.statistik-bund.de/basis/d/ vgr/vgrtab1.htm.
    2 OECD 2000g: 42.
    3 OECD 2000e: 19, 32-3.
    4 OECD 2001: 29.
    5 OECD 2000f: 37; Office of National Statistics; Business Investment, 24. May 2001, www. statistics.gov.uk.

Table 4. Social Security Contributions[*,†]

	Sickness		Old age pensions		Unemployment	
	employer	employee	employer	employee	employer	employee
Germany[‡]	6.76	6.76	9.65	9.65	3.25	3.25
France	12.80	0.75	8.20	6.55	3.97	2.71
Netherlands	6.35	1.75	/	19.15	3.75	6.25
Sweden	8.50	9.23	10.21	10.21	5.84	3.30
UK[§]	/	/	/	/	/	/

[*] percentage of gross income.

[†] data for Q4 2000.

[‡] contributions for sickness insurance only for the western German *Länder*; new *Länder* for both employers and employees: 6.91 per cent.

[§] Employers and employees pay global contributions to co-finance the public sickness insurance system, the National Health Service, that is primarily carried by tax-based state subsidies, however. Low income groups (with monthly incomes below GBP 264,-) have not to pay contributions at all. For higher incomes the global contributions, which cover also unemployment insurance, vary between 8.4 and 10 per cent of gross incomes for employees and between 9.2 and 12.2 per cent for employers.

Source: Germany: *Bundesversicherungsanstalt für Arbeitnehmer: Beitragssätze zur Sozialversicherung,* www.bfa.de/ger/ger_zahlenfakten.8/ger_rvwerte.81; The European Commission: *MISSOC: Common information system of social security in the member states of the European Union,* www.europa.eu.int/comm/employment_social/missoc2000

When it took over office, Labour reduced total public expenditures by GBP 3.5 billion (Parry 2000: 90). Consequently, public investment fell by 10 per cent points compared to the Tories' last year in government. Also the state's quota fell from 42 per cent under the Tories to 40.2 per cent thereafter (OECD 2000f: 37-8; BMFi 1999: 394). The trajectory of GDP shows that private sectors more than compensated this retreat of public expenditures. With an annual average GDP growth rate of 3.03 per cent since 1996, Britain ranks somewhat behind Sweden (3.58 per cent on average) but equals the Netherlands (3.04 per cent) and scores much higher than France (2.7 per cent since the *Parti Socialiste* is in government) and Germany (scarcely 2 per cent, see below). As in Sweden and the Netherlands this relative stable growth is primarily due to private investment. Favored by significant tax reductions in the course of consolidation efforts (see below), private investments into the British economy rose on average by 7.66 per cent per year – after Sweden this is the second highest growth in this sample (see Figure 4). Similar to the two other cases above, these investments flowed primarily into the private service sector. Since 1997 employment in the private service sector has increased absolutely by 470,000 people, a relative growth of 1.3 per cent (see Figure 3). Especially the sectors "transportation, logistics, telecommunication" (plus 117,000) and "financing, insurance and business services" (plus 289,000) proved to be the job machines. Yet, also the construction sector experienced higher investments and a job growth of about 140,000 so that losses in the manufacturing were more than compensated by these sectors (OECD 2000d: 276-9).

Beside supportive interest rates (see note 7), the positive labor market performance in Britain can be traced back to at least three reasons. First, the government left the labor market reforms which were introduced by its conservative predecessors untouched, e.g. highly deregulated labor relations, relative little job protection[14] and part time work. Atypical employment was even expanded – presently 23 per cent of the British labor force are working part time (see note 10). Second, the overall labor market benefited from rather moderate wage settlements. Wages and salaries grew moderately by some 4 per cent on annual average since 1997. Third, and with a look to the topic of this chapter may be most striking, the Labour government eased the tax burden for private investors and potential employers in general. Especially smaller companies were favored by different tax measures. For companies with profits up to GBP 300,000 the corporate tax rate was cut stepwise between 1996 and 1999 from 23 to 20 per cent. Smaller companies with reported revenues up to GBP 50,000 enjoy an even lesser rate, taxed with a new 10 per cent rate, whereas the general corporate tax rate was cut from 31 to 30 per cent (OECD 2000f: 71, 88; European Commission 2001: 485). In comparative view within this sample, British companies are taxed at the lowest level.[15]

Reductions of taxes and social security contributions are mirrored in Table 3. Although the share of income taxes on total taxation has increased slightly (column 2), what this is not due to tax increases on income but has to do with a broadening of tax bases[16] and the fact that the positive labor market performance brought about more income tax payers, the fall of the other three taxation measures reflects cuts in both taxation and social security contributions (columns 1, 3, and 4). In low wage sectors (up to GBP 264 per month) employers were discharged completely from social security payments (see Table 4). These cuts provided highly attractive incentives for private investors and potential employers either to invest in the British economy or to create new jobs.

To sum up, for the British case we can state that the retreat of the state as employer and investor has been more than just compensated by the private sector. The British economy owes the positive labor market development primarily the private sector – especially the job growth in the service sector – but to a big deal the government as well. It has made possible these positive developments, however with the exact opposite of what the Left traditionally did. After two years of a consequent restrictive fiscal course and the continuation of cuts in both public employment and labor market expenditures it was able to pay back its reserve to the economy by cuts in taxes and social security contributions. This really attracted new investors and gave private employers an incentive to create new jobs. Thanks to these approaches Britain enjoys the lowest unemployment rate since three decades.

For France and because of the quite short time of incumbency only sketchy for Germany we can see almost completely different attempts and outcomes. When the socialist-dominated

---

[14] The positive development of the British labor market, and partially in the Netherlands and Sweden, carries some problems, however. Beside cuts in welfare expenditures (see e.g. Parry 2000, Glyn and Wood 2000) the statistical success, i.e. reduction of the unemployment rate, is bought occasionally with insecure or bad paid jobs, often in the low skilled private service sector, e.g. in transportation, messenger jobs, jobs in restaurants, hotel- or cleaning services, telejobs etc. Whereas traditional social democratic labor market politics usually tried to link quantity (full employment) with quality (high job protection, full coverage of social security) we can presently state that "good quantity" is quite frequently achieved at the expense of quality.

[15] At present, France scores with a corporate tax rate of 33.3 per cent highest, followed by the Netherlands, where the corporate tax rate was cut in 1998 from 35 to 30 per cent too, Sweden (28 per cent since 1991) and Germany. In the context of the tax reform the corporate tax rate was reduced from 40 per cent to 25 per cent in 2001 (BMFi 2001; EU 2001). However, a positive impulse for both private investment and employment is not visible yet, because tax reductions usually need up to two years to cause the desired effects. Moreover, the German government had bad luck because their attempts fell into a period of a global cooling of growth, and finally, because tax policies were not paralleled with necessary labor market reforms, see below.

[16] For example tax discounts for married couples as well as income tax allowances have been changed. Since 1999 incomes over 100,000 GBP are taxed with at least 10 per cent (see OECD 2000f: 71-3).

French government took over office in 1997, it stopped immediately the restrictive fiscal path of its bourgeois-conservative predecessor. Instead, the Jospin-administration tried to fight the extremely high unemployment[17] with rather high state activities which find an expression in labor market expenditures. In relation to GDP, the Jospin-administration did not reduce the overall expenditures for labor market programs, except a slight turn to passive support, i.e. unemployment transfers (see Table 2). Moreover, the government left public employment completely untouched. After Sweden, where the SAP-government reduced public employment significantly, the French public sector is the second largest within this sample, with a share of roughly 25 per cent of the overall workforce.

Though the French government did not follow classical Keynesian ideas, given the experience of the failed experiment of trying "socialism in one country" in the early 1980s (see Hall 1985), its approaches in fiscal and labor market policies resembled clearly traditional socialist positions. In order to finance its activities, the administration increased public debts by .3 points to 59.5 per cent. Given the large public sector, it had to deal with higher consumptive expenditures (salaries for public sector employees, debt service). Moreover, public investment rose vice versa the international trend. Whereas the Swedish, the Dutch and the British governments cut public investment, it was rising since the PS is leading the coalition with the Greens and the Communist Party by 2.16 per cent per year. This comparatively high state activity is also reflected in the state's quota. Since 1997 it rose to 54.3 per cent, what is after Sweden – where this quota has fallen constantly yet – the second largest value in this sample (see BMFi 1999: 394). Fueled by these high state activities, France really experienced a quite stable GDP growth of an annual average of 2.7 per cent and the unemployment rate begun to fall – but is still far above EU-average (see Figure 2).

Yet, the fall of unemployment is primarily due to traditional left policies, especially public expenditures. Except that the public employment quota was left unchanged, the government introduced an employment program in order to create 700,000 new jobs either in public service or – supported with wage subsidies – in the private sector (see Cavallé 1998: ix; Merkel 2000a: 115, OECD 2000g: 32-5). A slight job growth was visible also in manufacturing, for example in automobile production, in construction and in the private service sector – here especially in low wage and low skilled sectors not least due to wage subsidies for employers (see below). However, the relative job growth in the private service sector was rather low with an increase of 1.4 per cent since 1997 (OECD 2000d: 148-51, see also Figure 3). This holds true also for private investments into the French economy. On annual average since 1997 private investments grew by only 5 per cent, what is the fourth of five places within this sample (see Figure 4).

The reserve of private investors can be explained by at least three reasons. First, the shift of interest sovereignty to the European Central Bank (ECB) diminished the management capacity of the government in terms of monetary policies. Although France experienced a

---

[17] Beside structural reforms, primarily privatization and succeeding lay offs in the industrial sector (automobile and chemical industries) in the late 1980s, this high unemployment has to be also explained by the macroeconomic orientation of the French governments. After the failure of the Keynesian experiment (1981-2), the French government returned to stabilization and anti-inflationary politics that contributed to an increase of unemployment, especially among younger people, immigrants, women and low skilled workers (see Hall 1996: Ch. 8; Lasserre, Schild, Utterwedde 1997: 124-5, 203). Faced with the ongoing European integration, the bourgeois governments Balladur (1993-5) and Juppé (1995-7) continued these politics. They handed over government to the socialists with a budget exactly in the range of Maastricht (minus 3 per cent) but with a peak unemployment rate of 12.3 per cent.

slight fall of interest rates since 1997 too, this decrease was rather low (see note 8) and explains why credit financed investments fall behind the average within the EU (OECD 2000g: 50-5). Second, the French government had not enough capacity to reduce taxes, especially for enterprises and capital gains. Even the contrary, in order to finance its expensive labor market activities the cabinet increased the corporate tax rate for companies with sales of more than 50 million Franc from 36.6 to 41.6 per cent (Schneider 1998: 789, Eichhorst et al. 2001: 326). Taxes on capital gains increased from 20.9 to 25 per cent whereas the peak level of income tax has been lifted from 54 to 61 per cent, what is the highest level of income taxation in the cases under study. These increases are mirrored in Table 3. Although the share of social security contributions as percentage of overall taxation fell,[18] the comparatively high tax burden for enterprises proved to be unfavorable for job creation by private investment.

A third reason for both the rather low private investment and the still high unemployment in France is – despite all state activities – the resistance of labor market institutions and social security systems against reforms which favor employers. In contrast to the Netherlands, Britain and partially Sweden, the French employers still have to carry the main part of social security contributions (see Table 4). Moreover, the percentage of part time workers has remained at a rather small level with only 17 per cent of the overall workforce (see note 10). Another point are working time regulations. The attempt of the government to reduce by law the weekly working time to 35 hours focused on the shortage of labor supply. Simultaneously it was an attempt to create vacancies that should be filled with unemployed work force. Yet, the government did not set on self regulation of labor market participants, i.e. negotiations of tariff partners. Instead it followed the expensive and highly regulative way of state subsidies. Employers who reduced the weekly working time to 35 hours and hired additional workers are rewarded with public subsidies of 9,000 Franc for each new worker for social security payments (see Uterwedde 2000: 114). These efforts were not totally without success, approximately some 40,000 jobs have been created by subsidies (ibid.). However, to promote job growth this way is expensive because the means for such subsidies have to be collected – among other taxes by the introduction of the new general social security fund (CSG, see note 18) at the expense of all sorts of incomes.

The French fiscal policy illustrates the fundamental trade off between socially "just" and economically efficient taxation. For the three well performing countries, as sketched above, we could observe a shift from direct to indirect taxation. In order to urge investment, the Dutch government cut corporation taxes but the need for the state's income was satisfied with a slight increase of the value-added tax (VAT). This holds true for Sweden where tax incentives for private investors are financed by a constantly high VAT. The British government compensated corporate tax reductions by broadening the general tax bases and reforms of tax allowances for married couples. These measures hit in principle all tax payers, yet, those with smaller incomes more than those with higher.

---

[18] This fall goes back to a reduction of sickness insurance payments for employees in 1991 (see Uterwedde 2000: 101). As for other reduction of side payments on wages, the intention was to increase real incomes without an increase of nominal wages. Since 1998, however, the new government introduced a social security fee of 7.5 per cent on all incomes (*Contribution sociale généralisée, CSG*) to stabilize the existing health care system. The CSG counteracts the earlier reductions and mirrors in the increases of income tax on overall taxation as reported in Table 3, column 2 (see also EC 2001: 210-11).

The French government, however, took the other way. Consumers and private households were eased from taxes by a VAT-reduction. Moreover, families were granted more payments, for example an increase of children's allowance. Though these measures may lead to both an increase of real income and a rise of domestic demand, it has been achieved only by tax increases for corporations and capital gains. Consequently, private investors[19] and potential employers were full of reserve as the investment data for France and the labor market performance illustrate (see Figures 3 and 4).

Since 1999 the government has changed its course somewhat. It cooled down public expenditures, and France ranges since then safely within the Maastricht criteria (see Figure 1). This standing was made possible by higher general tax revenues of the state thanks to the growth and employment policies that the French government conducted during its first two years (see OECD 2000g: 32-5). Simultaneously, the Jospin-cabinet is planning a tax reform in order to lower the high tax burden for corporations and incomes. This signal, connected with the rather high labor market expenditures and good overall economic conditions in 2000 let the unemployment rate fall. However, France still suffers an unemployment rate significantly above EU-average (see Figure 2). Moreover, the government is – like the other EU-partners – constraint by little autonomy in monetary politics and the stabilization pact that forces all Euro- participants not to exceed the general government's deficit of 3 per cent of GDP. And – like all the others too – France was hit by a global recession since the beginning of 2001.

Yet, unanswered is whether the Jospin-administration will be able to support a stable growth of the private sector if the limits of public expenditures are obviously reached. On the one hand this would include to improve business confidence through tax cuts and social security contributions for employers paralleled by a strict restrictive fiscal policy. On the other this would include the government's readiness to reduce expenditures for traditional social democratic approaches – e.g. a quite generous support for unemployed, expensive labor market programs, the further expansion of public employment to keep employment stable – even if this would result in a medium term "bitter cure" for those who are hit by lesser public expenditures. Although this would be a hard cure to prescribe and – for electoral reasons – a risky one because it would affect the Socialist's core constituency, especially in the public service, setting tax incentives for private investors in the track of a consequent restrictive fiscal policy seems to be a promising strategy to reduce unemployment as the experiences in Sweden, the Netherlands and Great Britain may suggest.

This holds true in a similar vein for *Germany*. Although we cannot draw on a full data set because the first legislation period of the SPD-led coalition with the Greens has not passed completely, a look at the existing data makes both policy approaches and labor market outcomes discernible. Similar to their French colleagues the German government stopped the moderate restrictive fiscal course of its bourgeois predecessor for one year (see Figure 1). Background for this pause was the attempt to fight the high unemployment (see Figure 2) with more public spending. Both public investment and consumption grew slightly by 0.2 percentage points between 1998 and 1999 and the state's quota was kept at constant 48 per cent. Though the total expenditures for labor market policies as percentage of GDP fell somewhat, the government exceeded spending for active measures, particularly for training

---

[19] Not only domestic but also investors from abroad were rather cautious in France. For example, in Britain foreign direct investment (FDI) grew by 40 per cent between 1997 and 2000 compared with only 20 per cent in France in the same period and 5 per cent since the SPD-led government has been ruling in Germany (see OECD 2000g: 30).

programs designed to reduce youth unemployment and subsidized jobs in eastern Germany. In the first year of the SPD-led government the number of participants in Employment Creation Measures (*Arbeitsbeschaffungsmaßnahmen, ABM*) in eastern Germany doubled to some 450,000, and rose moderately also in western Germany to approximately 70,000 (OECD 1999: 35-7). Moreover, the quota of public employment was kept almost constant (see Table 1). Together, these approaches correspond with traditional social democratic employment policies, i.e. they focus on employment maintenance by high state activities (e.g. Merkel 1993: Ch. 6.3). On the other hand, however, they are expensive and require rather high tax revenues of the state.

When the new government took over office in autumn 1998, German corporations were taxed with the top level within this sample of 40 per cent. One of the most ambitious measures of the Schröder-administration, that started with the chancellor's commitment to reduce unemployment below 3.5 million, has been to implement a tax reform that lowers the tax burden for business and private households. After roughly two years of legislation, intense debates in the cabinet that peaked in the exchange of the left-wing finance minister Oskar Lafontaine by the more pragmatic Hans Eichel and a turn back to a restrictive course in fiscal policy the first step of tax reform passed the parliament in 2000. The reform includes a reduction of income taxes from 53 per cent to 48.5 at the top rate and from 25.9 per cent to 19.9 at the entrance rate. Moreover, the corporate tax rate fell to nominally 25 per cent,[20] and large industrial companies were excluded from the energy tax that was originally introduced to keep the obligate overall contributions to old age pensions under 20 per cent of gross income (see below).

Given these positive tax signals for business, good global economic conditions between 1999 and 2000 that favored especially export oriented industries (which flourished because of the weak Euro against the Dollar as well), and the employment schemes of the government, unemployment began to fall (see Figure 2). However, the fall was slow and came to an end already in spring of 2001. This stagnation can be traced back to at least four reasons. First, despite the attempt to lower tax burdens for corporations, private investment into the German economy has been only weak with an annual increase since 1998 of 2.6 per cent (see Figure 4). This rather weak private investment activity is also reflected in an only small private service sector (see Figure 3) that proved to be the "job machine" of the well performing countries sketched above. Though Germany experienced a job growth in the private service sector of 2.7 percentage points since 1998 this sector is still comparatively small and could not compensate job losses in other labor market sectors, e.g. agriculture (minus 14,000), mining (minus 11,000), and the most striking case construction (minus 108,000). Second, in spite of tax reductions for corporations, the German system does not favor small corporations as, for example, the British system does (see above). Even worse, whereas industrial corporations could assert a lower taxation on energy consumption (20 per cent), smaller and medium sized firms, traders, all enterprises in the service sector and all private households are charged fully with that so-called environmental tax.[21] The third reason for both the only little

---

[20] In order to finance economic consolidation in eastern Germany, all incomes are taxed with an extra 5.5 per cent solidarity charge. This is added to the corporation taxes so that the taxation adds up to 30.5 per cent (see Eichhorst et al. 2001: 326).

[21] The energy tax was introduced by the new German government in April 1999, actually in order to keep the mandatory overall contributions for both employers and employees to old age pensions below 20 per cent of gross income. The basic tax rate for energy consumption was determined at DM 20,- per MWh. Up to 2003 it

job growth in private employment sectors and the stagnation in reducing unemployment is to find outside the assumed relationship between restrictive fiscal policy, tax cuts, an increase of private investment on the one hand and employment growth on the other. The stagnation in employment growth also goes back to comparatively high labor market regulations in combination with rather low *welfare to work*-components. In the Netherlands, Britain, and partially Sweden the pressure for job seekers has been increased by the threat of cuts in unemployment relief. This measure is only used in Germany in local models not as a nationwide policy, yet. Furthermore, the three well performing countries owe the fall of unemployment atypical forms of employment, especially part time work without full wage compensation or limited working contracts (see Eichhorst et al. 2001: 180; more generally Snower 1998). In contrast, Germany limps back in the creation of flexible jobs including a – possibly subsidized – low wage sector for low skilled workers (see Scharpf 1999). The whole German system is still designed to protect so-called insiders (e.g. Paqué 1996) and larger parts of both the left wing within the SPD and the leadership of the metal workers union (*IG Metall*) express constantly their reluctance against the introduction of any kind of low wage sectors or other measures which point to the creation of may be socially less secure but also less regulated jobs. This insider orientation at the expense of jobless workforce became impressively visible when the IG Metall opposed the introduction of a new flexible employment program in the Volkswagen plant, the so-called model "5,000 times 5,000".[22] Another example is the introduction of the new industrial relations scheme in 2001 that expands worker's co-determination rights, especially in smaller enterprises. Moreover, job creation is restrained by high social security contributions as percentage of gross income. In contrast to the Netherlands and Sweden where social security contributions, especially the employers' share to sickness insurance or old age pensions has been reduced, in Germany employers were not relieved from payments. Recently, the contributions for sickness insurance have been lifted again so that they mirror after a short term reduction the level of 1999.[23] Finally, the German government suffers to some extend simply "bad luck" that all the attempts to activate both private consumption and investment by tax reductions fell into a period of a global cooling. The expected job miracle of the New Economy broke when the Nasdaq bubble exploded, and consumer prices for groceries, especially meat, rose significantly in the track of *BSE* and mouth and claw disease. This contributed to a peak inflation rate of 3.5 per cent in spring of 2001 and counteracted all the efforts to improve the consumers' confidence and especially their spending.

---

doubles by a stepwise increase to DM 40,- (Euro 20.50) per MWh. Excluded from this kind of taxation are energy supplying enterprises. Industrial corporations and the whole agriculture sector enjoy a tax relief of 80 per cent.

[22] The idea was to create 5,000 new jobs including job training for unemployed who should receive a monthly gross income of DM 5,000 each. Because this is slightly under the average wage settings negotiated by the IG Metall for regular Volkswagen workers, the union opposed this plan. After long negotiations and an intervention of the German chancellor, the IG Metall accepted finally, so that meanwhile some 4,000 jobs are ready to be implemented.

[23] After the introduction of the energy tax, total social security contributions as percentage of gross income fell from 42.1 (spring 1999) to 40.8 per cent (January 2001). But faced with the disastrous budget of the public health system the government decided in summer 2001 to rise sickness insurance contributions to an average of 13.52 per cent (see Table 4). Consequently, the social security contributions as percentage of gross income rose back to the level of 1999. Given the rising unemployment, the suggestion of the Greens to reduce the contributions for unemployment insurance by 1 percentage point to 5.5 seems to be extremely unlikely and has been meanwhile erased from Green labor market proposals.

Presently the trajectory of Germany's labor market performance looks rather bad. The government tried to boost private consumption and investment by the tax reform that was introduced when the course was set back on restrictive fiscal policies in 1999. But it failed to accompany the tax incentives for private investors by comprehensive labor market reforms, e.g. support for atypical employment or the introduction of low wage sectors. Compared with Sweden, the Netherlands and Great Britain, the German government hesitated to expect of their core constituency – employees in the public service and its unions – to swallow the bitter pill of an earlier and more consequent budget consolidation. Though absolute employment in the public sector fell slightly (usually by non-filling of vacancies, particularly in schools, universities, and hospitals), the quota of public employment remained quite stable. Moreover, given the quite influential left wing of the party in government (especially in the ministry of labor and social affairs), it did not dare to exercise stronger constraints for job seekers similar to the models which are applied in the well performing countries, i.e. carry out more coercion to take part in active labor market measures at the expense of cuts in unemployment relief.[24] Instead the government pursued only a half hearted way of consolidation that tried to hurt no interest group but actually changed nothing on the labor market. Whether the government is ready to execute further labor market reforms scarcely one year before the next general election (and a strategically totally unorganized center-right opposition) that may be painful for its constituency – e.g. by a combination of unemployment and social relief payments or a stronger conditioning of wage compensation for job seekers – seems for electoral reasons quite unlikely. Given the feeble growth of the overall German economy and rising unemployment the government is rather going to expand public spending in order to promote growth and employment by traditional means. Due to these expansion and lesser tax revenues because of the unexpected low growth the government's fiscal deficit has increased again (see Figure 1) and limits the chance to set investment incentives by further tax cuts.

SUMMARY

Reducing unemployment by political measures is a difficult and multi-conditioned field for that no guaranteed solutions exist. Neither there is any certain way of macroeconomic management to return to full employment. This paper made discernible that not all measures that are seen from liberal labor market scholars as recipes to reduce unemployment can be treated as generally effective. For example, the Dutch labor market profited analogue to the British from flexible working regulations, particularly part time work without full wage compensation compared with full time jobs (see note 10). Yet, part time work alone is no sufficient condition for high employment because the Swedish labor market flourished too since the mid 1990s without a similar high percentage of part time work. The same is true for wage increase. Nominal wages did not rise faster in France and Germany than in the well performing countries (see note 11). But all countries which experienced a significant fall of unemployment have in common that employers were eased from social security contributions so that side payments on wages, i.e. labor costs for employers, could be reduced significantly (see Table 4). Moreover – with reference to the object of this chapter – we can see a strong relationship between budget consolidation, tax reductions and the fall of unemployment. The

---

[24] For proposals see e.g. Paqué (1996: 144-8).

Swedish, Dutch and the British governments pursued strictly restrictive fiscal policies and lowered tax burdens for corporations. This course led to a short term deterioration in employment figures because of lesser public spending that stroke both public employment and recipients of labor market subsidies. But after some delay it paid off by higher investment, particularly in the private service sector, and unemployment fell. In contrast, the two countries whose governments either adopted to the restrictive way later or less consequently (France) or failed to accompany tax incentives for employers with labor market reforms (Germany) suffer much higher unemployment because they did not have the capacity to improve private investment conditions.

The mechanisms behind this relationship become visible with a look at the development of taxes, investment data and unemployment figures. Table 3 portrays that since the SAP's incumbency all included tax items as percentage of overall taxation fell, followed by Great Britain with a relative reduction in three of four tax items and the Netherlands. This ranking corresponds exactly with the growth rate of private investment (see Figure 4) and the fall of the unemployment rate (see Figure 2). Compared with France and Germany, Sweden, the Netherlands and Britain not only display much lower unemployment rates today, but also higher employment ratios; Sweden 74 per cent, the Netherlands 72 per cent, United Kingdom 71 per cent, in contrast to Germany with 65 and France with 61 per cent. These data highlight that the well performing countries approximate much more to the originate social democratic ideal of "full employment with a high employment ratio", yet with the less social democratic means. Neither restrictive fiscal policy at the expense of the public sector and labor market subsidies nor tax cuts for corporations and reductions of social security contributions for employers do belong to the traditional social democratic agenda of employment policies. In other words, social democratic governments that abandoned traditional paths in employment policies show today much better records compared with countries whose governments hesitated to follow sometimes painful but in the longer run helpful employment policies.

The relationships sketched in this paper contradict common wisdom about social democratic budgetary and employment policies in two ways. First, not all social democrats have an almost "natural" tendency to reach full employment by expansive policy measures. Second, restrictive policy does not necessarily result in growth of unemployment (see Scharpf 1991: Ch. 2). For the first aspect it has been pointed to a paradigm change that was accepted by some social democrats as well (see Notermans 2000, Trautwein 2000, Uterwedde 2000, Schaar 2001). For the second I have argued throughout this paper that cuts in public expenditures may result in a short term increase of unemployment. But they open the chance of significant tax cuts and favor private investment and contribute – if paralleled with further labor market reforms – to job growth or a fall of unemployment respectively.

Given the domestic as well as the international economic constraints as sketched above (e.g. high interest burdens in case of large deficits, tax competition even among EMU members) a restrictive fiscal course seems to be without an alternative. Deficit spending as a strategy to keep the domestic labor market alive is no longer feasible. First, because the EU-stability criteria of Maastricht oblige the governments to stay above a budget deficit of minus 3 per cent vice versa GDP. Second, because higher deficits take away every scope for supply side oriented tax measures. Finally because financial markets usually react with higher interests and potential investors with relocation (see Ferner 1998, Kreile 1999: 615). The turn to restrictive policy and tax cuts for potential private employers are to be explained primarily with pragmatic considerations within the governments[25] which are exposed to constraints of a global economy. Even if this results in further losses of autonomy in policy choices for national governments this pragmatism can contribute not only to a statistic success (fall of the unemployment rate) but also to an overall increase of economic conditions.

To prescribe a whole economy a bitter cure of budget consolidation requires both courage and patience. It demands courage because cuts in public spending are highly unpopular. Governments that begin to reduce public spending have to calculate the risk of being punished by the electorate. This happened for example in the Netherlands where the PvdA lost approximately one third of its voters in the 1994 election when it supported plans to cut public expenditures for labor market and welfare spending (van Paridon 2000: 107). It requires patience too, because the effects are not visible immediately. Governments that turn strictly to restrictive policies and conduct tax cuts in the expectation that the private economy compensates job losses in the public sector have either to wait usually one or two years until these measures will become effective (e.g. Netherlands, Great Britain) or they have to stand even an intermediate deterioration of labor market figures (Sweden). Moreover, they have to defend its consolidation course against the opposition of unions, especially those that organize public sector employees.[26] However, where the unions behaved cooperatively and patiently, as in the Netherlands and Sweden, the labor markets recovered notably. Finally, tax cuts in the track of restrictive policies can hardly be labeled as sufficient condition for more private investment and job growth. Under the conditions of private ownership nobody can be forced to invest and not all investments translate necessarily into more jobs (see Scharpf 1991: Ch. 2, Merkel 2000a). But they provide strong incentives for private investors and proved to be empirically as an at least inductive confirmation for the positive relationship between restrictive policies, tax reductions, investment incentives and job growth in private sectors. Furthermore, restrictive policies set free financial resources that were used before to pay for public debts. These means can be utilized then for more goal-directed labor market measures, for example for the improvement of the employability of workers by active training measures (e.g. Snower 1998). Though the overall expenditures for labor market programs have been falling in four of the five cases under study (with the exception of France, see Table 2), the parallel increase for active measures reflects the attempt to improve the employability of the workforce. In accordance with the other approaches conducive for the

---

[25] More precisely, we have to consider what type of politician controls the governing parties or acts in the cabinet. If we consider the classification as given by Kitschelt (see Kitschelt 1994: Ch.5), the Swedish, the Dutch and the British governments contain much more so called pragmatists compared to France and Germany where pragmatists like chancellor Schröder or finance minister Eichel have to deal with influential lobbyists and ideologists in Kitschelt's sense. Other institutional variables which influence policy choices of governments are (i) the internal structure of governing parties, i.e. flexible cadre organizations vs. entrenched mass parties or (ii) the kind of government, i.e. single governmental party vs. coalition, and in case of a coalition, with which party. Here, Labour enjoys the best situation because it has not to consider interests of any coalition partner. Another institutional aspect that has been not deepened here is the degree of corporatism that contributes particularly in the Netherlands and Sweden to cooperative and favorable economic outcomes.

[26] This is exemplified in present German debates. Whereas the government is fighting with a constantly rising deficit, left-wing politicians within the SPD and the unions – after roughly two years of wage moderation – call for a soon return to more expansive policies, i.e. for more overall expenditures or higher public investment in order to promote both domestic demand and economic growth that slowed down significantly parallel to the cooling of the world economy since summer 2001. The return to expansive policies should be financed according to union officials by tax increases for wealthier social groups, e.g. an increase of inheritance tax rate and the re-introduction of the property tax that was abandoned in 1997 still by the former bourgeois-conservative government.

reduction of unemployment, as outlined in this chapter, active labor market programs seem to be not only one of the remaining fields that national governments can control in terms of employment policies – they seem to be also a promising strategy for the Left to keep both their domestic workforce competitive and their labor markets intact.

REFERENCES

Block, Fred. 1977. "The Ruling Class does not Rule. Notes on the Marxist Theory of the State". in: *Socialist Revolution,* No. 33/1977, 6-28.

BMFi (Bundesfinanzministerium). 1999. *Finanzreport 2000.* Bonn, Germany.

_____. 2001. *Steuerreform 2000 im Überblick.* www.bundesfinanzministerium. de/Referat IV A 1, Steuerreform2000imÜberblick170501.doc.

Callaghan, John. 2000. *The retreat of social democracy.* Manchester: Manchester University Press.

Cameron, David. 1984. "Social Democracy, Corporatism, Labor Quiescence, and the Representation of Economic Interest in Advanced Capitalist Society". in: John H. Goldthorpe. ed. *Order and Conflict in Contemporary Capitalism.* Oxford: Oxford University Press, 143-78 .

Cavallè, Carlos. 1998. "Preface". in: Jordi Gual. ed. *Job Creation. The Role of Labor Market Institutions.* Cheltenham: Edward Elgar 1998, ix-xii.

Eichhorst, Werner et al. 2001. *Benchmarking Deutschland. Arbeitsmarkt und Beschäftigung.* Heidelberg: Springer.

Esping-Andersen, Gösta. 1985. *Politics against Markets. The Social Democratic Road to Power.* Princeton: Princeton University Press.

_____. 1990. *The Three Worlds of Welfare Capitalism.* Princeton: Princeton University Press.

European Commission (EC). 2001. *Inventar der Steuern, die in den Mitgliedsstaaten der Europäischen Union erhoben werden.* Brussels, www.europa.eu.int/ comm/taxation .

Ferner, Anthony. 1998. "Multinationals, 'relocation', and employment in Europe" in: Jordi Gual. ed. *Job Creation. The Role of Labor Market Institutions.* Cheltenham: Edward Elgar, 165-96.

Financial Times. Dec. 4. 2000. "Financial Times Surveys: Sweden".

Funk, Lothar. 1999. *Institutionell verhärtete und politisch rationale Arbeitslosigkeit in der Bundesrepublik Deutschland.* Münster: LIT-Verlag.

Funk, Lothar and Albrecht Winkler. 1997. "Konsensmodell Niederlande. Ein sozial- und beschäftigungspolitisches Vorbild für Deutschland?" in: Eckhard Knappe and Albrecht Winkler. eds. *Sozialstaat im Umbruch. Herausforderungen für die deutsche Sozialpolitik.* Frankfurt am Main: Campus, 151-86.

Garrett, Geoffrey and Peter Lange. 1985. "The Politics of Growth". in: *Journal of Politics* 47, No. 3, 792-827.

Giddens, Anthony. 1999. *Der dritte Weg. Die Erneuerung der sozialen Demokratie.* Frankfurt am Main: Suhrkamp.

Glyn, Andrew and Stewart Wood. 2000. "Die Wirtschaftspolitik von New Labour". in: Eckhard Hein and Achim Truger. eds. *Perspektiven sozialdemokratischer Wirtschaftspolitik in Europa*. Marburg: Metropolis, 51-88.

Gual, Jordi. ed. 1998. *Job Creation. The Role of Labor Market Institutions*. Cheltenham: Edward Elgar .

Hall, Peter. 1985. "Socialism in One Country: Mitterand and the Struggle to Define a New Economic Policy for France". in: Philip G. Cerny and Martin A. Schain. eds. *Socialism, the state and public policy in France*. London: Routledge, 81-107.

_____ . 1986. *Governing the Economy. The Politics of State Intervention in Britain and France*. Cambridge: Cambridge University Press.

Hemerijck, Anton, Philip Manow and Kees van Keersbergen. 2000. "Welfare without Work? Divergent experiences of reform in Germany and the Netherlands". in: Stein Kuhnle. ed. *Survival of the European Welfare State*. London: Routledge, 105-27.

Iversen, Torben. 1998. "Wage Bargaining, Hard Money and Economic Performance: Theory and Evidence for Organized Market Economies" In: *British Journal of Political Science* 28, 31-61.

Kesselmann, Mark. 1996. "Sozialdemokratische Wirtschaftstheorie nach dem Ende des Keynesianismus". in: Jens Borchert et al. *Das sozialdemokratische Modell*. Opladen: Leske & Budrich, 135-67.

Kitschelt, Herbert. 1994. *The Transformation of European Social Democracy*. Cambridge: Cambridge University Press.

Kreile, Michael. 1999. "Globalisierung und europäische Integration". in: Wolfgang Merkel and Andreas Busch. eds. *Demokratie in Ost und West*. Frankfurt am Main: Suhrkamp, 605-23.

Lasserre, René, Joachim Schild and Henrik Uterwedde. 1997. *Frankreich. Politik, Wirtschaft, Gesellschaft*. Opladen: Leske & Budrich.

Merkel, Wolfgang. 1993. *Ende der Sozialdemokratie?* Frankfurt am Main: Campus.

_____ . 2000a. "Die Dritten Wege der Sozialdemokratie ins 21. Jahrhundert". in: *Berliner Journal für Soziologie*, 1/2000, 99-124.

_____ . 2000b. "Der 'Dritte Weg' und der Revisionismusstreit der Sozialdemokratie am Ende des 20. Jahrhunderts". in: Karl Hinrichs, Herbert Kitschelt and Helmut Wiesenthal. eds. *Kontingenz und Krise. Institutionenpolitik in kapitalistischen und postsozialistischen Gesellschaften*. Frankfurt am Main: Campus, 263-90.

Nickell, Stephen. 1998. "Employment dynamics and labor market institutions". in: Jordi Gual. ed. *Job Creation. The Role of Labor Market Institutions*. Cheltenham: Edward Elgar, 34-48.

Notermans, Ton. *Money, Markets, and the State. Social Democratic Economic Policies since 1918*. Cambridge: Cambridge University Press.

OECD. 1997. *Historical Statistics*. Paris: OECD Publications.

_____ . 1998. *Economic Surveys Sweden*. Paris: OECD Publications .

_____ . 1999. *Economic Surveys Germany*. Paris: OECD Publications, November 1999 .

_____ . 2000a. *Main Economic Indicators*. Paris: OECD Publications, December 2000.

_____ . 2000b. *Employment Outlook*. Paris: OECD Publications, June 2000.

_____ . 2000c. *Revenue Statistics 1965 – 1999*. Paris: OECD Publications.

_____ . 2000d. *Labour Force Statistics*. Paris: OECD Publications.

_____ . 2000e. *Economic Surveys Netherlands*. Paris: OECD Publications, March 2000.

_____. 2000f. *Economic Surveys United Kingdom*. Paris: OECD Publications, June 2000.

_____. 2000g. *Economic Surveys France*. Paris: OECD Publications, July 2000.

_____. 2001. *Economic Surveys Sweden*. Paris: OECD Publications, March 2001.

Offe, Claus. 1984. *Contradictions of the Welfare State*. Cambridge: MIT Press.

Paqué, Karl-Heinz. 1996. "Unemployment and the Crisis of the German Model". in: Herbert Giersch. ed. *Fighting Europe's Unemployment in the 1990s*. Heidelberg and New York: Springer, 119-55.

van Paridon, Kees. 2000. "Arbeitsmarktentwicklung in den Niederlanden seit 1983". in: Hartmut Berg. ed. *Arbeitsmarkt und Beschäftigung: Deutschland im internationalen Vergleich*. Berlin: Duncker & Humblot, 101-20.

Parry, Richard. 2000. "Exploring the sustainable limits of public expenditure in the British Welfare State". in: Stein Kuhnle. ed. *Survival of the European Welfare State*. London: Routledge, 88-105.

Przeworski, Adam. 1985. *Capitalism and Social Democracy*. Cambridge: Cambridge University Press.

Rothstein, Bo. 1996. *The Social Democratic State. The Swedish Model and the Bureaucratic Problem of Social Reforms*. Pittsburgh: University of Pittsburgh Press.

Sandholtz, Wayne. 1993. "Choosing union: monetary politics and Maastricht". in: *International Organization*, Winter 1993, 1-39.

Schaar, Enrico. 2001. "Makroökonomischer Regimewandel, Lohnverhandlungssysteme und Arbeitslosigkeit". in: *Politische Vierteljahresschrift*, Vol. 42, No. 2: 321-8.

Scharpf, Fritz W. 1991. *Crisis and Choice in European Social Democracy*. Ithaca: Cornell University Press.

_____. 1999. "Der Arbeitsmarkt im internationalen Wettbewerb". in: *Gewerkschaftliche Monatshefte* 7-8/99, 459-64.

Schneider, Michael. 1998. "Kleinmut kommt vor dem Fall. Oder: Was wir von den Franzosen lernen können". in: *Gewerkschaftliche Monatshefte* 12/98, 786-94.

Sweden. 2001. Regeringskansliet. Socialdepartment. *Detta är Socialdepartment*. www.social.regeringen.se/pressinfo/pdf/familij/ socialforsakring_en-pdf: Stockholm, August 2001.

Tanzi, Vito and Ludger Schuknecht. 2000. *Public Spending in the 20th Century. A Global Perspective*. Cambridge: Cambridge University Press.

Thomas, Sven. ed. 2000. *Texte zur europäischen Beschäftigungspolitik*. Frankfurt am Main: Peter Lang.

Trautwein, Hans-Michael. 2000. "Sozialdemokratischer Modellbau im Wandel? Das Beispiel Schweden". in: Eckhard Hein and Achim Truger. eds. *Perspektiven sozialdemokratischer Wirtschaftspolitik in Europa*. Marburg: Metropolis, 125-59.

Uterwedde, Henrik. 2000. "Linker Pragmatismus. Die Wirtschaftspolitik der französischen Sozialisten seit 1997". in: Eckhard Hein and Achim Truger. eds. *Perspektiven sozialdemokratischer Wirtschaftspolitik in Europa*. Marburg: Metropolis, 89-123.

Visser, Jelle. 1998. "Fünfzehn Jahre Bündnis für Arbeit in den Niederlanden". in: *Gewerkschaftliche Monatshefte* 10/98, 661-8.

Visser, Jelle and Anton Hemerijck. 1998. *Ein holländisches Wunder? Reform des Sozialstaats und Beschäftigungswachstum in den Niederlanden*. Frankfurt am Main: Campus.

Wagschal, Uwe. 2001. "Deutschlands Steuerstaat und die vier Welten der Besteuerung". in: Manfred G. Schmidt. ed. *Wohlfahrtsstaatliche Politik. Institutionen, politischer Prozess und Leistungsprofil*. Opladen: Leske & Budrich, 124-60.

In: European Economic and Political Issues, Volume 5
Editor: Frank Columbus. pp. 27-48.

ISBN 1-59033-322-5
© Nova Science Publishers, Inc.

Chapter 2

EXCHANGE RATE MOVEMENTS IN EUROPEAN TRANSITION ECONOMIES

Evžen Kočenda

ABSTRACT

This paper analyzes disparities among exchange rate movements across the Central and Eastern European (CEE) countries from 1991 to 1997. The results of this paper show that there exists an exchange rate convergence among the CEE countries in general, but its degree varies substantially. The countries are grouped based on a) criteria of prospective accession to the EU and b) exchange rate regime. When we compare two groups of countries seeking accession, we can conclude that the countries of the First Round are, from the point of their exchange rate conversion, better prepared for accession to the EU. Performance of the groups divided on the base of the exchange rate regime shows that countries with a float regime converge at the fastest pace, followed by those with a fixed regime. The countries favoring currency basket peg regime are the slowest ones. The First Round countries belong among those that favor the regimes showing faster convergence.

INTRODUCTION

This paper analyzes exchange rate movements across the Central and Eastern European (CEE) countries from 1991 to 1997. Investigating exchange rate convergence should enhance our knowledge of how transition economies adjust to changing economic environment over time. It should also provide concrete evidence when addressing the issue of the accession of the CEE countries to the European Union since stable exchange rate is one of pre-accession criteria.

Any country in transition must undergo a stage of macroeconomic stabilization, which is inevitably accompanied by large shocks to macroeconomic fundamentals. The nature and magnitude of these disruptions affect the progress of economic development. Research into the success of the stabilization programs in transition economies is especially important for policy makers. Owing to the relative openness and the close economic relations between transition economies in Central and Eastern Europe and between these countries and the EU, the exchange rate and the exchange rate regime play an important role in economic development.

This paper aims to address the question of whether the transition countries have achieved exchange rates' development eventually leading to a certain degree of convergence. The countries in question are the Czech Republic, Slovakia, Hungary, Poland, Slovenia, Romania, Bulgaria, Albania, Estonia, Latvia, and Lithuania. Currently ten of these CEE countries have formally applied for full membership in the European Union.[1] The issue of accession is debated in the Transition Report (1997) of the EBRD, which also provides extensive material for the discussion of this question.

The significance of the matter is related not only to the economic performance of each country but also to the expectations of the average citizen. Both aspects are crucial to the assessment of convergence with respect to the possible accession of the countries in question into the European Union. Therefore, studying whether and how the transition economies managed to reduce disparities among their exchange rates seems to be a relevant issue to investigate.

The paper is organized as follows. Section 2 provides a motivation for the research. Section 3 describes the data and conceptual approach. Section 4 describes the econometric methodology used in testing the convergence of exchange rate differentials. Section 5 presents the empirical findings. A brief conclusion follows.

MOTIVATION

From the very beginning of the transition process in Central and Eastern European economies, exchange rate behavior and associated exchange rate regimes were closely monitored. The choice of a particular exchange rate regime is one of the major policy decisions countries in transition had to make.[2] Exchange regimes and the evolution of nominal exchange rates relative to major currencies differ widely across these countries. The Czech Republic and Slovakia favored the semi-fixed regime of a basket peg, while Hungary moved from an adjustable peg to a pre-announced crawling band in 1995, and Poland moved from a fixed basket peg to a crawling basket peg. Many other countries in the region favored a managed float or currency board. Table 1 summarizes the types of exchange rate regimes that the CEE countries have adopted since their economic transition.

A fundamental issue is how the exchange rates themselves evolved during the transition process. Koch (1997) reviews and analyzes monetary and exchange rate policy issues in selected European transition countries and provides a timely and thorough survey of the monetary practices in the Czech Republic, Poland, and Hungary with cross references to other transition countries. Graphs that illustrate both nominal and real evolution of exchange rates are also presented later in this analysis.

---

[1] We include Albania in this research as well.
[2] For further discussion see Edison and Melvin (1990), Edwards (1993), Quirk (1994), Begg (1996), and Sachs (1996), among others.

Table 1. Exchange Rate Regimes

Country	Regime
Czech Republic	Fixed (basket peg) since January 1991 to May 1997
	Float from May 1997
Slovakia	Fixed (basket peg) since January 1991
	Managed float since October 1998
Hungary	Adjustable peg (basket peg) since before 1989
	Pre-announced crawling band (peg) since March 1995
Poland	Fixed (basket peg) from January 1990 to October 1991
	Pre-announced crawling peg from October 1991 to May 1995
	Float within crawling band from May 1995 to January 1996
	Pre-announced crawling peg from January 1996 to April 2000
	Float since May 2000
Slovenia	Managed float from October 1991
Bulgaria	Managed float from February 1991
	Currency board from July 1997
Romania	Managed float from August 1992
Albania	Managed float from July 1992
Estonia	Currency board from June 1992
Latvia	Managed float from July 1992 (in reality peg to SDR basket)
Lithuania	Float from October 1992 to April 1994
	Currency board from April 1994

A strength of a currency normally corresponds to the strength of an entire economy. Thus an exchange rate can be considered as a monetary mirror of a real side of an economy as a whole. When we take into the account a high degree of openness of the CEE economies we have to admit that exchange rate is an important variable within the scope of how these economies are becoming interconnected. This is, beside other facts, a reason why it is important to study exchange rate convergence. An innovative way of analyzing this process is to examine whether the differentials of exchange rate changes converge or diverge over time. Thus, the convergence of exchange rates should be reflected in a reduction of the exchange rate differentials across countries over time. Complete formal definition of exchange rate convergence is provided in section 4.

From the historical context the issue of the exchange rate convergence starts with a launch of transition reforms. At the beginning of the transition process most of the CEE countries devalued their national currencies. Halpern and Wyplosz (1995) suggest four main factors for the initially large undervaluation of transition currencies: (i) the existence of monetary overhang, (ii) pent-up demand for foreign assets, (iii) the lack of credibility on the part of the new authorities, and (iv) total uncertainty about the appropriate equilibrium exchange rate and, therefore, the tendency for risk-averse authorities to err on the side of undervaluation rather than overvaluation. The crucial reason for undervaluation seems to be more simple: the rates were undervalued in order to be long lasting and able to promote exports of local companies while discouraging imports of primarily consumer goods.

Massive devaluation was also meant to partially offset substantial inflation that the CEE countries were expected to experience. Indeed they did.[3] Thus, evolution of nominal exchange rates in the CEE countries might alone provide a misleading picture. Figures 1 - 11 comprehensively document the evolution of exchange rates in all the countries under consideration from 1991 to 1997 in nominal terms (thin line). The Czech Crown remained quite stable and depreciated in connection with the financial crisis in summer of 1997. The nominal exchange rates of Poland and Hungary depreciated over time. The Slovak Crown was devalued by 10% in July 1993, but remained more or less stable during the period. The nominal exchange rates of Slovenia and other Balkan countries also depreciated to a greater or lesser extent over the researched period. The Baltic countries offer interesting picture of evolution, as these countries were severing monetary ties with the former Soviet Union while gradually establishing different exchange rate regimes.

It is inflation that in case of transition economies substantially differentiates nominal and real sides of the story. In order to see the real evolution of the national currencies we explore the real exchange rates. For the purpose of econometric analysis the real exchange rates (Q_t) of national currencies in relation to the US Dollar and the Deutsche Mark were constructed in the usual manner as

$$Q_t = \left(E_t \cdot CPI_t * \right)/ CPI_t \tag{1}$$

where Q_t is the defined real exchange rate, E_t is a nominal exchange rate, CPI_t is a domestic consumer price index (CPI), and CPI_t is a foreign CPI.

In order to contrast nominal and real exchange rates' development Figures 1 - 11 also illustrate the evolution of currencies in real terms. The real exchange rates are plotted in levels (thick lines). The currencies of the countries belonging to the Visegrad Group[4] continuously appreciated in real terms over time, but the extent of appreciation varied. Koch (1997) claims that the empirical evidence indicates that the current level of the real effective exchange rates does not appear to be seriously out of line with the underlying fundamentals of the Czech Republic, Poland, and Hungary. The Baltic countries uniformly experienced a massive real appreciation during 1992. This movement, over next two years, transformed into an almost stable real exchange rate. The Balkan countries together with Slovenia offer the most varied picture of currencies, which appreciated and depreciated in real terms over time.

Koch (1997) argues that in general terms, in most of the CEE countries occurred a period when real appreciation has been stronger when measured in consumer rather than producer prices. The two most important factors that may explain such difference are phasing-out of consumer subsidies (affecting CPI) and an increased demand for services (affecting both CPI and PPI) combined with an initially small services sector. In any event it is a real exchange rate that in fact matters to deliver an information about a real strength of a national currency. This is the reason why it is only the real exchange rate that matters for analysis of exchange rate convergence.

---

[3] Transition Report (1997) of the EBRD serves as a compact reference. For other comparison among selected CEE countries see Kočenda (1998a).

[4] Visegrad Group consists of the Czech Republic, Slovakia, Poland, and Hungary.

Figure 1. Exchange Rate of Czech *koruna* per USD and DEM

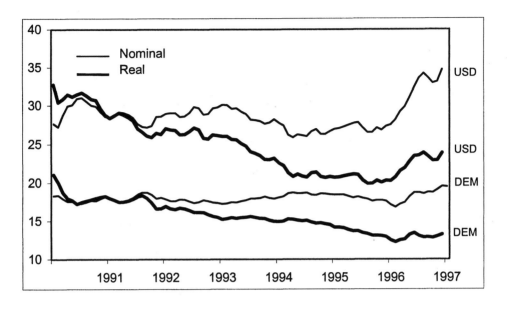

Figure 2. Exchange Rate of Slovak *koruna* per USD and DEM

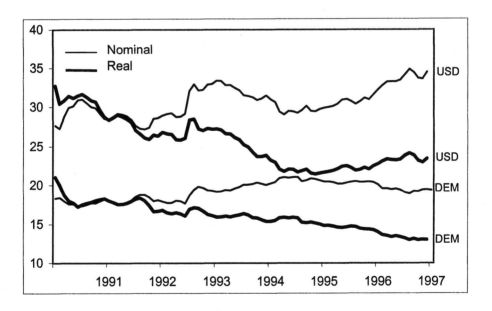

Figure 3. Exchange Rate of Polish *zloty* per USD and DEM

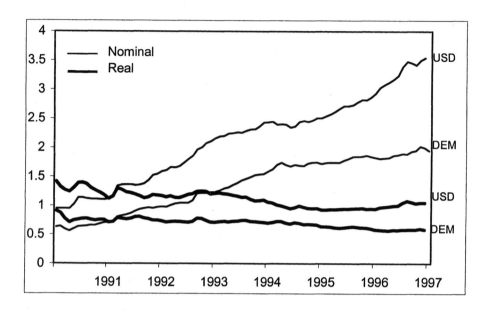

Figure 4. Exchange Rate of Hungarian *forint* per USD and DEM

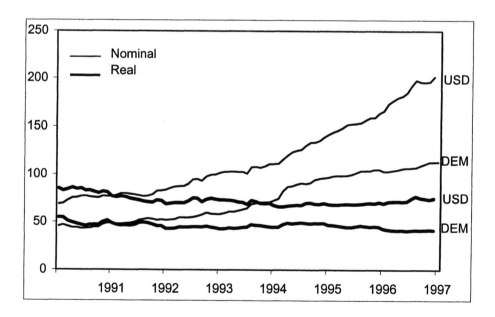

Figure 5. Exchange Rate of Slovenian *tolar* per USD and DEM

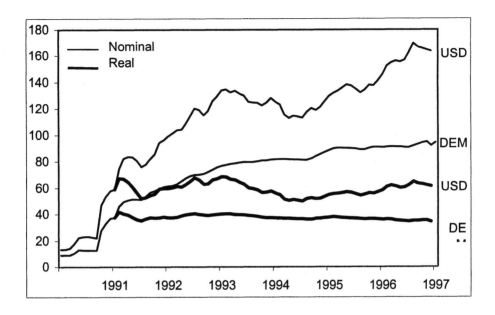

Figure 6. Exchange Rate of Romanian *leu* per USD and DEM

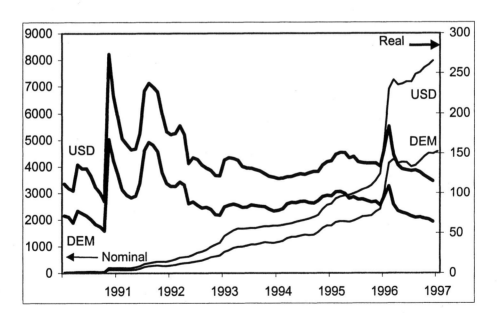

Figure 7. Exchange Rate of Bulgarian *leva* per USD and DEM

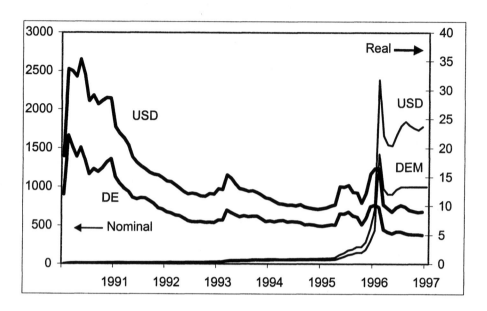

Figure 8. Exchange Rate of Albanian *lek* per USD and DEM

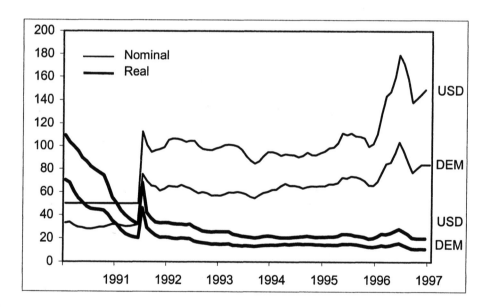

Figure 9. Exchange Rate of Estonian *kroon* per USD and DEM

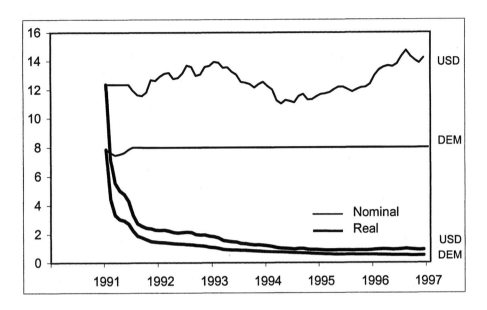

Figure 10. Exchange Rate of Lithuanian *lita* per USD and DEM

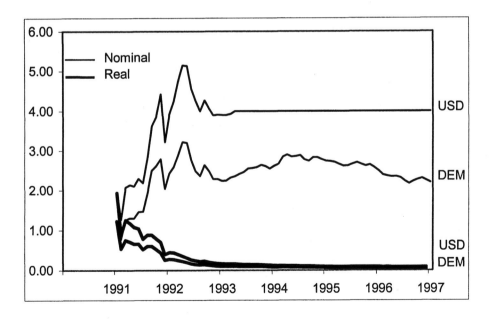

Figure 11. Exchange Rate of Latvian *lat* per USD and DEM

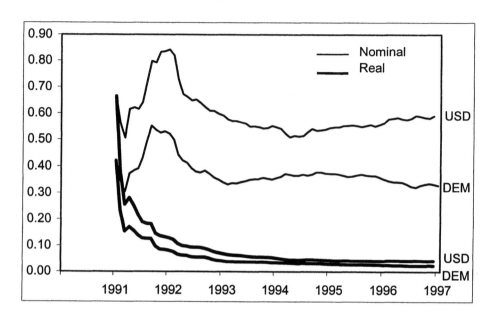

Real exchange convergence is especially important with respect to eventual accession of the CEE countries to the EU. As for the EU itself convergence has taken place within the framework of the European Monetary System (EMS) and has accelerated with the announcement of the Euro. Such process is expected to continue after the Euro (and its fraction cent) has become a sole and legal mean of payment within the member states of the EMU.

As it was hinted earlier an exchange rate convergence could not be discussed as a phenomenon isolated from other variables, specifically inflation that disguise the real picture. The EU countries participating in the European Monetary System (EMS) have already a record of their exchange rates convergence. Sarno (1997) found evidence of long-run convergence for both nominal and real exchange rates that was more frequent in cases of countries that adhered to the Exchange Rate Mechanism (ERM) than for the non-ERM countries. This suggests that the ERM of the EMS has been effective in reducing the tendency towards exchange rate misalignment, at least among its own members. Kočenda and Papell (1997) found evidence of dramatic convergence in inflation rates among the countries that adhered to the ERM. The results therefore suggest that a significant increase in policy convergence has been achieved within the former EMS.

Starting massive devaluation at the beginning of transition reforms was tied with new exchange regimes in respective countries. The choice of an exchange rate regime was an institutional decision of each country that often depended to various extents on the advice of an international institution (the IMF for example). Any form of non-free-float exchange regime (i.e. fixed, pegged, crawling-peg, managed float etc.) requires a certain degree of commitment from the monetary authorities. Such a commitment is a way of creating a consistent policy and establishing confidence in the policy actions of monetary authorities. For example the peg to a single currency may be the exchange regime with the greatest potential to gain credibility because it represent the simplest rule that is clear and understood by both the policy makers and the public.

Although the problem of exchange regime choice is of major concern for transition countries, the optimality of any such choice is subject to debate. The reason stems from two stylized facts: (i) no exchange regime has proven to be everlasting, and (ii) countries have tended to shift back and forth between exchange rate regimes. Despite the fact that the suitability of any adopted exchange rate regime remains an important topic in transition economies, its choice resulted from economic and/or political forces dominating each country at a time.

Currently ten countries in Central and Eastern Europe have formally applied for full membership in the European Union. In the future a crucial issue will be to harmonize exchange rate policies of the CEE countries with those prevailing in the European Union, especially with respect to European Monetary Union (EMU). In case of the CEE countries a relevant and related question arises. With so many varieties of exchange rate regimes, is there a link between the degree of convergence and a particular exchange rate regime? Or in other words, is convergence faster in countries that favored some kind of tight exchange regime opposite to a rather free one?

According to the recommendations of the IMF many transition economies adopted exchange rate regimes characterized by different degrees of flexibility and management. Several countries, including the Czech Republic, adopted an exchange regime based on a currency basket peg. Such a regime is, according to the IMF, characterized as a fixed exchange rate regime. However, a critical difference is that such an exchange rate is actually pegged to a currency basket rather than fixed to one foreign currency.[5]

In the case of the fixed regime, a country has by definition an exchange regime policy, gives up its own monetary policy, and the origin of a monetary base is purely a foreign one. The exact opposite is true for a floating exchange regime. A crucial difference arises in the case of a currency basket pegged regime whereby a country maintains both exchange rate and monetary policies. Under such an arrangement, eventual conflict between these two policies is likely to materialize due to the both domestic and foreign origin of the monetary base. Such a conflict may eventually evolve into a balance of payments crisis. The kind of exchange regime is thus likely to affect degree of exchange convergence as well.

The transition process in Central and Eastern Europe provides a unique opportunity to carry out quantitative analysis of exchange rate convergence within distinctive groups of the CEE countries based on different exchange rate regimes. This project addresses the question as to whether the transition countries have achieved exchange rate convergence and what are the implications for their eventual accession to the European Union.

---

[5] The essence of the argument comes from a possible dichotomy between exchange rate and monetary policies. For further details see Kočenda (1998b).

DATA AND DEFINITIONS

The study uses data from the following eleven countries: the Czech Republic, Slovakia, Hungary, Poland, Slovenia, Romania, Bulgaria, Albania, Estonia, Latvia, and Lithuania. The time span of the data is from January 1991 to December 1997. The monthly averages of exchange rates of respective national currencies were obtained from the Bank for International Settlements, Basel, the International Monetary Fund's International Financial Statistics, and the EBRD. The monthly consumer price indices were obtained from the latter two sources. The bulletins of the national banks of each country in question were consulted as well.

The prevalent view in the literature is that floating exchange rates follow a random walk.[6] Such behavior was not found in case of exchange rates of transition economies. This is apparently due to the nature of their exchange rate regimes and the fact that these economies are still undergoing huge structural shifts. The data (exchange rates of all countries in question) are not stationary but are integrated of degree one. The analysis is therefore performed on the changes in exchange rates between two consecutive periods. These changes are analogous to the first logarithmic differences. Such a method of how to achieve stationarity is preferred to that of detrending the data. By their nature the exchange rates contain polynomial trends of different degrees and thus a formerly described method is preferred to the latter one.

For the purpose of further analysis the countries were pooled in several logically differentiated groups. There are 84 observations per country and the dimension of each panel data structure changes accordingly. Table 2 shows all the countries that were included in our analysis and describes the composition of the various groups for which we tested the convergence hypothesis.

Table 2. Groups of Countries in Each Panel Data Set

Group	No[*]	Countries
Accession Rounds Groups		
First Round	5	Czech Republic, Hungary, Poland, Slovenia, Estonia
First Round w/o Estonia	4	Czech Republic, Hungary, Poland, Slovenia
Second Round	5	Bulgaria, Latvia, Lithuania, Romania, Slovakia
Exchange Rate Regime Groups		
Peg (A)	4	Slovakia, Hungary, Poland, Latvia
Peg (B)	5	Slovakia, Hungary, Poland, Latvia, Czech Republic
Fix	2	Estonia, Lithuania
Float (A)	4	Albania, Romania, Slovenia, Bulgaria
Float (B)	5	Albania, Romania, Slovenia, Bulgaria, Czech republic

* number of countries in a particular group.

---

[6] However, no strong statistical evidence has emerged to confirm or refute this view so far (see Brock, Hsieh, and LeBaron (1993), p. 130).

The institutional groups are defined with respect to eventual accession. Three groups were formed with respect to the analyses of progress in economic and political transition made by the EBRD about ten countries that have applied for the membership in the European Union. According to the European Commission five of the countries were identified as leading candidates in terms of the progress they have made so far. These are the Czech Republic, Hungary, Poland, Slovenia, and Estonia and form the First Round group. Removing Estonia makes a control group because this country maintained currency board exchange regime throughout the researched period.[7] The Second Round group was formed from Bulgaria, Latvia, Lithuania, Romania, and Slovakia.

Other groups were formed on the basis of the exchange rate regime prevailing in each country for the time span of our analysis. There are two groups with a currency basket based peg regime. One group, Peg A, contains Slovakia, Hungary, Poland, and Latvia. The other group, Peg B, includes also the Czech Republic. This country abandoned currency basket peg regime in May 1997 and therefore two peg groups were created. There is one group of countries that maintains fixed regime. The group is called Fix and contains Estonia and Lithuania. At last, we formed two groups of countries with float regimes. The Float A group contains Albania, Romania, Slovenia, and Bulgaria. The control Float B group in addition includes also the Czech Republic. Bulgaria is included in both groups because this country changed its regime from the managed float to a currency board in July 1997. Pooling countries in certain groups is meant to show not only the consistency, but also the sensitivity of our results.

A detailed description of the method to test for convergence follows in the next section. That section concentrates on investigating logically structured groups of countries to see how the differences in exchange rate differentials evolved over time, i.e. whether they increased or diminished.

CONVERGENCE OF EXCHANGE RATES: METHODOLOGY

The usual notion of convergence is that the difference between two or more variables should become negligible over time.[8] The following econometric methodology corresponds to the outlined notion of convergence. It utilizes a combination of cross-sections of individual time-series and was favorably exploited in several published empirical analyses.[9] Thus, a

---

[7] Elimination of Estonia from the First Round group is purely institutional step in this analysis.

[8] The formal way of describing the convergence is to say that the random variable x_n converges in probability to a constant c if $\lim_{n \to \infty} Pr\,ob(|x_n - c| > \varepsilon) = 0$ for any positive ε. Simply put, convergence in probability implies that the values that the variable may take that are not close to c become increasingly unlikely. Thus, if x_n converges in probability to c we can write $p \lim x_n = c$. A special case of convergence in probability is convergence in mean square or convergence in quadratic mean that can be characterize the following way. If x_n has mean μ_n and variance σ_n^2 such that the ordinary limits of μ_n and σ_n^2 are c and 0 respectively, then x_n converges in mean square to c, and $p \lim x_n = c$. It can be shown that convergence in probability does not imply convergence in mean square, however, convergence in mean square implies convergence in probability. The conditions for convergence in mean square are usually easier to verify than those for more general form. For details and proofs see Greene (1993), pp. 99-102.

[9] Ben-David (1995, 1996) performed an analysis of real per-capita income growth on numerous countries. Kočenda and Papell (1997) recently applied this methodology to study inflation convergence in the European

panel data analysis of the convergence of exchange rate differentials is conducted in order to fully exploit the effect of cross-variances in a pooled time series of moderate length. Previous econometric research has demonstrated the specific advantages of utilizing panel data in studying a wide range of economic issues. As shown by Levin and Lin (1992), the statistical power of a unit root test for a relatively small panel may be an order of magnitude higher than the power of the test for a single time series.

The analysis is performed for two types of exchange rates, which are measured as a change in the respective exchange rate over two successive periods. The individual nominal change in the exchange rate between two consecutive months (EX_t) or a first logarithmic difference is defined as

$$EX_t = \ln E_t - \ln E_{t-1} \tag{2}$$

where E_t denotes the nominal exchange rate at time t. In a consistent manner we define the change in the real exchange rate (QX_t) as

$$QX_t = \ln Q_t - \ln Q_{t-1} \tag{3}$$

where Q_t is a real exchange rate at a time t as defined earlier in equation (1).

We model the evolution of exchange rates (X_t) for a group of i individual countries with observations spanning over t time periods in the following way:

$$X_{i,t} = \alpha + \phi X_{i,t-1} + \varepsilon_{i,t} \tag{4}$$

The fact that the exchange rate is modeled as an autoregressive process is based on the common practice in the literature and does not represent any theory of how this variable is determined. It also constitutes a suitable form for the convergence test introduced later in this section. The inter-period changes in exchange rate were tested to have zero mean in case of all series. Therefore, we used equation (4) with a constant α not being significantly different from zero.

The convergence measure adopted here is based on a relationship that describes the dynamics of exchange rate differentials in a panel setting. Formally, we can transcribe this as follows:

$$X_{i,t} - \overline{X_t} = \phi\left(X_{i,t-1} - \overline{X_{t-1}}\right) + u_{i,t} \tag{5}$$

Union. Papell (1997) tested purchasing power parity for the real exchange rates of 20 developed countries. Kočenda and Hanousek (1998) tested for convergence and integration of Asian capital markets.

where $\overline{X_t} = \dfrac{1}{n}\sum_{i=1}^{n} X_{i,t}$. In the presence of pooling, the intercept α vanishes since, by construction, the exchange rate differentials have a zero mean over all the countries and time periods. How the countries are pooled into different groups was described in detail in the previous section.

Convergence in this context requires that exchange rate differentials become smaller and smaller over time. For this to be true, statistically significant ϕ must be less than one. From the construction of the test it follows, that as the coefficient ϕ approaches unity, the rate of convergence becomes smaller. On other hand, ϕ greater than one indicates a divergence of exchange rate differentials. The convergence coefficient ϕ for a particular group of countries can be obtained using the Dickey and Fuller (1979) test on equation (5). The augmented version of this test (ADF) is used in order to remove possible serial correlation from the data.[10] Since the analysis is performed on panel data of exchange rate changes, there will be no intercept by construction. Denoting the exchange rate differential as $d_{i,t} = X_{i,t} - \overline{X_t}$, and its difference as $\Delta d_{i,t} = d_{i,t} - d_{i,t-1}$, the equation for the ADF test is written as

$$\Delta d_{i,t} = (\phi - 1)d_{i,t-1} - \sum_{j=1}^{k} \gamma_j \Delta d_{i,t-j} + z_{i,t} \tag{6}$$

where the subscript $i = 1,...,k$ indexes the countries in a particular group. Equation (6) tests for a unit root in the panel of exchange rate differentials. The null hypothesis of a unit root is rejected in favor of the alternative of level stationarity if $(\phi - 1)$ is significantly different from zero or, implicitly, if ϕ is significantly different from one.

The number of lagged differences (k) is determined using the parametric method proposed by Campbell and Perron (1991) and Ng and Perron (1995). An upper bound of the number of lagged differences k_{max} is initially set at an appropriate level.[11] The regression is estimated and the significance of the coefficient γ_j is determined. If the coefficient is not found to be significant, then k is reduced by one and the equation (6) is reestimated. This procedure is repeated with a diminishing number of lagged differences until the coefficient is found to be significant. If no coefficient is found to be significant in conjunction with the respective k, then $k = 0$ and a standard form of the Dickey-Fuller test is used in the analysis. A ten- percent value of the asymptotic normal distribution (1.64) is used to assess the significance of the last lag. The advantage of this recursive t-statistic method over alternative procedures where k is either fixed or selected in order to minimize the Akaike Information Criterion is discussed in detail by Ng and Perron (1995).

---

[10] It was found that, in cases of both nominal and real exchange rates, the correlation sensitivity threshold was about 0.50. Employing the ridge regression of Hoerl and Kennard (1970) compensated for the encountered multicollinearity.

[11] $k_{max}=7$ since monthly data are used. We also wanted to incorporate up to half-year lags between monetary and real sides of economy.

To evaluate the statistical significance of the convergence coefficient ϕ we cannot use the standard critical values, which are used when such an analysis is conducted on panel data. The common critical values for panel unit root tests tabulated by Levin and Lin (1992) do not incorporate serial correlation in disturbances and are, therefore, incorrect for small samples of data. Using the Monte Carlo technique, Papell (1997) tabulated critical values taking serial correlation into account and found that, for both quarterly and monthly data in his data sets, the critical values were higher than those reported in Levin and Lin (1992). A similar result was found in Kočenda and Papell (1997).

Because of these findings, the exact finite sample critical values for the resulting test statistics were computed using the Monte Carlo method in the following way. Autoregressive (AR) models were first fit to the first differences of each panel group of exchange rate differentials using the Schwarz (1978) criterion to choose the optimal AR models. These optimal estimated AR models were then considered to be the true data generating process for errors of each of the panel group of data. Finally, for each panel, pseudo samples of corresponding size were constructed employing the optimal AR models described earlier with $iid(N(0,\sigma^2))$ innovations. The variance σ^2 is the estimated innovation variance of a particular optimal AR model. The resulting test statistic is the t-statistic on the coefficient $(1-\phi)$ in equation (6), with lag length k for each panel group chosen as described above.

This process was replicated 10,000 times and the critical values for the finite sample distributions were obtained from the sorted vector of such replicated statistics. The derived finite sample critical values are reported for significance levels of 1%, 5%, and 10% in the tables, along with the results of the ADF test conducted on different panel groups in the respective time periods.

EMPIRICAL FINDINGS

Earlier in the section 2 we argued that in the framework of transition economies it is the real exchange rate convergence that matters. Despite this fact we report results of nominal convergence as well. The reason is to provide reader with an institutional overview as well as with the data. We justify this by two reasons.

One reason why it is legitimate to analyze the nominal convergence is that in theory real exchange rate should behave the same way no matter whether the nominal rate is pegged or not because the price level should move as well. In practice, however, price level movements are much slower than nominal exchange rate movements and the convergence should be different as well. The second reason is that by fixing or pegging nominal exchange rate the authorities aim to lower inflation. By definition the fixed or pegged regimes should affect real exchange rate changes in a different manner than the floating regime.

The results of convergence tests for all constructed groups of countries are presented in four tables. Tables 3 and 4 show results for the nominal exchange rate differentials as an introduction to the principal part of real exchange rates. The results of the test performed on exchange rate differentials expressed in US Dollars and Deutsche Marks show that the values of coefficient ϕ are very similar, but not completely identical. Recall, that from the construction of the test it follows, that as the coefficient ϕ approaches unity, the rate of convergence becomes smaller. The tabulated coefficients are lower than one and significantly different from one. Thus, the differences in the differentials of all groups clearly diminish over time.

Table 3. US Dollar Nominal Exchange Rates (January 1991 - December 1997)

Group	No.[*]	ϕ	t-stat (ϕ)	k[†]	Critical Values 1%	5%	10%
Accession Rounds Groups							
First Round	5	0.5152[a]	-5.16	5	-3.19	-2.41	-1.93
First Round w/o Estonia	4	0.5109[a]	-4.70	5	-2.81	-2.07	-1.69
Second Round	5	0.4188[a]	-5.35	6	-3.34	-2.28	-1.80
Exchange Rate Regime Groups							
Peg (A)	4	0.5216[a]	-6.71	5	-2.80	-2.05	-1.66
Peg (B)	5	0.5716[a]	-6.53	6	-2.98	-2.22	-1.80
Fix	2	0.4988[a]	-4.12	5	-3.77	-2.40	-1.93
Float (A)	4	0.2861[a]	-5.26	6	-2.98	-2.16	-1.74
Float (B)	5	0.3296[a]	-5.86	6	-3.40	-2.23	-1.82

[*] number of countries in a particular group.
[†] number of lags.
[a] significance at 1% level.

Table 4. Deutsche Mark Nominal Exchange Rates (January 1991 - December 1997)

Group	No.[*]	ϕ	t-stat (ϕ)	k[†]	Critical Values 1%	5%	10%
Accession Rounds Groups							
First Round	5	0.5107[a]	-5.20	5	-3.20	-2.41	-1.95
First Round w/o Estonia	4	0.5061[a]	-4.74	5	-2.94	-2.19	-1.75
Second Round	5	0.4122[a]	-5.37	6	-3.37	-2.29	-1.80
Exchange Rate Regime Groups							
Peg (A)	4	0.5234[a]	-6.71	5	-2.79	-2.06	-1.66
Peg (B)	5	0.5413[a]	-7.47	5	-2.88	-2.15	-1.70
Fix	2	0.4996[a]	-4.12	5	-3.81	-2.42	-1.95
Float (A)	4	0.2717[a]	-5.32	6	-2.84	-2.14	-1.72
Float (B)	5	0.3181[a]	-5.92	6	-3.33	-2.24	-1.82

[*] number of countries in a particular group.
[†] number of lags.
[a] significance at 1% level.

When we compare the two groups seeking accession, we can see that both of them show comparable speed of convergence. However, the Second Round group fares somehow better. Performance of the groups divided on the base of the exchange rate regime is shown in the second part of both tables. Countries with a float regime converge at the fastest pace, followed by those with a fixed regime. The countries favoring peg regime stand at the last place.

The primary results of the convergence test on differentials of real exchange rates are presented in Tables 5 and 6. The countries of the First Round converge at slower pace than those from the Second Round. However, when Estonia is removed from the First Round group, than this group surpasses the Second Round group. These results may be caused by two reasons. First one is an extent of economic integration of the CEE countries with the EU. Such an extent should be greater for the countries of the First Group. This effect mirroring the real side of the economy should be even more pronounced in the later years of transition. The second reason stems from the monetary side and reflects the beginning situation when exchange rate and inflation in particular countries started to evolve from very different conditions. Unfortunately, both two effects tend to cancel each other with respect to the speed of convergence.

Table 5. Dollar Real Exchange Rates (January 1991 - December 1997)

Group	No.[*]	ϕ	t-stat (ϕ)	k[†]	Critical Values 1%	5%	10%
Accession Rounds Groups							
First Round	5	0.5575[a]	-8.04	6	-2.74	-2.07	-1.70
First Round w/o Estonia	4	0.1959[a]	-10.80	4	-2.76	-2.05	-1.68
Second Round	5	0.2163[a]	-4.98	7	-2.95	-2.20	-1.77
Exchange Rate Regime Groups							
Peg (A)	4	0.6958[a]	-4.38	6	-2.91	-2.15	-1.71
Peg (B)	5	0.6806[a]	-5.13	6	-2.88	-2.10	-1.74
Fix	2	0.4440[b]	-4.11	4	-4.46	-2.39	-1.90
Float (A)	4	0.1028[a]	-4.82	7	-2.87	-2.07	-1.65
Float (B)	5	0.1758[a]	-7.22	6	-2.79	-2.05	-1.69

[*] number of countries in a particular group.
[†] number of lags.
[a] significance at 1% level.
[b] significance at 5% level.

Table 6. Deutsche Mark Real Exchange Rates (January 1991 - December 1997)

Group	No.[*]	ϕ	t-stat (ϕ)	k[†]	Critical Values 1%	5%	10%
Accession Rounds Groups							
First Round	5	0.5552[a]	-8.14	6	-2.86	-2.06	-1.64
First Round w/o Estonia	4	0.2008[a]	-10.88	4	-2.79	-2.05	-1.69
Second Round	5	0.2061[a]	-5.01	7	-2.90	-2.15	-1.70
Exchange Rate Regime Groups							
Peg (A)	4	0.6398[a]	-5.13	5	-2.87	-2.11	-1.73
Peg (B)	5	0.6239[a]	-5.96	5	-2.83	-2.11	-1.72
Fix	2	0.4395[b]	-4.10	4	-4.47	-2.43	-1.91
Float (A)	4	0.0978[a]	-4.86	7	-2.90	-2.15	-1.70
Float (B)	5	0.1807[a]	-7.28	6	-2.85	-2.09	-1.74

[*] number of countries in a particular group.
[†] number of lags.
[a] significance at 1% level.
[b] significance at 5% level.

In order to investigate the extent of both effects, the test was performed on First and Second Round groups again but this time the time span was divided to two periods of equal length of three and half years (1991:1 – 1993:6 and 1993:7 – 1997:12). We opted for such division because of the necessary requirements for panel data format. The panel has to have a certain dimension given by the number of countries and time periods to yield reliable results. Investigation that would account for time periods that are determined by regime switches in individual countries would lead to identification problems and/or unreliable parameter estimates. Such panels would then simply yield incorrect results.

The results for periods January 1991 – June 1993 and July 1993 – December 1997 are reported in Tables 7 and 8. For both currencies we can see that the Second Round group converges during the earlier period of transition at the faster pace than the First Round group. The monetary effect representing the beginning conditions thus prevails since the degree of real integration was quite limited in that time. However, during the later period of transition the First Round group converges faster then the Second Round group. This is presumably due to the higher degree of real economic integration of the CEE countries with the EU that was achieved at the advanced stage of the transition period. Thus we can conclude that the countries of the First Round are, from the point of their exchange rate conversion, better equipped for accession to the EU.

Table 7. US Dollar Real Exchange Rates (Two Period Division)

Group	No.[*]	φ	t-stat (φ)	k[†]	1%	5%	10%
					Critical Values		
January 1991 – June 1993							
First Round w/o Estonia	4	0.4145	-8.23[a]	4	-3.55	-2.46	-2.01
Second Round	5	0.2498	-2.98[b]	7	-3.22	-2.39	-1.94
Second Round w/o Lithuania	4	0.1680	-2.92[b]	7	-2.99	-2.21	-1.76
July 1993 – December 1997							
First Round w/o Estonia	4	0.1205	-6.08[a]	4	-3.04	-2.28	-1.89
Second Round	5	0.1616	-4.26[a]	6	-3.63	-2.52	-2.00
Second Round w/o Lithuania	4	0.2001	-4.29[a]	7	-3.45	-2.41	-1.91

[*] number of countries in a particular group.
[†] number of lags.
[a] significance at 1% level.
[b] significance at 5% level.

Additional information about real convergence is contained in the second part of the Tables 5 and 6. When we compare countries according to their exchange rate regimes, then countries with the float regime show greater degree of convergence than those with fixed regimes. The groups of countries with peg regimes converge at the slowest pace.

We conclude that the currency basket based peg regime is the least effective regime to promote convergence in both nominal and real terms. On other hand, the float regime seems to be one that is most effective in this sense. Fixed regime lies between. The policy implication of these facts is that the countries with a float or fixed exchange rate regimes are cutting disparities among the exchange rates of their currencies faster than those with a peg regime. It comes as a no surprise that the First Round countries also favor the regimes that allow for faster convergence.

Table 8. Deutsche Mark Real Exchange Rates (Two Period Division)

Group	No.[*]	ϕ	t-stat (ϕ)	k[†]	Critical Values 1%	5%	10%
January 1991 – June 1993							
First Round w/o Estonia	4	0.4284	-8.34[a]	4	-3.50	-2.47	-2.01
Second Round	5	0.2346	-3.02[b]	7	-3.20	-2.37	-1.92
Second Round w/o Lithuania	4	0.1556	-2.95[b]	7	-2.99	-2.21	-1.77
July 1993 – December 1997							
First Round w/o Estonia	4	0.1253	-6.07[a]	4	-3.12	-2.32	-1.93
Second Round	5	0.1735	-4.24[a]	6	-3.62	-2.52	-2.00
Second Round w/o Lithuania	4	0.1816	-4.26[a]	7	-3.46	-2.40	-1.90

[*] number of countries in a particular group.
[†] number of lags.
[a] significance at 1% level.
[b] significance at 5% level.

Quite interesting conclusion stems from comparison of results that come from two different currencies in which exchange rates are expressed. The exchange rates in Deutsche Mark show higher degree of convergence than those expressed in US Dollars. The difference is not large but consistent across all the groups. This fact hints on the stabilizing effect of Deutsche Mark for the exchange rates of the CEE countries.

Convergence of nominal exchange rates is an indicator of increasing stability of the currencies. It is not an incidental event that majority of the CEE countries included Deutsche Mark in their exchange rate regimes in a form of direct peg or heavily weighted currency in a currency basket. This can be viewed from the perspective of eventual accession to EU and further joining the EMU. The policy implication is that convergence of exchange rates to some long-run equilibrium is likely to be faster in case of real exchange rates rather than nominal ones. The reason is a higher rate of inflation in the CEE countries than that in Germany or the USA. This is connected with the process of decreasing disparities of the inflation rates among the CEE countries and Germany. Only after the inflation rates in transition economies come near to that of Germany, there will be more pronounced convergence of the nominal exchange rates.

There is certain portion of institutional noise that has to be taken into account when presenting results of our analysis. Changes in exchange regimes are the most important ones. In addition, at the beginning of transition reforms exchange rates in some transition economies were official rates for currencies that were not fully convertible yet and thus were not really free market exchange rates. The potential impact of non-convertibility on exchange rate convergence in this analysis is not likely to be large. The CEE countries early during the transition reforms realized that convertibility of currency benefits its real strength. Non-negligible effects certainly also played wild Ponzi games in Albania and Bulgaria. Such pyramid schemes considerably disturbed the financial sector and, naturally, the exchange rates as well. To analyze the hypotheses outlined above is a task for further research.

CONCLUDING COMMENTS

The results of this paper show that there exists an exchange rate convergence among the CEE countries in general. The degree of convergence varies substantially among the groups of countries though. The primary division of countries is done based on criteria of prospective accession to the EU and exchange rate regime prevailing in specific countries during transition.

When we compare two groups of countries seeking accession, we can see that both of them show comparable speed of convergence. When time span of the data is divided to two equal periods then the Second Round group converges during the earlier period of transition at the faster pace than the First Round group. The monetary effect representing the beginning conditions thus prevails since the degree of real integration was quite limited in that time. However, during the later period of transition the First Round group converges faster then the Second Round group. This is presumably due to the higher degree of real economic integration of the CEE countries with the EU that was achieved at the advanced stage of the transition period. We can conclude that the countries of the First Round are, from the point of their exchange rate conversion, better prepared for accession to the EU.

Performance of the groups divided on the base of the exchange rate regime significantly differs. Countries with a float regime converge at the fastest pace, followed by those with a fixed regime. The countries favoring a currency basket based peg regime are the slowest ones. The policy implication of these facts is that the countries with a float or fixed exchange rate regimes are cutting disparities among the exchange rates of their currencies faster than those with a peg regime. The First Round countries belong among those that favor the regimes showing faster convergence. Further, the exchange rates in Deutsche Mark show higher degree of convergence than those expressed in US Dollars. This fact hints on the stabilizing effect of Deutsche Mark for the exchange rates of the CEE countries.

Due to the long-term nature of the transformation process in the CEE countries, the presented findings provide arguments for further monetary policy debate on how exchange rate management or mismanagement can be related to economic development during transition. Before the CEE countries join the EU, and later the EMU, they will have to manage more open and more credible pegging to the euro.

REFERENCES

Begg, D. 1996. "Monetary Policy in Central and Eastern Europe, IMF Working Paper, 96/108.

Ben-David, Dan.1996. "Trade Convergence Among Countries," *Journal of International Economics* 40: 279-298.

Ben-David, Dan. 1995. "Measuring Income Convergence: An Alternative Test," Tel Aviv University, *Foerder Institute Working Paper*, 41-95.

Brock, W. A., Hsieh, D. A., and LeBaron, B., 1993, *Nonlinear Dynamics, Chaos, and Instability: Statistical Theory and Economic Evidence.* The MIT Press, Cambridge, Massachusetts.

Campbell, J. Y. and Perron, P. 1991. "Pitfalls and Opportunities: What Macroeconomist Should Know About Unit Roots," *NBER Macroeconomics Annual.*

Dickey, D. and Fuller, W. A. 1979. "Distribution of the Estimators for Time Series Regressions with a Unit Root," *Journal of the American Statistical Association* 74: 427-431.

Edison, H. J., and Melvin, M. 1990. "The Determinants and Implications of the Choice of an Exchange Rate System," in W.S. Haraf and T.D. Willet (eds.), *Monetary Policy for Volatile Global Economy*, Washington, DC, The AEI Press, 1-44.

Edwards, S. 1993. "Exchange-rate Regimes as Nominal Anchors," *Weltwirtschaftliches Archiv*, 129(1), 1-32.

Greene, R. 1993. *"Econometric Analysis"*, 2nd Edition, Macmillan Publishing Company, New York, New York.

Halpern, L. and Wyplosz, C. 1995. "Equilibrium Real Exchange Rates in Transition," CEPR Discussion Paper No. 1145.

Hoerl, A. E. and Kennard, R. W. 1970. "Ridge Regression: Biased Estimation for Non-Orthogonal Problems," *Technometrics* 12: 55-82.

Koch, E. B. 1997. "Exchange Rates and Monetary Policy in Central Europe-A Survey of Some Issues," *MOCT-MOST,* 7(1), 1-48.

Kočenda, E. 1998a. *"Macroeconomy,"* III: 20-27. In: Turnovec, F. (ed.), Czech Republic 1997: The Year of Crisises. Praha: CERGE UK.

Kočenda, E. 1998b. "Discrepancy between Exchange Rate Regime and Monetary Policy" (in Czech), *Politická ekonomie*, 46(5), 661-666.

Kočenda, E., and Hanousek, J.1998. "Integration of Emerging Equity Markets: MajorAsian Players", *Korean Economic Review*, 14(1), 99-114.

Kočenda, E. and Papell, D. 1997. "Inflation Convergence within the European Union: A Panel Data Analysis," *International Journal of Finance and Economics* 3, 189-198.

Levin, A. and Lin, Chien-Fu. 1992. "Unit Root Tests in Panel Data: Asymptotic and Finite-Sample Properties," *University of California - San Diego Discussion Paper*: 92-23.

Ng, S. and Perron, P. 1995. "Unit Root Tests in ARMA Models with Data-Dependent Methods for the Selection of the Truncation Lag," *Journal of the American Statistical Association* 90: 268-281.

Papell, D. 1997. "Searching for Stationarity: Purchasing Power Parity Under the Current Float", *Journal of International Economics* 43: 313-332.

Quirk, P.J. 1994. "Fixed or Floating Exchange-rate Regimes: Does it Matter for Inflation?", IMF Working Paper 94/134.

Sachs, J. 1996. "Economic Transition and the Exchange-rate Regime," *American Economic Review Papers and Proceedings*, 86(May), 147-152.

Sarno, L. 1997. "Policy Convergence, the Exchange Rate Mechanism and the Misalignment of the Exchange Rates," *Applied Economics* 29, 591-605.

Schwarz, G., 1978. "Estimating the Dimension of a Model," *Annals of Statistics*, 6, 461-464.

Transition Report, 1997. European Bank for Reconstruction and Development.

In: European Economic and Political Issues, Volume 5　　ISBN 1-59033-322-5
Editor: Frank Columbus. pp. 49-69.　　© Nova Science Publishers, Inc.

Chapter 3

THE REDISTRIBUTIVE EFFECTS OF THE EU BUDGET: 1986-2000[*]

Rafael Doménech and Juan Varela

ABSTRACT

In this paper we analyze the redistributive effects among European countries of the EU budget, exploring the relationship between income and fiscal flows, both in per capita terms. As redistribution policies imply transferring income among members to alleviate persistent differences in per capita income levels, they can increase the speed of convergence of beneficiary countries to similar steady states. Using a new data set on EU budget data from 1986 to 1998, we find that the EU budget has a redistributive character, though only on its expenditure side. Of all expenditure categories we do consider, the most redistributive one is the regional fund, followed by the social fund and by the guarantee section of the EAGGF. All of them become increasingly redistributive in time. As far as total budgetary revenues are concerned, they show proportionality with income. When we consider the net financial balance, our analysis allows us to identify three groups of countries, given the treatment they get from the EU budget that cannot be explained by their per capita income levels.

INTRODUCTION

With the current process of monetary unification among European countries, the analysis of fiscal policy has attracted considerable attention in the last few years. The standard approach in this literature (Sachs and Sala-i-Martin, 1992, von Hagen, 1992 or Bayoumi and

---

[*] This is an updated version of the paper by Doménech, Maudes and Varela (2000) to 1989 and 2000, the first year of application of the European Council agreement on the Agenda 2000 (Berlin, March 1999). This paper has benefited from the valuable suggestions by José E. Boscá, Alberto Cerdán, Teresa Dabán, Ana de la Fuente, Angel de la Fuente. R. Doménech acknowledges the financial support of CICYT SEC99-0820 and Instituto de Economía Internacional (UV-EG). Address for comments: R. Doménech, Dpto. Análisis Económico, Universidad de Valencia, 46022-Valencia (SPAIN). e-mail: rafael.domenech@uv.es.

Masson, 1995) has consisted in the analysis of the experience in the United States or Canada to infer some empirical lessons for monetary union in Europe. Among the questions involved in this research line, two main issues have emerged. The first one relates to the need of a Community-wide fiscal arrangement to deal with asymmetric shocks affecting the members of the new monetary federation, in a similar way to the federal system in the United States or to the national fiscal systems in European countries, which allow to partially offset asymmetric cyclical fluctuations at the regional level (see Fatás, 1998). The second issue refers to the ability of federal or national systems to implement redistributional transfers between their members, and it has received a special attention by the European Commission since, in the end, nominal convergence imposed by the Maastricht Treaty was aimed to promote and to enhance real convergence among member states in the long run.

Although on some occasions no distinction is made between stabilization or redistribution policies, some authors, as von Hagen (1992) or Bayoumi and Masson (1995), have pointed out the convenience of analyzing them separately. Stabilization policies are often justified by the existence of transitory or cyclical deviations from trend output, that may be mitigated by the redistribution of income from regions or countries having a temporary expansion to those experiencing a transitory recession. Redistribution policies imply transferring income among members to alleviate persistent differences in per capita income levels and implementing policies that stimulate long-run growth in poorer countries or regions to reduce economic inequalities.

Redistribution policies are nowadays of greater importance in the EU budget. Over time, economic and social cohesion has become one of the pillars of the European Union, giving rise to policies aimed at the reduction of regional disparities, at the support of regions affected by economic change and at the development of human resources throughout the Union. These objectives have not only implied a firm political will by the Commission, but they have also been reflected in the treaties signed by member countries. Thus, Article 2 of the Treaty of the European Union states that "the Community shall have as its tasks, by establishing a common market and an economic and monetary union and by implementing common policies,... to promote throughout the Community a harmonious, balanced and sustainable development of economic activities, a high level of employment and of social protection, ... convergence of economic performance, ... and social cohesion and solidarity among Member States".

Over and above, when the Maastricht Treaty laid down the basis for establishing an Economic and Monetary Union by 1999, it was also decided to reduce some of the existing economic disparities among future members that could endanger this ambitious project, and also to address the risk that EMU could deepen regional disparities. Additionally, the Treaty's requirement (extended in the Stability and Growth Pact signed in Dublin in 1996) that limits budget deficits by a maximum of 3 percent of gross domestic product (GDP), also constrains the possibilities of poorer states of increasing their investments to catch up with their richer partners. In response to these questions, the Maastricht Treaty established a new Cohesion Fund to channel financial assistance to the four poorest states, which had a per capita GDP below the 90 percent of the Union's average in PPP terms. More recently, the European Commission has kept its willingness to maintain and even further increase in the future the weight that structural policies have in the European project.

This paper contributes in several respects to the existing literature on the analysis of fiscal policy in the EU. First, we present an exogenous growth model which allows us to simulate some of the effects of these policies upon the convergence process. Second, and probably more important, we use EU budget data. As far as we know, this is the first attempt to evaluate the redistributive effect of fiscal policy in Europe, through the usual econometric setup implemented to analyze the evidence in the United States and Canada, with this kind of data which make it possible to distinguish between different classes of revenues and expenditures.[1] Third, we provide a systematic examination of the correlations between EU budget aggregates for each country and relative income from 1986 to 1998. This allows us to analyze changes on the finance and the expenditure sides of the EU budget, and to undertake a preliminary evaluation of the effects of the enlargement of the EU to Austria, Finland and Sweden upon redistribution policies. Fourth, in contrast with the US experience where federal taxes play an important role in redistributing income across states (see, for example, Bayoumi and Masson, 1995), we find that member contributions to the EU budget are proportional to per capita incomes and that redistribution across European countries is mainly achieved through the different types of expenditures.

The structure of the paper is as follows. In section 2, we sketch a simple growth model in which we can analyze the impact of redistribution policies through a federal budget upon the convergence rate to the steady state. In section 3 we explain the source and characteristics of the data used in our empirical exercises and present preliminary evidence on fiscal flows among European countries through the EU budget. In section 4 we further explore the relationships between per capita income and countries' transfers from and contributions to the EU budget. Finally, section 5 concludes with the main results.

SOME THEORETICAL ISSUES

European countries have many reasons to justify the existence of redistribution policies. In particular, as stated in different treaties, the European Community shall aim at reducing disparities between the levels of development of member states and the backwardness of the least favored regions. However, it can be argued that these policies do not aim to support a continuous and constant transfer from richer to poorer countries, but to establish appropriate conditions in which a backward economy can catch up with the leading ones more quickly than in the absence of such policies. In the long run, the financial assistance to a given country or region vanishes as disparities with the rest of the Union disappear. In other words, we can say that redistribution policies aspire to speed up the convergence process of poorer countries or regions to the average Community level.

Since European redistribution policies aim to accelerate the transition of backward economies to richer countries, the neoclassical growth model with exogenous growth can be extended conveniently to analyze this kind of policies.[2] The way in which we cope with this question is by allowing for the existence of net foreign transfers when a country has a per capita income below the Union average, which accelerates the convergence process among Union members. Our approach is somewhat similar to the one proposed by Barro et al.

---

[1] There are in the literature other papers that use this kind of data, although with different purposes or approaches. For example, Martín (2000) uses data from the Annual Report of the Court of Auditors to compute Gini coefficients in 1986 and 1996, showing that redistribution is mainly achieved through the regional fund.

[2] As Temple (1999) has pointed out, it is difficult, at the empirical level, to distinguish between endogenous growth and long transitional dynamics in a model of exogenous growth. In our case, it is important to notice that this redistribution policies do not aim to have permanent effects upon growth rates.

(1995), in the context of open economies with partial capital mobility. In their model, borrowing on world markets can only partially finance the accumulation of capital, allowing for a slightly faster convergence rate than in closed economies.

For simplicity, we focus on a country or region in which per capita income is below the average Union level, and we let aside questions related with the federal budget balance.[3] According to the main priorities of fiscal policy in the EU, we assume that this country will receive transfers from the federal budget only during the transition to a steady state that is similar for all Union countries.[4]

The available technology for this economy is given by the following production function:

$$Y = A K_p^{\alpha} K_g^{\beta} \left(L e^{gt} \right)^{1-\alpha-\beta} \tag{1}$$

where Y is aggregate output, K_p is the private capital stock in a broad sense (that is, it may include, not only physical capital, but also human or R&D capital, in line with Mankiw et al., 1992 or Nonneman and Vanhoudt, 1996), K_g is the public capital stock, L is labor supply, and g is the exogenous rate of growth, A is a technology scale parameter, $\alpha>0$, $\beta>0$ and $\alpha+\beta<1$.

Equation (1) can be rewritten in units of effective labor as:

$$y = A k_p^{\alpha} k_g^{\beta} \tag{2}$$

where

$$y = \frac{Y}{L e^{gt}}, k_p = \frac{K_p}{L e^{gt}} \text{ and } k_g = \frac{K_g}{L e^{gt}}.$$

Now, we assume that, in units of effective labor, all transfers from and contributions to the federal budget tr^{UE} can be synthesized by three different kinds of flows.[5] The first one comprises all transfers this economy receives to accumulate public capital. The second type of flows are related to the accumulation of private capital, such as agricultural machinery, R&D funds or labor training funds. The third one comprises the net balance between contributions to the federal budget and the rest of transfers such as, for example, non structural agricultural funds. If we assume that, for simplicity, these types of flows are only explained by the difference between the average per capita income level of the Union and that of this country, we have: [6]

---

[3] These two assumptions could be relaxed in a two country model that accounts explicitly for a balanced federal budget. Given the purpose of this paper, these extensions to the model presented here do not change the main implications that we want to address.

[4] It is obvious that European countries present similar, although not identical, determinants of their long run per capita income levels. Nonetheless, the assumption of similar steady states that we make for simplicity can be relaxed to allow for the existence of small differences in the per capita incomes of the Union countries.

[5] Because of the presence of these transfers, the budget restriction for this economy in efficiency units is given by: $y=c+i+xm$, where c and i include private and public expenditures in consumption and investment respectively, and $xm=- tr^{UE}$.

[6] Accepting that all countries have access to the same technology (that is, a common A and g), differences in per capita income are proportional to differences in income in efficiency units. For simplicity, the relations between fiscal flows and income in this equation are linear. In section 4 we consider a more convenient log-linear relationship.

$$tr^{EU} = tr_{k_g}^{EU} + tr_{k_p}^{EU} + tr_y^{EU} = \left(\phi_{k_g} + \phi_{k_p} + \phi_y \right) \left(y^{EU} - y \right) \tag{3}$$

In this economy there are two production factors which can be accumulated. The first one is public capital. We assume that

$$\dot{k}_g = \tau \left[y + \phi_y \left(y^{EU} - y \right) \right] - (n + g + \delta) k_g + \phi_{k_g} \left(y^{EU} - y \right) \tag{4}$$

where τ is the income tax rate, n is the growth rate of labor and δ is the depreciation rate. As we can see, if $\phi_y > 0$ and $\phi_{kg} > 0$ this economy accumulates more public capital than in the closed economy case. It is also important to notice that, since there is public capital accumulation, this factor is used in the production of goods as a conventional stock and not like the services from public goods, as in Barro's (1991) model.

Private capital accumulation is given by the following law of motion:

$$\dot{k}_p = s(1-\tau) \left[y + \phi_y \left(y^{EU} - y \right) \right] - (n + g + \delta) k_p + \phi_{k_p} \left(y^{EU} - y \right) \tag{5}$$

where s is the saving rate. As we focus on fiscal transfers and we want to compare our results with the standard growth model for a closed economy, we do not consider the possibility of borrowing on world markets as Barro et al. (1995), although this extension, as well as the analysis of its implications upon the convergence rate, is straightforward.

Given the parameter values in the production function (1) the model exhibits exogenous growth. Therefore, changes in s or τ have only level effects on income measured in units of effective labor. In the steady state the growth rate of the variables in efficiency units is zero, $y^{EU} = y*$ and income in efficiency units is given by:

$$y^* = A^{\frac{1}{1-\alpha-\beta}} \left(\frac{\tau}{\delta + g + n} \right)^{\frac{\beta}{1-\alpha-\beta}} \left(\frac{s(1-\tau)}{\delta + g + n} \right)^{\frac{\alpha}{1-\alpha-\beta}} \tag{6}$$

Finally, using the production function, by Taylor approximation of (4) and (5) we can obtain the convergence equation of per capita income ($\tilde{y}_t$) to its steady state:

$$\frac{\dot{\tilde{y}}}{\tilde{y}_t} = g - \lambda \left[\ln \tilde{y}_{t-1} - \ln A - gt - \alpha \ln k_p^* - \beta \ln k_g^* \right] \tag{7}$$

where

$$\lambda = (1 - \alpha - \beta) \tilde{\delta} + \alpha \left[s(1-\tau) \phi_y + \phi_{k_p} \right] \frac{\tilde{\delta}}{s(1-\tau)} + \beta \left(\tau \phi_y + \phi_{k_g} \right) \frac{\tilde{\delta}}{\tau} \tag{8}$$

and

$$\tilde{\delta} = \delta + g + n$$

As we can see, if fiscal flows are not related with income ($\phi_y = \phi_{kp} = \phi_{kg} = 0$), then (8) simplifies to the usual convergence rate in an extended Solow model (see Barro and Sala-i-Martin, 1996).

Now, it is possible to calibrate this model to evaluate some implications of these fiscal flows upon the convergence process. In order to compare the performance of this model with the existing results in the literature, we have chosen conventional parameter values. In particular, as we want a convergence rate of 2 percent for the closed economy without fiscal flows, we impose $\alpha = 2/3$ and $\delta = 0.05$, $g = 0.02$ and $n = 0.01$. The choice of β is more problematic given the range in the estimates of public investment returns (see Gramlich, 1994, and Sturm, Kuper and de Haan, 1997). In accordance with the estimations of Otto and Voss (1998) and De la Fuente (1997), we set β at 0.08. On the other hand, if we assume an optimal tax finance then τ should be equal to $\beta/(\alpha+\beta)$.[7] The saving rate has been set at 0.2, taking into account not only private physical investment but also education and R&D expenditures. Finally, as we estimate in section four, the aggregate value of $\phi_y + \phi_{kp} + \phi_{kg}$ is close to 0.05. Therefore, we analyze different values of ϕ_y, ϕ_{kp} and ϕ_{kg} maintaining constant $\phi_y + \phi_{kp} + \phi_{kg}$ at 0.05.[8]

In Figure 1 we present the transitional dynamics of a country that is 10 percent below its steady state in three different environments. The first one is the closed economy environment in which $\lambda = 0.02$, that we use as a benchmark case, taking approximately 35 years to close half of the gap with the steady state. In the second one, net transfers are only used in private capital accumulation, so $\phi_{kp} = 0.05$ and $\phi_y + \phi_{kg} = 0.0$. In this case, the convergence rate is higher than in the previous environment, and it takes approximately 18 years to close half of gap with the steady state. Finally, we assume that $\phi_{kg} = 0.05$ and $\phi_y + \phi_{kp} = 0.0$, that is, net transfers from the Union budget are only used in public capital accumulation. In this case, the economy close half of the gap in 28 years. Since the coefficients of ϕ_y and ϕ_{kg} are equal in (8) when τ is set at its optimal level $\beta/(\alpha+\beta)$, the convergence rate is not affected by changes in ϕ_{kg} holding $\phi_y + \phi_{kp}$ constant. These convergence rates can also be increased if it is possible to finance the accumulation of private capital by borrowing from world markets, in the presence of some credit constraints as in Barro, Mankiw and Sala-i-Martin (1995) model, to avoid an infinite speed of convergence. It is worth noting that convergence rates larger than the traditional 2 per cent have been recently estimated in the empirical growth literature, as for example, in the contributions of Islam (1995), Caselli, Esquivel and Lefort (1996), and Lee, Pesaran and Smith (1997).

The model can be easily extended to consider the possibility of bureaucratic inefficiencies, corruption of other distortions affecting the contribution of redistribution policies upon accumulation rates. We can interpret the preceding model as a particular case in which we imposed the maximum effectiveness of Union transfers. In the extreme case in which transfers do not increase accumulation rates in (4) and (5), even with redistribution policies, the model collapses to the standard exogenous growth model with no effects upon

---

[7]   In this model τ has level but not growth effects. The optimal tax level is easily obtained maximizing income in units of effective labour.
[8]   Since A is only a scale parameter, we choose its value to satisfy $y^{UE} = 1.0$.

the convergence rate. Therefore, administrative controls and meticulous evaluations of projects are as important as generous transfers in order to accelerate the convergence process.

Figure 1. Convergence paths to the steady state under different redistribution policies.

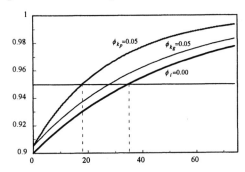

As a summary, the main properties of the model that we have presented are the following. First, because of the assumptions we have made, steady state income levels are not affected by redistribution policies. Second, as in any exogenous growth model, changes in the saving rate or in the income tax rate have only level effects upon long run per capita income levels, although they affect the rate of growth during the transition. Third, and more important, the convergence rate to the steady states is higher when ϕ_y, ϕ_{kp} or ϕ_{kg} are positive, even though for reasonable parameter values it is preferable to finance private capital accumulation. Given the importance of the values of these parameters upon convergence rates, in the rest of the paper we focus precisely on the analysis of the relationships between per capita income levels and country transfers from and contributions to the EU budget.

DATA AND PRELIMINARY EVIDENCE

In order to analyze the redistribution effects emanating from EU's budget policy, we need complete information about the geographic distribution of European revenues and the allocation of operating expenditure among EU member states. Although the basic information for this exercise is available at national level we call the attention to some qualifications which condition our analysis. As the European Commission (1998) has pointed out, the fiscal balance of each country does not account for all the economic benefits that they derive from the Union due, at least, by three main reasons. First, there are some important indirect gains which are not taken into account when comparing fiscal balances between countries, such as spillover effects stemming from, for example, the development of European transport networks. Second, there are some difficulties in determining the nationality of the final beneficiaries of the different expenditures of the EU budget. Finally, the EU funds are heterogeneous across countries and direct comparisons between diverse categories of these expenditures are not easy.

With respect to the time dimension of the information used, this paper draws its conclusions from the budgetary information of the 1986 to 2000 period, in which the EU budget has exhibited important changes. It must be remembered that the political and institutional equilibrium of the Community's financial regime was being eroded from 1975 to 1987. This euroskeptic period was characterized by a stalled budget procedure and a rapidly growing gap between resources and expenditures in the EC. To solve this institutional crisis, an interinstitutional accord was approved in 1988, in which the European Parliament, the Council of Ministers and the Commission reached an agreement dealing with the budgetary procedures of the EU that made it possible to define the main budgetary priorities for a multi-year period. The first agreement was reached in Brussels in February 1988 and it concerned the Financial Perspectives for the 1988 to 1992 period, the so-called Delors's package, which was closely related to the Single European Act. Taking into account that this programming tool was one of the most successful reforms, the European institutions reached a new institutional agreement at the European Council of Edinburgh in December 1992, the Delors II proposal.

As far as the raw data are concerned, there is a wide variety of sources providing accounting information about the European Union. Nevertheless, the most reliable information unanimously uses the Commission accounting system (SINCOM) as the source for data on resources and allocations. This is the system used by the *Annual Report* of the Court of Auditors and by the *Allocation of Operating Expenditure by Member State* of the European Commission, which constitute the most complete EU budget data sets.[9]

On the revenue side, given the relative magnitudes of the contributions of each member state to the EU budget, we classify the available information in four different groups: net traditional own resources, VAT and GNP revenues and total resources. The latter comprises aggregate resources coming from each member state, which also include the budget adjustments from the previous financial year and miscellaneous revenue. Similarly, on the expenditure side, in order to simplify our analysis, we only distinguish four different groups: the guarantee section of the European Agricultural Guarantee and Guidance Fund (EAGGF), Social Funds, Regional Funds and total expenditures. It should be noted that Regional Funds include structural actions but not the Cohesion Fund, that appears as part of total expenditures.

All the Court of Auditors information is provided in current ECUs or euros. As we discuss in the next section, given the econometric specifications that we use (variables are in logarithms and regressions include time dummies), working with current variables in ECUs or euros is not a drawback. Nonetheless, from an economic point of view it is also relevant to conduct some of the analysis with variables expressed in PPPs, since they provide complementary information to gauge the economic gains that a given country gets from EU fiscal flows.

In Table 1 we present the average EU countries' fiscal flows from and contributions to the European budget, from 1995 to 2000, expressed as a percentage of their GDPs, and their relative per capita incomes in PPPs.[10] As we can see, agricultural funds (x^{ag}) represent less than 1 per cent of GDP on average, but in the case of Greece and Ireland this percentage is around 3 percent. Among richer countries, Denmark could also be considered an outlier since,

---

[9] The data used in this paper and its technical details are available at http:/iei.uv.es/~rdomenec/EUbudget.html.

[10] We compute these average for this period because the enlargement of the EU to Austria, Finland and Sweden in 1995. Contributions from the EU budget for these countries in 1995 show a clear different pattern to that observed in 1996 and 1998. Per capita income is defined as the ratio of GDP to population. Data for these variables, as well as for PPPs, come from OECD's *National Accounts* and *Purchasing Power Parities and Real Expenditures*, Volume I, 1993.

in per capita terms, it is receiving above twice as much funds as other countries with similar incomes. Greece and Ireland, jointly with Portugal and Spain, are again well above the EU average in the case of regional funds (x^r). Social funds expenditures (x^s) only represent 0.15 percent on average, with the same group of countries above this level. The preceding magnitudes do not include the Cohesion Fund. When we compare total EU expenditures among member states (x^G), we can evaluate the importance of this fund relative to the GDP of the four poorest countries: Spain, Portugal, Greece and Ireland receive at least more than twice as much as any other EU country. When we focus on the contribution side, we get a very different picture.

As far as the VAT contribution (x^{VAT}) is concerned, there are no clear outliers from the EU average, with the exception of the United Kingdom, that is well below due to the British check or compensation introduced in the 1984 Fontainebleau summit.[11] As expected, the GNP contribution (x^{GNP}) of each member state in GDP percentage points is approximately the same, being the EU average 0.31 percent.[12] With respect to the own traditional resources contributions (x^{own}), there is more variability among member states, notably because the performance of Belgium and the Netherlands, explained by the so called "Rotterdam effect" which states that in small open economies the EU's traditional own resources contribution is large, in per capita terms, due to the fact that they are foreign trade oriented and non EU goods pay duties in the country where they are introduced in the Community's territory, which is not necessarily the country where they are consumed or transformed.[13] When we aggregate these revenues, total contributions as a percentage of GDP (x^T) range from 0.85 of Italy and 1.47 in the case of the Netherlands.

Finally, the net financial balance in terms of the GDP (x^{G-T}) shows that Ireland, Greece, Portugal and, to a lesser extent, Spain are the main beneficiaries of the EU budget, while the Netherlands, Germany, Luxembourg and Sweden present the largest transfers as a share of their domestic production. The negative budget position of some of these countries has been a main concern of the European Commission (1998), and it partially explains that, according to the Agenda 2000 approved at Berlin in 1998, Austria, Germany, the Netherlands and Sweden will benefit in the future with a reduction of a 25 per cent in their contributions to finance the British check.

ECONOMETRIC RESULTS

In this section we further explore the relationships between per capita income levels and country transfers from and contributions to the EU budget that, as we have seen in the second section are crucial to quantify the effects upon convergence rates to countries' steady states.

---

[11] The British check is the United Kingdom's abatement to its EU budget contribution calculated as two-thirds of the difference between its VAT share and its EU allocated expenditure share.

[12] In principle, GNP contributions must be strictly proportional to the GNP levels, that in most European countries are fairly similar to their GDPs. However, on a cash basis, this may not happen for a given year t since these contributions are subject to ex-post adjustments due to several factors such as revisions in GNP estimates or differences between the exchange rates in February t-1, used in the EU budget for year t passed by the EU Parliament, and the exchange rates in December t-1, which is the one finally used to make the payments in year t.

[13] The Berlin Council in 1998 decided an increase of the collection fees in traditional own resources from 10 to 25 per cent. This change will mitigate the Rotterdam effect in the total contributions of Belgium and the Netherlands.

We do not perform a formal test of our model. First, given the small length of the sample period (from 1986 to 2000) it is difficult to evaluate the long run effects of these redistribution policies. Second, given the information available, it is not possible to distinguish the part of the transfers that finance private or public capital. In other words, we cannot get estimates of ϕ_y, ϕ_{kp} and ϕ_{kg} separately. Instead, we concentrate in the estimation of relationships as the one stated by (3) in the model analyzed in the second section for different categories of expenditures and contributions. Therefore, the objective of this section is to end up with an estimate of $\phi=\phi_y+\phi_{kp}+\phi_{kg}$ for the net balance, as a way of testing a necessary condition to accelerate the convergence process among European countries.[14]

Table 1. Principal EU Budget Magnitudes as a Percentage of the GNP for each Member. 1995-2000

Country	Code	Expenditures				Resources					
		x^{ag}	x^r	x^s	x^G	x^{VAT}	x^{GNP}	x^{own}	x^T	x^{G-T}	y_i/y_{EL}
Austria	A	0.43	0.03	0.05	0.69	0.55	0.38	0.13	1.07	-0.38	1.09
Belgium	B	0.49	0.05	0.05	0.87	0.48	0.39	0.48	1.33	-0.46	1.16
Germany	D	0.30	0.07	0.06	0.51	0.54	0.38	0.18	1.10	-0.60	1.05
Denmark	DK	0.86	0.02	0.04	1.03	0.45	0.37	0.19	1.01	0.02	1.15
Spain	E	0.95	0.54	0.27	2.25	0.52	0.37	0.14	1.03	1.22	0.81
Finland	SF	0.47	0.07	0.08	0.92	0.48	0.38	0.13	0.99	-0.07	0.97
France	F	0.71	0.06	0.06	0.93	0.54	0.37	0.12	1.03	-0.11	1.07
United Kingdom	GB	0.33	0.06	0.07	0.54	0.27	0.38	0.27	0.90	-0.36	1.02
Greece	GR	2.40	1.30	0.28	4.80	0.56	0.39	0.15	1.10	3.70	0.66
Ireland	IRL	2.67	0.66	0.48	4.62	0.59	0.39	0.33	1.31	3.31	0.95
Italy	I	0.44	0.19	0.07	0.81	0.43	0.37	0.12	0.91	-0.11	1.00
Luxembourg	L	0.12	0.02	0.03	0.65	0.59	0.39	0.13	1.11	-0.46	1.84
Netherlands	NL	0.45	0.02	0.05	0.61	0.53	0.37	0.48	1.38	-0.77	1.10
Portugal	P	0.69	1.52	0.57	3.83	0.56	0.36	0.18	1.10	2.73	0.70
Sweden	S	0.29	0.03	0.04	0.54	0.50	0.38	0.18	1.07	-0.53	0.99
Average EU (weighted)		0.53	0.15	0.09	0.94	0.49	0.37	0.19	1.05	-	1.00

Before estimating ϕ, it is illustrative to analyze the way EU redistribution policies are implemented. We do so estimating the following regressions:

$$\ln \tilde{x}_{it}^j = \gamma_{0t}^j + \gamma_{1t}^j \ln \tilde{y}_{it} + \varepsilon_{it}, \qquad (9)$$

---

[14] As we have shown in the second section, notice that this condition is necessary but not sufficient.

where $\bar{y}_{it}$ is per capita income of country i in year t, $\bar{x}_{it}^{j}$ are the different categories of transfers and revenues considered in per capita terms, and t=1986,...,1998. In general, we could think of different economic or socio-political variables, that for convenience we include in vector **z**, explaining the per capita levels of transfers and contributions for each European country, that is,

$$\ln \bar{x}_{it}^{j} = f(z_{it}^{j}) \tag{10}$$

For example, z_{it}^{j} could contain information about the share of agriculture in GDP, unemployment rates, population in regions that are classified as Objective 1 by the European Commission, the outside-EU trade for each country, etc. In other words, z_{it}^{j} summarizes the European legislation, shaped by a large number of rules which have changed over the years, concerning each transfer and contribution. However, we do not want to recover these rules used by the European Commission to calculate different aggregates. Instead, we want to uncover the intensity of redistribution through different expenditures and contributions, that is, (9) just tests one hypothesis: to what extent does all this legislation have a redistributive effect between European countries. Therefore, the empirical results we present in this section should not be evaluated in terms of the fit of the regressions but by the value and the significance of per capita income coefficients.

It is important to point out some issues related with the estimation of (9). First, this equation is estimated in levels. As it is usual in this literature (e.g., in Bayoumi and Masson, 1995), with this specification we analyze redistribution, whereas estimation in growth rates evaluate fiscal stabilization. Second, by estimating cross-sectional regressions in different years, we can analyze the stability of the coefficients of $\ln \bar{y}_{it}$. If these coefficients remain constant across periods we can impose the restriction $\gamma_{1t}^{j} = \gamma_{1}^{j}$, allowing the estimation of an equation with different intercepts using pooled data. Another possibility is that γ_{1t}^{j} may show a trend pattern. In this case we can estimate the following equation using again pooled data:

$$\ln \bar{x}_{it}^{j} = \gamma_{0t}^{j} + \gamma_{1}^{j} \ln \bar{y}_{it} + \gamma_{2}^{j} \ln \bar{y}_{it} \, t + \gamma_{3t} \, d_{t+} \, \varepsilon_{it}, \tag{11}$$

where d_t are time dummies and t is a trend. If γ_{2}^{j} is positive (negative) the elasticity of $\bar{x}_{it}^{j}$ with respect to $\bar{y}_{it}$ increases (decreases) when moving from 1986 to 2000 .

The acceptance of the hypotheses $\gamma_{1t}^{j} = \gamma_{1}^{j}$ opens the possibility of testing other kind of restrictions once we have sufficient degrees of freedom. For example, pooled regressions allow to analyze the sensitivity of our results to the exclusion of some countries. These exercises are interesting because we can analyze the importance of redistributing EU budget flows when we exclude from the sample clear outliers, if they exist, or countries that benefit exceptionally from Community transfers, as well as countries that have recently become EU members. In the latter case, we can test whether the enlargement of the European Community to Austria, Finland and Sweden in 1995 has implied any change upon the redistributive effects of fiscal flows between prior members, from which we may infer some lessons to future enlargements.

Besides the differences in the data used (fiscal flows between EU countries instead of regional or state data for the United States or Canada), our approach differs somewhat from other related researches in the literature. Bayoumi and Masson (1995) implement a strategy consisting in running different regressions with pooled data from 1969 to 1986, both in growth rates and in levels, to analyze fiscal stabilization and long term redistribution respectively. In their article the regressor is per capita personal income, before federal taxes and transfers, and dependent variables are different combinations of personal income after taxes and before or after social insurance, transfers or grants. They also test for the stability of their results for three subperiods, with no evidence of statistically significant changes in the estimated coefficients. Although the approach of von Hagen (1992) is more similar to ours because the main regressor is real gross state products and dependent variables are real federal income taxes and expenditures, he mainly focuses on regressions in growth rates using data for the period from 1981 to 1986 and estimates a system of seemingly unrelated regressions with one equation for each year. Finally, Sala-i-Martin and Sachs (1992) estimate one equation for each region relating relative (to the US) real income to relative taxes and transfers for the sample period 1978-88, in per capita terms, rejecting the hypothesis of regional equality in transfers responses to income but not in taxes responses to income. Instead of holding constant the elasticity across countries (as von Hagen, 1992) or across periods (as Sala-i-Martin and Sachs, 1992), we analyze the sensitivity of our results to changes in the sample in both directions.

In Figure 2 we show the OLS estimated values of γ_{1t}^{j} in (9) and their confidence intervals for the expenditure side using variables in ECUs or euros.[15] The estimated coefficients for agricultural funds (γ_{1t}^{ag}) show a slight downward trend from 1986 to 1992 and subsequently they stabilize around a value of -0.60, although we cannot reject the hypothesis that γ_{1t}^{ag} are all equal to zero. In the case of regional funds (γ_{1t}^{r}), these coefficients are negative and statistically significant and there is a clear downward trend from 1986 to 2000. These findings indicate not only that regional funds are negatively related with per capita income but also that this redistributive effect has increased over time. Social funds' coefficients (γ_{1t}^{s}) are also negative and statistically significant for most of the years, although their redistributive effects remain practically constant around a smaller value in absolute terms (-1.40) than that for regional funds. Finally, total expenditures show a negative relationship with per capita income. The estimated coefficients (γ_{1t}^{G}) are not statistically different from zero but, with the exception of 1986 and 1994, they are statistically different from 1.0. The average value of γ_{1t}^{G} is equal to -0.43, implying that on average a 1 percent increase in a country's per capita income decreases the per capita funds it receives from the EU budget by 0.43 percent.

---

[15] Confidence intervals do not change very much when we use White's heterokedasticity correction.

Figure 2. Estimated Values of γ_{it} and Their Confidence Intervals at 95 Percent for Different Expenditure Categories

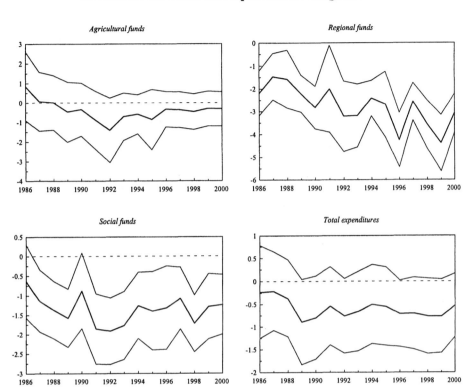

In Figure 3 we present a similar exercise for the revenue side of the EU budget. The estimated coefficients of VAT contributions (γ_{1t}^{VAT}) are, in general, not statistically different from one.[16] GNP contributions started in 1990, although in that year this resource had a negligible importance because it only represented on average 0.62 percent of countries' total contributions. This explains that our regressions initiate in 1991. In this year, and also in 1992, the coefficients of GNP contributions (γ_{1t}^{GNP}) are statistically significant and larger than one, implying that in those years this resource was not proportional to income. Nonetheless, in successive years we can safely accept the hypothesis of proportionality. The coefficients of own traditional resources (γ_{1t}^{own}) are in general less than 1.0 (the average value is 0.94), although they are not statistically different from this value. Finally, the elasticity of total contributions to income in per capita terms (γ_{1t}^{T}) is on average equal to 1.03, and we can accept again that this elasticity is time invariant and equal to 1.0, that is, if a country's per capita income increases by 1 percent its total per capita contribution to the EU budget increases by the same amount. This result is in contrast with the evidence shown by

---

[16] The exception is 1987, although in this case we can accept the hypothesis γ_{1t}^{VAT} =1.0 at a 10 percent significant level.

Bayoumi and Masson (1995) for the United States, where the contribution of each state to the federal budget have a redistributive character.

Figure 3. Estimated Values of γ_{it} and Their Confidence Intervals at 95 Percent for Different Countries' Contributions to the EU Budget

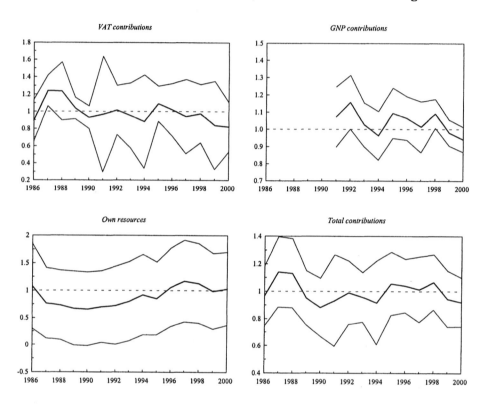

In summary, we have found that per capita contributions increase proportionally to per capita income as a country becomes richer, but the Community funds received remain constant or even decrease. This result implies that the EU budget has a clear redistributive effect on the income of its members in per capita terms, and that this effect is driven by expenditure criteria but not by revenue ones, confirming the results of other researches that use alternative methodologies (see, for example, Martín, 2000). Figure 4 summarizes these findings and shows the estimated coefficient ϕ_1 in the following regression:

$$\ln \bar{y}_{it} = \phi_0 + \phi_1 \ln(\bar{y}_{it} - \bar{x}_{it}^G + \bar{x}_{it}^T) + v_{it} \tag{12}$$

where ϕ_1 is the elasticity of the observed per capita GDP to income before transfers from and taxes to the European Union. The interpretation of this coefficient is straightforward. If $\phi_1 \geq 1$ fiscal flows among EU members have no redistributive effects, while if $\phi_1 < 1$ the EU budget reduces per capita income in rich countries and increases that of poor ones. In fact, we can approximate (12) by:[17]

$$\frac{\tilde{x}_{it}^G - \tilde{x}_{it}^T}{\tilde{y}_{it}} = \frac{1-\phi_1}{\phi_1} \frac{\tilde{y}_t^{EU} - \tilde{y}_{it}}{\tilde{y}_{it}} + v_{it} \tag{13}$$

that has the same interpretation as (3) in our model of the second section. For example, in 1993 we find that $\phi_1 = 0.955$ and it is statistically different from 1, so $\phi = \dfrac{1-\phi_1}{\phi_1} = 0.047$. As the confidence interval for ϕ is given by (0.022, 0.071) we can accept the necessary condition $\phi > 0$ to accelerate the convergence process among European countries.

Figure 4. Estimated Values of Coefficient ϕ_1 in (12)

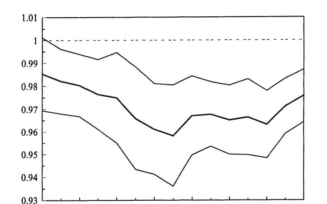

In Table 2 we present the estimated values of γ_1^j and γ_2^j in (11) for the four categories of expenditures and revenues, expressed in ECUs or euros and in per capita terms.[18] The first three columns of results refer to the current fifteen EU members. At the beginning of our sample, agricultural funds were positively correlated with income although the negative value of γ_2^{ag} implies that these funds became negatively correlated with income after 1988. This result was also pointed out by Figure 2. As we can see, γ_1^j is also significant for regional and social funds, having in both cases a negative sign. The trend in the coefficients of these variables is no longer present when we consider total expenditures, confirming again the results displayed in Figure 2. It is also meaningful to note that the coefficient of γ_1^G is negative although not different from zero.

---

[17] We assume that when $\ln \tilde{y}_{it} = \ln \tilde{y}_{EU}$ then $\tilde{x}_{it}^G + \tilde{x}_{it}^T = 0$ so $\phi_0 = (1-\phi_1)\ln \tilde{y}_{EU}$.

[18] These regressions include time dummies for each year in the sample. The inclusion of these dummies has the advantage that, as the variables appear in logarithms, we do not need to express them in constant terms (e.g., using a GDP deflator for the EU).

When we exclude Ireland from these regressions we find that γ_1^j increases for the four expenditure categories.[19] The differences between the estimates in column (5) and (2) give an approximation to the magnitudes of the specific budgetary benefits for this country. In the case of Luxembourg we find mixed results. The exclusion of this country increases the elasticity between agricultural funds and income (through γ_1^{ag}, that becomes positive), but, with the exception of 1986 and 1987, also decreases the elasticity between regional funds and income (through the increase in the absolute value of γ_2^r). In other words, the exclusion of Luxembourg increases the redistribution effects of regional funds but decreases those of agricultural funds. Finally, when comparing the results for the EU15 with those of the EU12 we do not find any remarkable difference, suggesting that the enlargement in 1995 of the EU did not have any effects upon fiscal flows between European countries and the EU budget.

On the revenue side, the comparison of the results for the four country samples considered does not yield any noteworthy difference, with the exception of the own traditional resources coefficient that increases notably (by 20 percent) when we exclude Luxembourg. Although Luxembourg is a small open economy, the Rotterdam effect does not apply because most of its imports coming from non EU countries enter the Union through foreign customs.

When we estimate the same equations as in Table 2 with the variables expressed in PPPs, the overall results of the comparisons across country samples remain valid.[20] However, there are some interesting variations in the estimated coefficients of (11) when we change from variables in ECUs to variables in PPPs. In general, there is a stronger negative correlation between per capita expenditure variables and income. Agricultural funds are negatively correlated with income from the beginning of the sample, and the estimated coefficients for the other two funds and for total expenditures are larger in absolute value. On the revenue side, the estimated coefficients are slightly higher but, interestingly, per capita income explains a smaller variance of per capita contributions to the EU budget. This result suggests that the financing of the Community budget takes into account differences in countries' per capita incomes using current exchange rates of national currencies to the ECU or the euro, while expenditures are based upon income differentials after accounting for disparities in price levels.

Another way of analyzing the implications of using current exchange rates or PPPs is through the estimation of (12) twelve times (given the insufficient number of observations we exclude Austria, Finland and Sweden from this analysis), including a single country dummy each time. In Figure 5 we present the estimated values of these dummies using both types of conversion rates. Countries outside the grey areas have statistically significant dummies. The dummies for Portugal and United Kingdom are statistically significant when we express variables in ECUs or euros but not in PPPs. In other cases, there are some differences in the estimated values of country dummies. Thus, the ranking of countries that specially benefit from the EU budget in per capita terms (Ireland, Greece and Luxembourg), after accounting for per capita income differentials, changes when we use variables expressed in PPPs instead

---

[19] The exclusion of Ireland and Luxembourg in these regressions is justified by the fact that these are two small countries which, given their specificities, can bias the results for the whole sample. In fact, the results obtained when we exclude these two countries are similar to those obtained weighting the observations by population size.

[20] These results are available upon request from the authors.

of in ECUs or euros. Something similar happens in the ranking of countries for which the estimated dummies are negative (Portugal, Spain and United Kingdom).

Table 2. Redistribution through fiscal flows. Variables in ECUs

	EU15			EU15-IRL		EU15-LUX		EU12	
	γ_1^j	γ_2^j	R^2	γ_1^j	γ_2^j	γ_1^j	γ_2^j	γ_1^j	γ_2^j
$\ln \bar{x}_{it}^{ag}$	-0.01	-0.06	0.11	0.26	-0.07	1.04	-0.11	-0.01	-0.05
	(0.01)	(1.44)		(0.92)	(1.91)	(3.75)	(3.11)	(0.01)	(1.28)
$\ln \bar{x}_{it}^{r}$	-1.76	-0.14	0.67	-1.57	-0.15	-2.22	-0.14	-1.77	-0.14
	(6.60)	(4.11)		(6.31)	(4.63)	(8.75)	(4.16)	(6.43)	(3.74)
$\ln \bar{x}_{it}^{s}$	-0.01	-0.01	0.33	-0.01	-0.01	-0.02	-0.01	-0.01	-0.01
	(2.57)	(2.59)		(2.63)	(6.51)	(2.33)	(2.80)	(2.50)	(2.31)
$\ln \bar{x}_{it}^{G}$	-0.42	-0.03	0.29	-0.21	-0.03	0.01	-0.10	-0.43	-0.02
	(2.21)	(1.02)		(1.30)	(1.68)	(0.04)	(3.60)	(2.20)	(0.73)
$\ln \bar{x}_{it}^{VAT}$	1.10	-0.01	0.76	1.12	-0.02	1.06	-0.02	1.10	-0.02
	(14.0)	(1.46)		(13.7)	(1.49)	(11.9)	(1.88)	(13.4)	(1.53)
$\ln \bar{x}_{it}^{GNP}$	1.15	-0.01	0.98	1.14	-0.01	1.27	-0.02	1.16	-0.01
	(16.3)	(1.63)		(15.9)	(1.50)	(15.8)	(2.77)	(15.3)	(1.60)
$\ln \bar{x}_{it}^{own}$	0.75	0.02	0.37	0.83	0.02	1.14	0.01	0.73	0.03
	(4.83)	(1.00)		(5.33)	(0.88)	(7.11)	(0.27)	(4.60)	(1.24)
$\ln \bar{x}_{it}^{T}$	1.02	-0.01	0.91	1.06	-0.01	1.08	-0.01	1.02	-0.01
	(19.8)	(0.62)		(20.8)	(0.96)	(18.3)	(1.26)	(18.9)	(0.49)
$Obs.^a$	198			183		183		180	

^{a} Sample period 1986-2000, except for $\ln \bar{x}_{it}^{GNP}$, 1991-2000

Finally, we have also tested if there has been any remarkable change in the estimated coefficient of these country dummies during the sample period we are analyzing. We have considered two different periods taking 1993, when the transfers associated to cohesion fund begun, as the partitioning year. As we can see in Figure 6, there is a clear positive relationship between the estimated values of these dummies in both periods, when we express the variables in ECUs. However, for some countries there are some important changes since their dummies become significant from 1993 to 1998. Thus, taking into account their per capita incomes, Portugal and Luxembourg clearly improve their final balance with the EU budget in the second part of the sample, while for the United Kingdom and Italy we observe the opposite. It is also important to notice that in the four countries these changes seem to be mainly explained by variations in the expenditure side rather than in the revenue side.

Figure 5. Estimated Values of Country Dummies in (12).

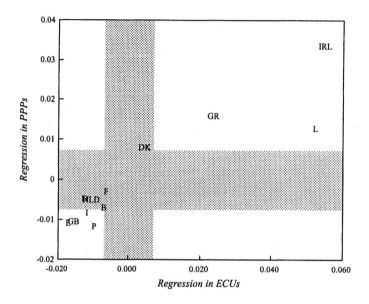

Figure 6. Changes in Estimated Values of Country Dummies in (12).

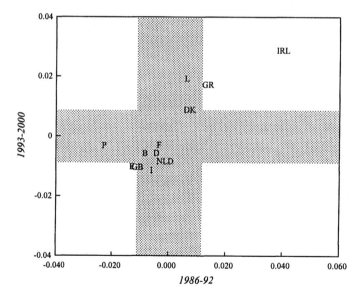

CONCLUSIONS

In this paper we have analyzed the redistributive effects of the EU general budget. This issue is particularly important because redistribution policies are nowadays of greater importance in the EU budget. In fact, when the Maastricht Treaty was signed it was also decided to reduce some of the existing economic disparities that could be deepened by EMU.

Redistribution policies imply transferring income among members to alleviate persistent differences in per capita income levels and, as our growth model shows, these policies can increase the speed of convergence of beneficiary countries to common steady states. However, the small size of the EU budget limits the magnitude of these effects. In any case, it must be understood that these policies do not account for all the gains EU countries derive from the Union.

Using EU budget data on a cash basis from 1986 to 2000, we obtain as the main result that the EU budget has a redistributive character, though only on its expenditure side. For instance, the elasticity of total per capita expenditure in current ECUs with respect to per capita income is less than one with a point estimate of -0.23 for the EU15, although not statistically different from zero. Of all expenditure categories we do consider, the most redistributive one is the regional fund, followed by the social fund and by the guarantee section of the EAGGF. All of them become increasingly redistributive in time. These findings do not basically change when the regressions are run in PPPs. Nonetheless, they are altered when we exclude some countries from the sample. For example, excluding Ireland greatly reduces the redistributive power of the expenditures, since all the elasticities of the four expenditure categories increase. Likewise, if we exclude Luxembourg from the sample, the common agricultural policy becomes regressive.

As far as total budgetary revenues are concerned, in contrast with the results for the United States, they show proportionality with income. Surprisingly, the only exception seems to be the GNP resource, which apparently shows a redistributive effect in the early nineties, but at the end of the period it has an elasticity equal to one.

Finally, when we consider the net financial balance, we find that the EU budget has a remarkably redistributive effect on the income of its members. This result is a necessary condition to speed up the convergence process among European countries. Our results show that the EU budget redistributes the 5 per cent of any difference between richer and poorer countries. Although this number is well below the estimates for the United States (federal taxes and transfers redistribute approximately a 20 per cent), it is important to notice that this redistributive effect is achieved with budget resources that represent less that 1.27 per cent of the European GNP. However, not all EU countries are treated alike, since we identify three different groups of countries. Firstly, those that benefit by more than what would correspond to their per capita income level. Secondly, those whose per capita financial balance is in line with their per capita income level. It is interesting to note that, surprisingly, in this group we find some of the countries that have been questioning the current system of distribution policies implied by the EU budget. The third group comprises those countries which get a poorer treatment.

There are several natural extensions to the findings of this paper. First, although we have analyzed the redistributive effects of EU budget at national level, most fiscal policies in the expenditure side are determined by principles of regional cohesion and solidarity. Certainly, some revenues cannot be easily redistributed at regional level and, therefore, this kind of analysis would be only partial. A second possible extension is related to the analysis of level and growth effects for the EU as a whole of these redistributive policies. Our model could be easily modified to consider some kind of spillover effects across countries which can not only affect the convergence paths but also the steady state levels of European countries. Thus, at the empirical level, instead of looking for the winners and the losers of these policies, it is also relevant to study if redistribution has also positive effects upon countries that are net contributors to the EU budget.

REFERENCES

Artis, M. and Lee, N. (1995): *The Economics of the European Union, Policy and Analysis.* Oxford University Press.

Barro, R. J. (1990): Government Spending in a Simple Model of Endogenous Growth. *Journal of Political Economy*, 98, S103-125.

Barro, R. J., N. G. Mankiw, and X. Sala-i-Martin (1995): Capital Mobility in Neoclassical Models of Growth. *American Economic Review*, 85(1), 103-115.

Barro, R. J. and X. Sala-i-Martin (1995): *Economic Growth*. McGraw Hill.

Bayoumi, T. and P. R. Masson (1996): Fiscal Flows in the United States and Canada: Lessons for Monetary Union in Europe. *European Economic Review*, 39, 253-274.

Caselli, F., G. Esquivel and F. Lefort (1996): Reopening the Convergence Debate: A New Look at Cross-Country Growth Empirics, *Journal of Economic Growth*, 363-389.

De la Fuente, A. (1997): Fiscal Policy and Growth in the OECD. D. 97007. DGAPP. Ministerio de Economía y Hacienda. Madrid.

Doménech, R.; A. Maudes and J. Varela (2000): Fiscal Flows in Europe: The Redistributive Effects of the EU Budget, *Weltwirtschaftliches Archiv,* 136 (4), 609-634.

EC Commission (1997): *Informe Anual sobre los Fondos Estructurales 1996*, COM(97) 526 final.

EC Commission (1998): *Financig the European Union. Commission Report on the Operation of the Own Resources System.*

EC, Annual Report of The Court of Auditors, *Official Journal of the European Communities*, various issues.

Fatás, A. (1998): Does EMU Need a Fiscal Federation?, in D. Begg, J. von Hagen, C. Wyplosz and C. F. Zimmermann (eds.), *EMU: Prospects and Challenges for the Euro.* CEPR.

Gramlich, E. M. (1994): Infraestructure Investment: a Review Essay. *Journal of Economic Literature*, 32, 1176-1196.

Islam, N. (1995): Growth Empirics: A Panel Data Approach, *Quarterly Journal of Economics*, CX, 1127-1170.

Lee, K., M. H. Pesaran and R. Smith (1997): Growth and Convergence in a Multi-Country Empirical Stochastic Solow Model. *Journal of Applied Econometrics*, XII, 357-392.

Mankiw, N. G.; D. Romer and D. N. Weil (1992): A Contribution to the Empirics of Economic Growth. *Quarterly Journal of Economics*, 107(2), 407-37.

Martin, C. (2000): *The Spanish Economy in the New Europe.* Macmillan Press.

Nonneman, W. and P. Vanhoudt (1996): A Further Augmentation of the Solow Model and the Empirics of Economic Growth for OECD Countries. *Quarterly Journal of Economics*, 111, 943-953.

Otto, G. D. and G. M. Voss (1998): Is Public Capital Provision Efficient?. *Journal of Monetary Economics*, 42, 47-66.

Sachs, J. and X. Sala-i-Martin (1992): Fiscal Federalism and Optimun Currency Areas: Evidence from Europe and the United States, in M. Canzoneri, V. Grilli and P. Masson (eds.), *Establishing a Central Bank: Issues in Europe and Lessons from the US*, Cambridge University Press.

Sturm, J. E., G. H. Kuper and J. de Haan (1997): Modeling Goverment Investment and Economic Growth on a Macro Level: A Review, in D. Brakman, H. van Ees and S. K. Kuipers (eds), *Market Behaviour and Macroeconomic Modeling*. Macmillan.

Von Hagen, J. (1992): Fiscal Arrangements in a Monetary Union: Evidence from the US, in D. E. Fair and C. de Boissieu (eds.), *Fiscal Policy, Taxation and the Financial System in an Increasingly Integrated Europe*, Kluwer Academic Publishers.

In: European Economic and Political Issues, Volume 5   ISBN 1-59033-322-5
Editor: Frank Columbus. pp. 71-89.   © Nova Science Publishers, Inc.

Chapter 4

TURKEY AND EUROPE – ECONOMIC ASPECTS OF A DIFFICULT RELATIONSHIP

Astrid-Marina Lohrmann

INTRODUCTION

The European Union has manifold agreements with third countries, which led to the expression of a "European Spaghetti Bowl" in economic literature (Panagariya/Srinivasan, 1998). Beside of all these Free Trade, Association and Non-reciprocal agreements, there is one with a special character: The European Union and Turkey form a Customs Union. This form of integration goes beyond free trade, it requires the adoption of a Common External Tariff (CET). In case of Turkey, the Customs Union Decision, in the following: CUD, (EC-Turkey Association Council, 1995), additionally, required Turkey to approach to European fiscal and competition policy and to accede to the Stockholm Act of the Paris convention on the protection of industrial property, the Patent Co-operation Treaty, the Nice convention on the international classification of goods and services for the purposes of registering marks, the Paris Act of the Bern convention on the protection of literary and artistic works and the Rome convention of performers, producers of phonograms and broadcasting organisations. Beside of all that, Turkey had to adopt EU legislation with respect to industrial property, copyright and neighbouring rights, Turkey implemented the EU regulation on the prohibition of counterfeit goods, and she had to implement the GATT Uruguay Round decision on TRIPS (Trade Related Aspects of Intellectual Property Rights). By 1999, Turkey acceded the Protocol of the Madrid Agreement on the international registration of marks, the Budapest treaty on international recognition of micro-organisms for the purposes of patenting and the international convention on the protection of new varieties of plants (Togan 2001).

The far-going regulations and declarations in the CUD are not necessarily for a Customs Union, so one might conclude that the relation between Turkey and the EU are approximating to a Common Market than to a Customs Union only (Kramer, 1994) In 1999, at the Helsinki summit, the European Council accepted Turkey as a potential new member, among the Central and Eastern European countries, Cyprus and Malta. But Turkey does not belong to first group of candidates: Czech Republic, Estonia, Hungary, Poland, Slovenia and Cyprus (Schröder 2001). Turkish media like CNN Türk believe that the country may become a member at 2015 latest (Şen 2001). In the meantime, she has to adjust her economic and political structure to the requirements of the EU. Whether the Customs Union will Turkey's economy prepare for membership is the focal point of the following analysis.

THE CUSTOMS UNION AGREEMENT AND ITS IMPLICATIONS

On December, 13, 1995 the European Parliament ratified the decision about the implementation of a Customs Union with Turkey by a plurality of 2/3. The Customs Union was set into force on January, 1, 1996. This decision was hardly discussed on both sides. On the European side there were objections about human rights and democracy in Turkey, on the Turkish side there were in particular economic doubts. Supporters of the decision in Turkey were especially among the representatives of the textile sector, which hoped to increase their exports due to the abolition of European quotas, and representatives of the tourism- and banking sector, which thought to increase transactions. On the other hand, representatives of the automobile industry, the so-called white industry (refrigerators, washing machines) and the brown industry (electronic commodities like colour TVs) hesitated, because they feared the increase of competition and increased low-price imports (Hic, 1995, p. 18). But in general, the Customs Union was mostly seen as a kind of "safe-haven" with market access to Turkeys major trading partner.

Basis of the Customs Union is the Association Agreement ("Ankara Agreement") of 1963 and the Additional Protocol of 1970. The aim of the Agreement is to take care of peace and freedom and to foster trade and economic relations between the contracting parties in order to accelerate the development of the Turkish economy and increase the living standard of the Turkish population. For this purpose, a Customs Union was to be implemented in three stages:

- The preparatory stage (until 1973) was to support the Turkish economy. The EEC granted unilateral concessions to Turkey, while Turkey did not change her trade regime.
- The transitional stage aimed at forming a Customs Union. Therefore the parties signed the Additional Protocol in 1970.
- In the final period of the association the Customs Union is implemented and stronger economic coordination should be enforced.

The Agreement does not contain any promises about the accession of Turkey to the EC, but the examination of the possibility of an accession in case of a functioning agreement and the ability of Turkey to adopt all obligations of the Rome Treaty (Art. 28 of the Agreement). So there is no automatic Turkish entry into the EC (now EU), but Turkey always believed to have a privileged role among other Mediterranean countries and saw the customs Union as a stepping stone to full membership.

In 1987 Turkey applied for membership, but it was rejected in 1989. According to the European Commission there were several important reasons (Commission of the EC, 1989):

Because of the creation of the Single European Market in 1992, negotiations with new members should begin in 1993 earliest. Turkey's economic problems were seen as too big to manage the adjustment problems of membership. In particular, the Commission mentioned the structural disparities between Europe and Turkey in the industrial and agricultural sector, macroeconomic instabilities, high industrial protection rates and a low social standard. "As long as these disparities continue to exist, there will be reason to fear that Turkey would experience serious difficulties in taking on the obligations resulting from the Community's economic and social policies" (Commission of the EC, 1989, p. 6). Due to the Commission, the accession of Turkey would have meant a severe financial burden for the EC at that time. Additionally, a considerable inflow of Turkish labour was feared at a time of increasing tensions at the European labour market.

It was recommended that Turkey enters into the Customs Union first and then negotiate again about membership.

The details of the Customs Union were settled in the Additional Protocol. The EC abolished all duties on industrial products in 1973, with some exceptions. Hale (1990) states that the EC used restrictions especially in the textile and clothing sector, because European producers "were feeling the pinch of third-world competition" (Hale, 1990, p. 156) due to the competitiveness of Turkish enterprises. On the other hand, this practice was in the context of worldwide regulated restrictive trade policies on textile goods. Usually the European Commission and the Istanbul Textile and Apparel Exporters Associations (ITKIB) negotiated about so-called Voluntary Export Restraints (VER) since 1982 (GATT, 1994). Also the market access restrictions on agricultural products ran up against Turkish criticism. At the beginning of the 1970s, Turkeys main export items were agricultural. So one may conclude that the opening of the European market did not meet Turkeys trade structure and therefore could not help accelerate economic development, as stated in the Ankara Agreement. Since January 1987 the EC has abolished all Customs Duties on industrial and manufactured agricultural products from Turkey.

On the Turkish side, the Customs Union should have been implemented stepwise. Within 22 years, she had to abolish all customs duties towards the EC and to adopt the Common External Tariff (CET). Therefore a detailed time schedule was created. On a so-called 12-years-list commodities of the electronic and metal industry were included. These goods were seen as in the need of protection in an average way. The 22-years-list included all commodities which needed a longer protection, and these concerned nearly all relevant Turkish industries. Table 1 shows the scheduled customs duties on the percentage basis of initial duties.

Table 1. Time Schedule for Customs Duties Reductions

Time	12-years-list	22-years-list
1.1.1973	90	95
1.1.1976	80	90
1.1.1978	70	
1.1.1979	60	85
1.1.1980	50	
1.1.1981	40	
1.1.1982	30	
1.1.1983	20	80
1.1.1984	10	
1.1.1985	0	70
1.1.1986		60
1.1.1988		50
1.1.1990		40
1.1.1991		30
1.1.1993		20
1.1.1994		10
1.1.1995		0

Source: Manegold, 1988.

But the establishment of the Customs Union could not be finalised in time due to serious macroeconomic problems in Turkey. She did not fulfil her obligations. There were only two negligible reductions of customs duties for products of the EC of 10% each. An adjustment on the CET was not begun at all. In 1978, the Turkish government asked for a five year "moratorium" of the association regime. With the application for membership in 1987 Turkey started again to follow her obligations, and especially in the 1990s she made big efforts to complete the Customs Union on time and it was completed with only one year delay to the schedule foreseen in the Association Agreement.

The Association Agreement contains agreements on stepwise liberalisation of free movement of labour (art. 36-40), removal of restrictons on the freedom of location and services (art. 41-42) and of facilitation of capital movements (art. 50-52). Additionally, there are decisions on the approximation of tax systems and competition laws.

One may suppose that the Association Agreement was not suitable to prepare Turkey to become integrated closer (Hine, 1995). The double strategy of trade preferences and financial aid is impressive at the first glimpse, but regarding the enormous disparities between the partners reveals its insufficiency. As far as the duty free access for industrial products was concerned, Turkey had only a small industrial basis to get an advantage of the European preferences. And the EC had even preferential agreements with some other developing nations, so that the intended advantage of preferential access eroded. A special aspect is the European reaction to Turkish export success: "Even when Turkey did succeed in developing its exports to the Community, the EC's response in some cases was to bring measures to restrain them, as with the introduction of import quotas and restrictions in 1977 (especially on cotton yarn and T-shirts)" (Hine, 1995, p. 144).

Turkey did not use the transition period to prepare herself on further integration. One important factor was that Turkey followed an import-substitution strategy until the end of the 1970s instead of liberalizing the high protected economy. This led, due to the deterioration of exports, to a massive financial crisis. After the 1980s military intervention, there was a sharp economic reorientation, fostered by IMF and Worldbank and under the guidance of Turgut Özal, the later Prime Minister. But this so-called Stabilization and Structural Adjustment programme (SSAP) cannot delude about the fact that the Turkish economy still was highly protected. In the 1980s, Turkey created so-called "fund levies" on imports in order to raise money. These funds were established to finance large infrastructure, housing projects and Turkeys defense industry. According to the EC, this was a violation of the Association Agreement which forbid the implementation of new barriers to trade. The Customs Union Decision (CUD) from 1995 brought important changes for Turkeys trade policy. Chapter 1 of the Agreement deals with the free movement of goods, except primary goods and manufactured agrarian goods. Turkey had to abolish all customs duties and similar duties on imports from the EU, from January 1, 1996. For Turkey this meant a radical reduction of import duties. In 1993, the average duty on EU-imports was at 4.44%. Including the funds, this amount increased up to 22.66%. Towards third countries, Turkey charged an average duty of 9.28% resp. 27.48%. (Lohrmann, 1999). According to the GATT Secretary, the average customs duties for European/EFTA imports was 5%, on imports from third countries 9.5% (GATT, 1994). An exception for the free trade of commodities was made for European used cars, with respect to Turkish producers which feared a massive import wave.

Turkey had to adopt the Common External Tariff, with a 5-years transition period for several commodities like tractors, minivans and cars. Another transition period of 5 years concerns the adoption of the European Preferential System.

Referring to the textile and clothing sector, the EU wanted clear efforts in the adoption of European policy, before abolishing textile qoutas on Turkish imports. Turkey did follow this rather fast, so that the quotas could fall with the beginning of the CU. But that does not meant an automatical free market access for Turkeys producers. The EU pointed out that in case of a violation of European laws at a later point of time, the Community will implement anti-dumping measures. In Turkey, this was seen as a new protection instrument. According to this believe, only to institute proceedings against a Turkish producer would have been sufficient to supersede him for years from the European market. Hine stated: "....., that EC producers are using the anti-dumping rules to prevent their domestic cartels from being undermined." (Hine, 1995, p. 147)

The CUD is quiet on rules concerning the movement of labour and capital. It only deals with commodity trade between the partners and the general European trade policy. As far as migration of Turkish workforce is concerned, there is under the topic "Cooperation of social matters" in an appendix on cooperation in sciences, environment and culture the only sentence: "A regular dialogue will be set up on the situation of Turkish workers in regular employment and vice versa. The two parties will explore all possibilities for a better integration of such workers." (Turkey-EC-Association Council Decision, 3.3.1995, p.4) So this problem is adjourned for an unknown period, which led to disappointment on the Turkish side. The same held true for the agrarian sector; the Association Council noticed that there is an additional period required to adjust Turkeys agrarian policy, but any hinds about a time schedule are missing.

The EU's financial support before the completion of the Customs Union (according to the financial protocols I to IV) had an official amount of € mio.1.427, but the fourth of € 600 mio. was blocked in 1981 by the suspension of the bilateral relations. The CU brought new financial aid for Turkey. It is about € mio. 376 within the period from 1996 to 1999 and access to EIB loans for infrastructure (about € mio. 300-400). The amount depends on the suggested projects. Additional loans were provided by the EIB for the improvement of Turkeys competitiveness during 5 years, and Turkey had access to special credit programs (funding facilities for Mediterranean countries, the MEDA programme). But in 1997, the € mio. 376 financial aid was frozen due to a resolution of the European Parliament. At the Luxemburg Summit in December 1997 Turkey was not included in the group of accession countries. Due to Turkey's negative reaction, the document "European Strategy for Turkey" was changed into "Pre-Accession Strategy" in 1998. From 2000 onwards there should be a doubling of financial resources on an annual basis to Turkey, which should be seen as an attempt to reinforce Customs Union and the funds foreseen. After the Helsinki summit (Turkey was finally accepted as an accession country) EU Foreign Affairs Ministers adopted a Commission proposal to provide a € 15 million grant to Turkey during a 3-year-period, and later the Commission adopted another € 150 million adjustment grant facility under the MEDA programme to support economic reforms in Turkey as a necessary condition of accession. According to a Commission's press release, this was "tailor-made towards speeding up Turkey's pre-accession strategy" (EU Commission, Nov. 30, 2000).

Regarding all this, we have to pose the question whether the Association Agreement between Turkey and the EU had any positive developments in terms of structural adjustment and specialization.

A BRIEF THEORETICAL SURVEY

Beginning with Viner (1950), Meade (1955) and Lipsey (1960) the Customs Union Theory focused mainly on welfare effects. Regional integration was seen as a second-best solution, due to contrary effects of "Trade Creation", which is welfare improving, and "Trade Diversion", which decreases welfare. The main issue is the shift from a low-cost producer to a high-cost supplier in the Union because of a discrimination of third-countries. Although the theory points out the importance of dynamic effects (competition effects, economies of scale effects, learning effects) its main interest were the so-called static effects. This may be due to this special situation: at that time, regional integration occurred between high developed countries. In a second phase, regional integration was seen as a means for development for underdeveloped countries. These attempts all failed because of similar production structures in the member countries and a so-called import-substitution strategy which led to severe balance-of-payment crisis. Now, in a third phase of regionalism, we have to face heterogeneous blocs with smaller, less developed countries seeking agreements with large countries or blocs. Although in literature the question "Stepping stone" or "Stumbling stone" in the sense of a step towards or away from free trade is hardly discussed (so-called "Memorial Drive School" versus "GATT-School"), the development effects in heterogeneous blocs have still to be evaluated. Neo-classical theory of factor/proportions, the product-cycle hypothesis and the catching-up hypothesis predict a positive economic development through specialization and trade. Economists like Myrdal (1956) instead point out a circle of cumulative causation, which may be supported by the New Growth Theory (Lohrmann 1999b). Some models describe the possibility of lagging behind due to a "wrong" specialization: the industrialized country is specialized in high-tech industries and accumulates human capital via learning by doing, the poor country specializes in low-tech goods with no skill-accumulation. The underdeveloped country gets into the "Heckscher-Ohlin-Trap" (Lohrmann, 2000). Other models show how exports from a leading region will crowd out the industry in the lagging region, which may lead to a form of "Mezzogiornofication" (Krugman, 1991).

In the next section, we will give a survey on the Structural Adjustment Programme and Turkeys macroeconomic development. Subsequently, her trade and specialization structure towards the EU is analyzed.

STRUCTURAL ADJUSTMENT PROGRAMME AND MACROECONOMIC DEVELOPMENT – SUCCESS AND FAILURE

Turkey was the first developing country which implemented a so-called Stabilization and Structural Adjustment Programme (SSAP), supported by World Bank and IMF, in 1980. The first objective of this programme was the opening of the economy and had two main components: a balance-of-payments adjustment and a structural adjustment of the economy to increase efficiency. The balance-of-payments measures contained a depreciation of the lira and a restrictive financial and money policy. This led to a decrease of economic activities and lowered the internal absorption. The structural adjustment measures aimed at accelerating growth and improving the trade balance via export-orientation and import-liberalisation. The programme of 1980 followed the main line of IMF and World Bank (export-orientation, liberalization, deregulation and priority of the private sector) and represented a fundamental break of the former policy with extensive state intervention (Önis, 1991) In the medium range, the programme had 8 main objectives (Lohrmann, 1997):

- Reduction of inflation
- Increase of exports
- Decrease of the balance-of-payments deficit
- Increase of savings and private investment
- Opening and restructuring of Turkish industry
- Restructuring of the public sector
- A change in income-distribution
- Solution of social problems

Table 2. Main Economic Indicators

Years	Export	% chg.	Import	% chg.	Ex/Im%	Growth Rates %	Cap.util. Rates
1980	2910	-	7909	-	36,8	-1,1	55,2
1981	4702	61,6	8933	12,9	52,6	4,2	56,6
1982	5745,973	22,2	8842,664	-1,0	65,0	4,6	59,3
1983	5727,833	-0,3	9235,001	4,4	62,0	3,3	60,2
1984	7133,602	24,5	10756,923	16,5	66,3	5,9	75,2
1985	7958,008	11,6	11343,475	5,5	70,2	5,1	70,3
1986	7456,724	-6,3	11104,77	-2,1	67,1	8,1	70
1987	10190,047	36,7	14157,805	27,5	72,0	9,8	77,5
1988	11662,021	14,4	14335,396	1,3	81,4	1,5	76,8
1989	11624,692	-0,3	15792,143	10,2	73,6	1,6	69,5
1990	12959,288	11,5	22302,126	41,2	58,1	9,4	74,4
1991	13593,462	4,9	21047,014	-5,6	64,6	0,3	75,6
1992	14714,629	8,2	22871,055	8,7	64,3	6,4	77,3
1993	15345,067	4,3	29428,37	28,7	52,1	8,1	80,5
1994	18105,872	18,0	23270,019	-20,9	77,8	-6,1	72,9
1995	21637,041	19,5	35709,011	53,5	60,6	8.0	78,5
1996	23224,465	7,3	43626,642	22,2	53,2	7,1	78
1997	26261,072	13,1	48558,721	11,3	54,1	8,3	79,4
1998	26973,952	2,7	45921,392	-5,4	58,7	3,9	76,5
1999	26587,225	-1,4	40686,746	-11,4	65,3	-6,4	72,2
2000	27485,438	3,4	54149,795	33,1	50,8	6,1	75,9
2001[*]	2169,121	2,2	3972,717	23,0	54,6	-	70,2[1]

[*] January, 2001.

[1] February, 2001.

Source: Undersecretary of Foreign Trade, Republic of Turkey (2001), http://www.foreigntrade.gov.tr.

Turkey has made a remarkable export success, but in general, the positive impression of growth and dynamic is impaired by structural problems. Turkey is characterized by an unstable macroeconomic performance, boom-recession cycles in the real economy, persistent inflation, high public sector debt and a deterioration of the balance-of-payments. One problem is due to the state sector and its fiscal and monetary policy, which led to fluctuations in the value of the Turkish Lira and affected the balance-of-payments. An estatist policy and a strategy of industrialization through state enterprises has led to a massive burden for the Turkish financial household. These state enterprises do still not work according to market-oriented principles and need long-term subsidies. Even an initiative of privatization was only successful partly; 143 of 218 state enterprises were privatized between 1986 and 2000 (Şen, 2001). The latest efforts to sell 51% of Turkish Airlines and 33,5% of Türk Telekom are connected with a banking scandal, which led to a state intervention of US$ 13 Billion. To overcome massive liquidity problems, Turkey negotiated an IMF credit of US$ 10 Billion in December 2000. At the beginning of 2001 Turkey went into a massive crisis, although in 2000 was an impressive successful year for Turkey: Growth rates increased remarkably after the catastrophic earthquake in 1999, and the unemployment rate was at the lowest level in the 1990s with 7%.

The crisis of 2001 led to a massive depreciation of the Turkish Lira of 40% (iwd, 2001). International capital avoids investment in Turkey due to corruption and mismanagement. According to a report by "Price Waterhouse Coopers" Turkey ranks place 4 in world-wide mismanagement, behind China, Russia and Indonesia (Şen, 2001). The high social dualism which seperates the country in a rich and a very rural and poor part constitutes another problem: the migration from Eastern Anatolia to the developed regions leads to massive social problems in the economic centres of the west.

TRADE STRUCTURE IN THE CUSTOMS UNION

Turkeys main success due to the Stabilization and Structural Adjustment Programme was a remarkable export boom. Exports rose from US$ 2910 million in 1980 to US$ 27485 in 2000 (see table 2). Europe's share of Turkey's exports and imports is more than 50%. Turkeys biggest trading partner is Germany. The trade between the Turkish and European partners has risen significantly in the Customs Union. But Turkish exports increased not as much as imports, the trade balance worsened. On the other hand, there is a tendency of reorientation: exports to the former Soviet Republics increased, while remained stable to Europe. Another factor is the co-called "suitcase trade" of Russian tourists, which is not counted officially.

Turkey's main export items are textiles and apparel, and for a few years now in Europe there is a market for so-called white consumer products like washing machines and brown products (consumer electronics like TV), which are exported for selling at catalogue suppliers in Europe. But especially the performance of the textile and clothing sector was disappointing for Turkish producers, since they expected an increase of their sales after the abolishment of quotas and increased their investment in textile and apparel industries (Lohrmann, 1997b). Indeed, Turkish producers did not fulfill the EU-quotas in the textile and apparel sector even before the implementation of the CU (Lohrmann, 1997b), so there was no real chance to increase exports remarkably. Decreasing textile exports to the EU due to slow growth in the partner countries affected the trade deficit for Turkey remarkably.

Table 3. EU-import quotas towards Turkey and fulfilment before the CU (in %)

Commodity	Unit	Quota 1995	% 1995	% 1994	% 1993
Cotton yarn	kg	100317850	22,3	42,2	25,5
Cotton fabric	kg	39284000	70,9	90,7	80,6
T-Shirts	pcs.	112783716	91,3	93,6	93,7
Pullover	pcs.	Surveillance		93,5	95,2
Shorts	pcs.	27801610	87,2	92,9	89,4
Blouses	pcs.	28952932	99,5	96,4	96,1
Shirts	pcs.	24824328	82,2	93,8	96,7
Terry towelling	kg	Surveillance		83,0	98,6
Bed-linen	kg	12852750	56,9	45,5	62,5
Socks	pair	264677401	98,3	99,7	97,9
Underwear	pcs.	56048655	93,1	93,0	91,7
Singlets	kg	8733760	78,2	99,9	60,6
Dresses	pcs.	30403926	65,4	49,6	75,8
Coats	kg	2589189	98,9	97,6	94,7
Bags	kg	Surveillance		100,0	98,0

Source: Lohrmann, 1997, p. 133.

Turkish consumers enjoyed the new freedom and imported shoes and knitting ware from Italy. According to a study of ITKIB (Istanbul Textile and Apparel Exporters Association, 1999) the T&A sector is still the biggest in the economy, it earns 38% of Turkeys export earnings and occupies 21% of Turkish labour force. On the other hand, the problems became obviously: Especially labour, energy and raw material costs are much cheaper in competing countries from Asia and (partly) in Italy (ITKIB, 1996). So Turkey gets under pressure from both sides: high quality imports from Europe, low price competition with East Asean countries (Lohrmann, 1997b).

So, the CU ended up in disappointment by the Turkish side, mainly because it was seen as a "cure-at-all that would impose discipline on the domestic market, correct the foreign trade imbalance, provide financial resources and promote foreign investment." (Balkir, 1998).

Turkey's main import items are capital goods (machinery and transport equipment) and consumption goods like TV's, furniture, apparel and household articles, so that one may conclude that an income increase in Turkey led to a demand boom, especially in the early 1990's. As the representative of the US Department of Commerce stated in 1994: "The Turkish market is ripe for greatly increased consumption spending in many areas." (Corro, 1994, p. 24) But disparities between rural and urban areas, and upper an lower income groups are very high in Turkey. The persistent inflation worsens the social situation of lower income groups further.

TURKEY'S COMPETITIVENESS TOWARDS THE EU

A first indicator of competitiveness is the so-called Revealed Comparative Advantage (RCA). Indices are calculated according to Balassa (1965):

$$RCA = LN \left[\left(X_i / M_i \right) / \left(\Sigma X_i / \Sigma M_i \right) \right] \times 100$$

Turkey's industrial commodities were divided into five different groups (Yilmaz, 1998):

- Raw material-intensive goods
- Labour-intensive goods
- Capital-intensive goods
- Easily imitable research-oriented goods
- Difficultly imitable research-oriented goods

Striking is the errative changing of values over the period. There is no tendency which may lead to the conclusion of an improvement or deterioration of competitiveness before and after the implementation of the CU. Labour-intensive goods like travel bags (SITC 83) dropped from 266 in 1991 to 194 in 1995 and improved slightly again to 253 at the end of the century, apparel shows its highest value in 1991. A tendency of improvement may be seen for rubber manufactures, iron/steel, non-ferrous metals (capital-intensive commodities). Interesting is the improvement of group 52 (inorganic chemicals) and 75 (office machines), which belong to easy imitable research-oriented goods.

INTRA-INDUSTRY-TRADE AND HORIZONTAL AND VERTICAL SPECIALIZATION

Another indicator of economic development is the value of intra-industry-trade. A high value of IIT occurs mostly between countries with similar economic structures and development levels. So, an increase of IIT may be interpreted as a catching-up process between an less developed country like Turkey and the EU. Here, instead of using the standard Grubel-Lloyd index, we calculated the Marginal Intra-Industry Trade (MIIT) according to Brülhart (1994), which should be seen as a dynamic analysis of trade (Lohrmann, 2002). Therefore we chose the periods 1991-1995 and 1995-1999.

The so-called A-index is calculated as follows, using the 3-digit SITC-level for industrial commodities:

$$A = 1 - \left[\left| \Delta X - \Delta M \right| / \left(\left| \Delta X \right| + \left| \Delta M \right| \right) \right],$$

with X and M standing for Turkey's exports and imports from the EU respectively.

Table 4. Turkeys RCA towards the EU

SITC	1991	1995	1999
Raw-material intensive goods			
56	72	-69	-295
Labour-intensive goods			
61	-273	-213	-143
63	-120	-15	-41
64	-265	-217	-258
65	130	98	110
66	104	76	97
69	-88	-30	-22
81	67	29	93
82	1	26	-50
83	266	194	253
84	446	441	367
85	89	54	-45
Capital-intensive goods			
53	-417	-454	-368
55	-228	-217	-259
62	38	111	88
67	-131	-26	59
68	-32	-32	28
78	-176	-104	-106
Easily imitable research-oriented goods			
51	-142	-133	-196
52	-69	19	65
54	-307	-243	-280
58	-215	-179	-156
59	-409	-351	-388
75	-194	-349	37
76	29	-49	-262
Difficultly imitable research-oriented goods			
57	-126	-198	-278
71	-168	-76	-88
72	-366	-360	-249
73	-208	-200	-92
74	-265	-206	-180
77	-116	-38	4
79	-143	-9	0
87	-238	-208	-180
88	-363	-340	-270

Source: Eurostat, authors calculations.

The A index reveals the structure of changes in import and export flows. It varies between 0 and 1. 0 indicates trade to be inter-industrial and 1 represents intra-industrial trade. In the latter case, both imports and exports have grown or shrunk to an equal extent, so that neither the domestic nor the foreign industry has achieved a better trade performance compared to the competitor.

The B index links MIIT with the analysis of sectoral trade performance (Brülhart 1994):

$$B = \Delta X - \Delta M / |\Delta X| + |\Delta M|$$

It varies between −1 and 1. The closer B is to 0, the higher is MIIT, while −1 and 1 represent trade pattern of the inter-industry type. A positive B index appears when the increase of exports was higher than the increase of imports in a sector during a specified period, so one may interprete B as a indicator of sectoral specialization. (Lohrmann, 2002).

Table 5. A-Indices, Aggregated at the 1-Digit Level

SITC	A9195	A9599
5	0,17	0,07
6	0,32	0,45
7	0,14	0,25
8	0,07	0,13

Source: Lohrmann, 2002.

In general, the A-index reveals a low amount of MIIT, which may lead to the conclusion of a "traditional" inter-industry trade pattern betweeen Turkey and the EU. Interesting are the changes during the analyzed periods. Except in sector 5 (chemicals and related products) there is an increase of MIIT in the period 1995-1999, which should be seen as the "Customs Union period". We may interprete that as an improvement of trade pattern after the implementation of the CU and a slight catching-up process.

As stated above, the B-index is an indicator of sectoral performance. Because it is impossible to aggregate B meaningfully, we computed the ratio of positive to negative values for SITC 5,6,7 and 8 for the two periods 1991-1995 and 1995-1999 at the 3-digit level.

Table 6. Ratio of Positive to Negative B Indices

SITC	B1991-1995	B1995-1999
5	8	0,12
6	3,5	0,8
7	3,5	0,14
8	1,6	0,5

Source: Lohrmann, 2002.

B ratios declined sharply in the second period, which is an indicator of a deterioration of international "competitiveness". Turkey seems to specialize "out-of" chemicals especially. At a more disaggregated level (Lohrmann, 2002), the picture is very ambigous. A positive development (in the sense of a specialization "into") is revealed for textile yarns, glass/ceramics, apparel, accessories and sanitary equipment, while all commodities of group 7 (machines and transport equipment) show negative indices. This is a rather disappointing result for trade in the Customs Union.

In order to get more information about the price structure of Turkey's exports, we calculated the ratio of export price over import price on a bilateral basis at the 3-digit SITC level and classified all commodity groups of manufactured products into 3 intervals according to Greenaway, Hine, and Milner (1994) and Rossini and Burattoni (1999). If the unit value of export over unit value of import was below 0.85, Turkey exported goods of lower quality than those imported. Between 0.85 and 1.15, we call it horizontal differentiation, which can be seen as trade in homogenous goods. Above 1.15, we have higher export prices than import prices in the same 3-digit category. This second kind of so-called vertical trade can be seen as advantaged vertical trade, while the first one represents disadvantaged vertical trade (Rossini/Burattoni 1999).

Table 7. Horizontal and Vertical Specialization

Year	Vertical I	Horizontal	Vertical II
1991	68%	8%	24%
1995	75%	5%	20%
1999	71%	5%	24%

Source: Lohrmann, 2002

Striking is the high amount of disadvantaged trade for Turkey with the European Union in the nineties. Turkey is still specializing in low-quality products, although we can see an improvement in 1999. If we have a look at several disaggregated commodity groups, we can see some changes during the observation period. While in 1991 products of the chemical sector had a high share in commodities which could be classified as advantaged, in 1999 especially commodities of the apparel sector, glass/ceramics, iron/steel products and textile yarns appeared in this category (Lohrmann 2002). But, a high amount of vertical trade reveals a trade structure which is rather inter- than intra-industry style. This may cause severe adjustment problems rather than indicated by an improvement of standard or dynamic intra-industry trade indices.

FOREIGN DIRECT INVESTMENT

In general, the amount of foreign direct investment (FDI) has increased in the last decade. This was connected to liberalization and industrialization strategies in developing countries worldwide.

Turkey hoped to attract an increasing amount of FDI due to the improved market access to the EU. Indeed, the performance was disappointing, although not uniform in the 1990s. The most striking increase was in 1996, when the total amount rose from US$ 2,938 million to US$ 3,837 million. Today, the FDI inflow remains at 0.5% of GDP (European Commission, 2001) and is about US$ 27,488 million (Hazine Müsteşarliği Yabanci Sermaye Genel Müdürlüğü 2000). This situation is very disappointing for Turkey, especially in comparison with other countries in Southeast Asia and Latin America. One of the reasons is macroeconomic instability with high inflation and high interest rates. The chairman of the Turkish Foreign Investors Association (YASED) blamed the incessant crisis atmosphere and the lack of confidence in Turkey for that situation (Economist Intelligence Unit, 1996). But, additionally, it is a question of productivity, energy, infrastructure, and education. Although we can see an improvement in the latter (so, the compulsory schooling has been increased from 5 to 8 years), there are still serious difficulties in providing staff and facilities. The main problem is still a lack of stability in the economic and legal framework. This instability is not only due to material conditions: "In the eyes of foreigners, this image arises from a frequent failure to honour contracts, a failure to be sufficiently cautious when making contracts." (Ariman, 1996) Barham statet in The Financial Times (Dec. 6, 1996): "Investing in Turkey is always a hazardous business". The outcome of this is that FDI in not going to flow in. This represents missed opportunities in modernising the Turkish capital stock and to transfer know-how.

Analysis of the sectoral distribution reveals an increase in services (1999: 32.5%, 2000 (until September) 70.8%), while the share of industrial investment declined in the same period (66.05% resp. 26.08%)) (Hazine Müsteşarliği Yabanci Sermaye Genel Müdürlüğü 2000). The distribution of FDI shows a domination of labour-intensive sectors. Noticeable is the increased investment of worldwide acting multinational companies (like Pepsi, Coca-Cola, Beiersdorf or Colgate-Palmolive) which are crowding-out domestic producers with softdrinks and hygienic household products. These companies satisfy the need for brands, which is supported by an aggressive marketing strategy. (Lohrmann 1997). Important is the development in services, especially in commerce and financing. Restaurants and Hotels rank at the top, which is also not an indicator for increased transfer of know-how, since in these branches unskilled cheap labour is a pillow of economic success.

CONCLUSION

After a long period of transition, the Customs Union between the EU and Turkey is in force since January 1996. In 1999 Turkey was accepted as a potential new member among transition economies in Central and Eastern Europe, Cyprus and Malta, but the Customs Union will be the legal status for the near future, supported by a so-called "Pre-Accession Strategy for Turkey". Although it is quite early to make exact statements about the impact of the CU on Turkey's economy, existing data provides information about tendencies. The analysis has shown that Turkish industry is still specialized in labour-intensive goods, with a significant negative competitiveness in skill-intensive, easily and difficultly imitable research-oriented goods towards the European Union. Horizontal and vertical specialization shows that Turkey's exports are mostly represented by so-called disadvantaged trade, which means specialization in low-quality products. The low amount of Marginal Intra-Industry Trade (MIIT) can be interpreted as an indicator of a laying behind of the Turkish economy in comparison with the EU, although a slight improvement in the second period (the CU-period) gives hope for a catching-up process.

The lack of human capital is a main problem for Turkey's competitiveness. Although there is a favourable demographic structure, the facilites for schooling and training are not enough. The literacy rate is very low when compared to international standards. The dualism of the Turkish economy, with an industrial and educational concentration in urban areas, while a considerable share of the population lives in rural areas, is to be seen as a reason for insufficient human capital resources. The low inflow of foreign direct investment and the concentration on low-skilled production may foster a development which leads to a "Heckscher-Ohlin-Trap", a circle of cumulative causation in the sense of low skilled production – low wages - low skilled production.

Despite all remarkable success in the completion of the Customs Union and the preparation for accession, there is still a lot to do (European Commssion, 2001): macroeconomic stability, a sustainable market-based economic development, significant restructuring in various sectors like state enterprises and banking, and a redifinition of budgetaty priorities in favour of investment in education and public infrastructure.

APPENDIX
SITC Classification

5	**Chemicals and related products, n.e.s.**
51	Organic chemicals
52	Inorganic chemicals
53	Dyeing, tanning and colouring materials
54	Medicinal and pharmaceutical products
55	Essential oils & perfume materials; toilet polishing and cleansing preparations
56	Fertilizers, manufactured
57	Explosives and pyrotechnic products
58	Artificial resins, plastic materials, cellulose esters and ethers
59	Chemical materials and products, n.e.s.
6	**Manufactured goods classified chiefly by material**
61	Leather, leather manufactures, n.e.s. and dressed furskin
62	Rubber manufactures, n.e.s.
63	Cork and wood manufactures (excluding furniture)
64	Paper, paperboard, articles of paper, paper-pulp/board
65	Textile yarn, fabrics, made-up articles, related products
66	Non-metallic mineral manufactures, n.e.s.
67	Iron and steel
68	Non-ferrous metals
69	Manufactures of metal, n.e.s.
7	**Machinery and Transport Equipment**
71	Power generating machinery and equipment
72	Machinery specialized for particular industries
73	Metalworking machinery
74	General industrial machinery & equipment, and parts
75	Office machines & automatic data processing equipment
76	Telecommunications & sound recording apparatus
77	Electrical machinery, apparatus & appliances n.e.s.
78	Road vehicles (including air-cushion vehicles)
79	Other transport equipment
8	**Miscellaneous Manufactured Articles**
81	Sanitary, plumbing, heating and lighting fixtures
82	Furniture and parts thereof
83	Travel goods, handbags and similar containers
84	Articles of apparel and clothing accessories
85	Footwear
87	Professional, scientific & controling instruments
88	Photographic apparatus, optical goods, watches
89	Miscellaneous manufactured articles, n.e.s.

REFERENCES

Ariman, A. (1996), Developments in Foreign Investment in Post-1996 Turkey, YASED (Yabanci Sermaye Koordinasiyon Derneği, Association for Foreign Capital Coordination), Istanbul 1996.

Balassa, B. (1965), Trade Liberalization and "Revealed" Comparative Advantage, The Manchester School of Economic and Social Studies, Vol. 33, Manchester 1965, p. 99-123.

Balkir, C. (1998), The Customs Union and Beyond, in: Rittenberg, L. (Ed.), The Political Economy of Turkey in the Post-Soviet Era, Westport 1998, p. 51-78.

Barham, J. (1996), Riskier than usual, Financial Times, Turkey: Investment and Finance, Dec. 6, 1996, p. III.

Commission of the EC (1989), Commission Opinion on Turkey's Request for Accession to the Community, Brussels, December 1989, SEC (89) 2290 final.

Corro, A., (1994), Turkey – Economic Future is Bright, Business America, Vol. 115, Iss. 3, March 1994, p. 24.

EC-Turkey-Association Council, Decision No. 1/95 (Customs Union), CE-TR 106/95, Brussels, March 1995.

Economist Intelligence Unit (1996), Country Report, Turkey, 4th quarter 1996.

EC-Turkey-Association Council Decision, 3.3.1995, Draft Resolution, 1995.

European Commission (1999), Enlargement, Progress Report, Turkey, Luxemburg, October 1999, www.eu.int./comm/enlargement.

European Commssion (2001), Regular Report on Turkey's Progress towards Accession, Luxemburg, November 2001, www.eu.int./comm/enlargement.

GATT (1994), Trade Policy Review, The Republic of Turkey, Vol. 1, Geneva, March 1994.

Greenaway, D./ Hine, R.C./ Milner, C., (1994), Country-Specific Factors and the Pattern of Horizontal and Vertical Intra-Industry Trade in the UK, Weltwirtschaftliches Archiv, 130, 1994, pp. 78-100.

Hale, W. (1990), Turkish Industry and the Common Market, in: Evin, A. / Denton, G. (Eds.), Turkey and the European Community, Opladen 1990, p. 153-166.

Hazine Müsteşarliği Yabanci Sermaye Genel Müdürlüğü (2000), Yabanci Sermaye Raporu, Ankara, 2000, III. çeyrek.

Hic, M. (1995), Turkey's Customs Union with the European Union, Stiftung Wissenschaft und Politik, Ebenhausen 1995.

Hine, R. C. (1995), Turkey and the European Community: Regional Integration and Economic Convergence, in: Togan, S. (Ed.), The Economy of Turkey since Liberalization, Aldershot 1995, p. 131-154.

ITKIB, (1996), (Istanbul Textile and Apparel Exporters Associations), unpublished internal report, Istanbul 1996.

ITKIB, (1999), (Istanbul Textile and Apparel Exporters Associations), unpublished internal report, Istanbul 1999.

Iwd – Informationsdienst des Instituts der deutschen Wirtschaft (2001), Türkei: Sturmtief über dem Bosporus, Nr. 19, p. 2, May 10., 2001.

Kramer, H. (1994), EC-Turkish Relations: Unfinished Forever?, in: Ludlow, P. (Ed.), Europe and the Mediterranean, London 1994, p. 190-249.

Krugman, P. (1991), Geography and Trade, London 1991.

Lipsey, R.G. (1960), The Theory of Customs Unions: a general survey, Economic Journal, Vol. 50, 1960, p. 496-513.

Lohrmann, A.-M. (1997), Handels- und Entwicklungseffekte der Zollunion zwischen der EU und der Türkei, Frankfurt 1997.

Lohrmann, A.-M. (1997b), Der Textil- und Bekleidungssektor in der Türkei und die Auswirkungen der Zollunion mit der Europäischen Union, Zeitschrift für Türkeistudien (Journal of Turkish Studies; in German), H. 2, 1997, p. 203-223.

Lohrmann, A.-M. (1999), Trade and Welfare Effects of the Customs Union between Turkey and the EU, Zentrum für Türkeistudien (Ed.): Turkey in the EU Customs Union, Münster 1999, p. 47-57.

Lohrmann, A.-M. (1999b), Neuere Entwicklungen in der Konvergenzdiskussion – die EU-Kohäsionspolitik aus theoretischer Perspektive, Zeitschrift für Wirtschaftspolitik, (Journal of Economic Policy, in German), 48. Jg., 3, 1999, p. 323-343.

Lohrmann, A.-M, (2000), Development Effects of the Customs Union between Turkey and the EU – Catching-up or the Heckscher-Ohlin-Trap, Russian and East European Finance and Trade, Vol. 36, No. 4, July-August 2000, p. 26-44 .

Lohrmann, A.-M., (2002), A Dynamic Analysis of Turkey's Trade with the EU in the 1990s, Russian and East European Finance and Trade, forthcoming, March/April 2002.

Manegold, D. (1988), Die wirtschaftspolitischen Beziehungen der Türkei zur Europäischen Gemeinschaft und die Entwicklung der türkischen Volkswirtschaft, IflM-Arbeitsbericht, , FAL Braunschweig 1988.

Meade, J.E. (1955), The Theory of Customs Unions, Amsterdam 1955.

Myrdal, G. (1956), Development and Underdevelopment, reprinted in: Meyer, G.M. (Ed.), Leading Issues in Economic Development, 3. Ed., New York 1976, p. 688-692.

Önis, Z. (1991), Political Economy of Turkey in the 1980's: Anatomy of Unorthodox Liberalism, in: Heper, M. (Ed.), Strong State and Economic Interest Groups, Berlin 1991, p. 27-40.

Panagariya, A. / Srinivasan, T.N. (1998), The New Regionalism – a Benign or Malign Growth?, in: Bhagwati, J. /Hirsch, M. (Eds.), The Uruguay Round and Beyond, Berlin 1998, p. 221-240.

Rossini, G./ Burattoni, M. (1999), Italy, in: Brülhart, M./ Hine R.C (Eds.): Intra-Industry Trade and Adjustment, pp. 213-224.

Schröder, P.J.H. (2001), Eastern Enlargement: The New Challenge, in: Hansen, J.D. (Ed.), European Integration – An Economic Perspective, Oxford 2001, p. 193-225.

Şen, F. (2001), Die Türkei zu Beginn der EU-Beitrittspartnerschaft, Aus Politik und Zeitgeschichte, B 13-14 / 2001, p. 27-39.

Togan, S. (2001),The Turkish Economy and the European Economies in Transition, in: Togan, S. / Balasubramanyam, V.N. (Eds.), Turkey and Central and Eastern European Countries in Transition, Basingstoke, 2001, p. 7-50.

Undersecretary of Foreign Trade, Republic of Turkey (2001), Ankara 2001, www.foreigntrade.gov.tr.

Viner, J. (1950), The Customs Union Issue, New York / London 1950.

Yilmaz, B. (1998), International Competitiveness of Turkey with the European Union: A Comparison with Greece, Portugal, Spain and the EU/9, in: Rittenberg, L. (Ed.), The Political Economy of Turkey in the Post-Soviet Era, Westport 1998, p. 79-93.

In: European Economic and Political Issues, Volume 5
Editor: Frank Columbus. pp. 91-104.

ISBN 1-59033-322-5
© Nova Science Publishers, Inc.

Chapter 5

HOW DOES FOREIGN DIRECT INVESTMENT INFLUENCE POLAND'S EXPORTS TO THE EU

Marzenna Anna Weresa[1]

ABSTRACT

The favorable climate for inward investment in Poland resulted in a dynamic growth of foreign capital flows in terms of both quantity and value. The number of firms with a foreign capital stake reached nearly 45 thousand, rising six-fold during the nineties. The total value of foreign direct investment (FDI) stock amounted to $36.475 billion at the end of 2000, and was nearly 350 times larger than in 1990.

The objective of this paper is to examine the links between foreign direct investment in Poland and trade performance with the European Union, and, in particular, to find out how the activity of firms with foreign capital influences the competitiveness of Polish exports to the EU. The problem seems to be important, as the EU predominates in Poland's foreign trade, as well as in exports and imports of foreign investment enterprises (FIEs).

The importance of FDI in shaping the pattern of Poland's foreign trade with the EU has been growing in the 1990s, as FDI companies accounted for more than half of Poland's overall trade turnover in 2000, compared with one-fourth in 1995.

The inflow of FDI does not substitute for Poland's trade with the EU. On the contrary, it creates trade flows, as foreign investment is made mainly in sectors where Poland already has a comparative advantage in trade. Export creation, through the multiplier, has a positive effect on the pace of economic growth.

On the other hand however, the quality level of Polish exports is still lagging substantially behind that of the EU countries. In the short run the Polish trade pattern seems to be relatively stable. There are no significant shifts in Poland's export specialization towards the EU. Poland is increasingly specializing in traditional, price sensitive sectors, and this process is, to some extent, supported by inward FDI. The

[1] World Economy Research Institute, Warsaw School of Economics, Al. Niepodległosci 162, 02-521 Warsaw, Poland, tel./fax +48 22 848 91 32, e-mail: mweres@sgh.waw.pl.

Polish trade pattern will probably be changing in the long run. Externalities created by trade and FDI inflow will cause gradual upgrading of local production and influence specialization patterns. There have already been some positive shifts in high-tech trade competitiveness, which may result in changes of Poland's specialization pattern.

INTRODUCTION

Foreign capital is acknowledged as essential to the development and modernisation of the Polish economy (see for instance: Olesiński, 1998; Sadowski, 2000; Weresa, 2000). Since 1989, successive Polish governments have sought to attract and maintain foreign capital. Despite some debate about the appropriate level of foreign ownership in certain strategic sectors, all mainstream political parties and social groups generally welcome foreign direct investment (FDI). One exception is foreign ownership of agricultural land, which remains a sensitive issue subject to strict control.

The favourable climate for inward investment in Poland resulted in a dynamic growth of foreign capital flows in terms of both quantity and value. The number of firms with a foreign capital stake reached over 40 thousand, rising six-fold during the nineties. The total value of FDI stock amounted to $36.475 billion at the end of 2000, and was over 300 times larger than in 1990.[2]

It has been widely discussed that foreign direct investment has a significant impact on a country's foreign trade performance (for the theory see: Mundell, 1968; Puvis, 1972; Kojima, 1978; Bhaghwati & Brecher, 1980). At least two aspects of this interrelationship have to be taken into account. One is FDI influence on the volume and value of trade, and the other is connected with qualitative parameters of trade reflected in the competitiveness of tradables.

The objective of this paper is to examine the links between foreign direct investment in Poland and trade performance with the European Union, and, in particular, to find out how the activity of firms with foreign capital influences the competitiveness of Polish exports to the EU. The problem seems to be important, as the EU predominates in Poland's foreign trade, as well as in exports and imports of foreign investment enterprises (FIEs).

FDI AND EXPORT PROPENSITY: FOREIGN INVESTMENT ENTERPRISES (FIES) AND DOMESTIC FIRMS COMPARED

The different theoretical studies on the impact of FDI on country's trade volume suggest that there can be either substitution or complementation between these two phenomena. Furthermore, it is expected that with the opening of the economy for capital some quality or technology caching –up will occur (for the review of different theoretical approaches to FDI and trade links see for instance Weresa, 2001). The interrelationship depends mainly on the motives of international production and on the relevant type of FDI (Stern, 1997). Thus, the impact of foreign capital inflow on exports and imports can not be determined *a priori*. It

---

[2] This data related to FDI in Poland is based on National Bank of Poland balance of payments statistics.

must be determined empirically on the case-by-case basis. Table 1 summarizes possible impacts of FDI on export performance.

Table 1. Main FDI Motives and their Impacts on Export Performance

Main FDI Motives	Type of investment	Channels of FDI impact on trade	Possible improvements in the export sector
Local market penetration	Market–oriented investment	Spill over of technology from FIEs to local Polish exporters Competition effect	Quality upgrading of exports Increasing quality competition
Cost reduction	Resource seeking investment or Component-outsourcing investment	Demonstration effect. "Learning by doing" effects. Technological upgrading of exports created by firms with foreign capital	Productivity gains in the export sector Inter-industry or intra-company trade creation
Improvement of investor's global competitiveness (including export expansion)	Efficiency-seeking investment	Spill over of technology & imitation Direct technological and quality improvements in the exporting FIEs	Creation of intra-industry trade

The Polish case confirms that the relationship between FDI and foreign trade cannot be reduced to a dichotomy of substitution and complementation. FDI has both direct and indirect effects on trade. The indirect impact of FDI on foreign trade embraces a wide variety of effects, both micro and macroeconomic, which are associated with the use and diffusion of technology, the extent and direction of knowledge-transfer regarding production, management or distribution.

As a rule however, firms with foreign stakes are more export–oriented than "pure" Polish companies. Throughout the whole transition period export propensity, measured, as a share of export sales in the total sales, has been nearly two times higher for companies with foreign participation than for domestic firms. The companies with foreign participation seem to be more export oriented, although export propensity has been declining for both groups of enterprises since 1994. They have become relatively more oriented towards the internal market, which is to some extent a result of growing domestic absorption in 1996 and 1997. The picture changed in 1998, when FIEs improved the export performance in terms of its value related to the value of total sales, and after a slight swing in 1999 export propensity rose again, reaching 16.2% in 2000 (table 2).

Table 2. Export propensity of FIEs in Poland (export sales/total sales in %), 1994-2000

	1994	1995	1996	1997	1998	1999	2000
FIEs	15.6	15.3	13.9	13.8	14.1	13.2	16.2
Domestic firms	9.0	9.5	8.8	8.0	7.1	6.4	6.2

Source: Author's calculations from Poland's Main Statistical Office (GUS) data.

Moreover, FIEs are more effective in their export activity. In 1995-2000 export per employee has been continuously increasing, while it has been rather stable for domestic firms. In 1995 export per employee in FIEs amounted to 24,715 zlotys, compared with 8,557 zlotys in domestic enterprises. In 2000 these results were 71,024 zlotys and 12,926 zlotys respectively, so the gap widened in real and relative terms.

There is also a growing difference in productivity of both groups of enterprises, measured by income per employee. Figure 1 illustrates the statistical findings.

The influence of FIEs on the volume of Poland's total exports, as well as on Polish exports to the EU is relatively large. Since 1994, both the exports and the imports of FIEs have been increasing at a higher pace than Poland's total exports and imports. Their share in Poland's foreign trade has been constantly growing. In 1995 FIEs exported to the EU $6,130.1 million, creating 32.8% of Poland's exports, while in 2000 their export to the EU reached $13,468.2 million, which is 60.8% of the total. Import from the EU has been developing even more rapidly. In 1995 FIEs imported $9,140.7million worth of goods (48.7% of Poland's imports from the EU), while in 2000 their imports rose to $18,890.8 million, constituting 63.1% of Poland's total imports from the EU countries. During the whole transition period exports to the EU created by the companies with foreign participation have doubled, while exports of "pure" Polish firms have decreased (Figure 2).

Figure 1. Income and export per employee: FIEs and Polish firms compared, 1995-2000

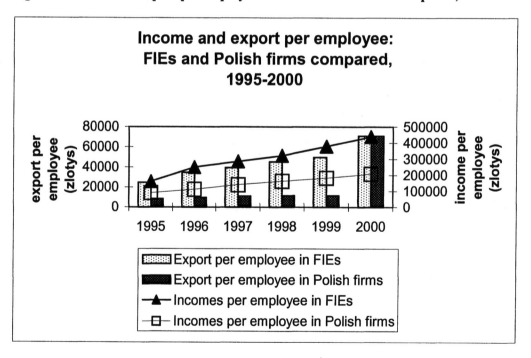

Source: Author's calculations based on GUS data.

Figure 2. Polish Exports to the EU: FIEs and Polish firms compared (in $ m), 1995-2000

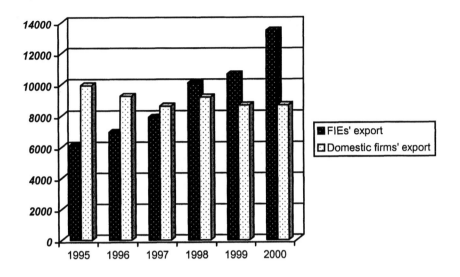

Source: Tabulated from GUS and IKiCHZ data.

FDI AND GEOGRAPHY OF POLISH EXPORTS TO THE EU

There is some similarity between the structure of the FDI stock in Poland by individual EU countries and the geographical composition of Poland's foreign trade with the EU.

In terms of value, Germany predominates in Poland's foreign trade with the EU, while in terms of capital stock value it is the second biggest investor in the Polish market. In respect to exports and imports, Italy places behind Germany, although its investment position in the Polish market measured by FDI stock is relatively lower. For both Germany and Italy, the absolute value of trade (exports as well as imports) considerably exceeded the value of capital invested by companies from these countries. The same applies to their relative value. Their shares in the total export of FIEs are higher than the percentage of their total FDI stock in Poland. In 2000 export to Germany constituted 35.8% of total export of FIEs, while the stock of German capital invested in Poland reached only 12.8% of the total FDI stock. The gap between share in export compared with the share in total capital stock is even wider for Italy: export of FIEs to Italy constituted 11.3%, while Italian FDI stock was 7.5% of the total.

The biggest investor in the Polish market in terms of capital stock value is France, but it is not the leader in terms of exports. French capital share in total capital stock in Poland originated amounted to 17.3%, while France's share in FIEs' export reached in 2000 only 6.4%.

There is no statistical evidence that a country's share in FDI stock is correlated with its share in exports to the home country.

On the other hand, however, in case of four EU countries, namely Italy, Belgium, France and UK, the share of FIEs in total Poland's export to these countries was relatively high, exceeding the average for all EU countries. In case of Italy, for example, nearly 80% of total Polish export is created by FIEs (figure3).

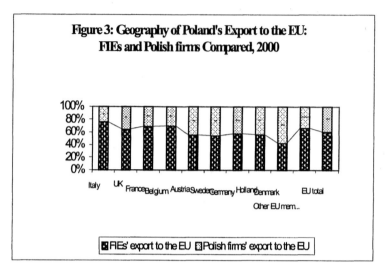

Source: Based on GUS data.

MEASURING EXPORT COMPETITIVENESS

Some quality or technology catching up is expected to follow the opening of an economy for goods, capital and technology. A catching up process, in relation to foreign trade, can be seen in some improvements in competitiveness of exports. How far has this process progressed in the case of Poland's export and what role has FDI played there?

There are some indicators, which may reflect the impact of foreign capital inflow on competitiveness of exported products. Theoretically, the growth of competitiveness could be expected, where foreign investors possess the ownership advantages, which sooner or later are acquired by domestic firms. Ownership advantages can be defined as managerial or technological know-how, patents, trading expertise, trademarks or other intangible assets (Dunning, 1993). As long as FDI leads to the diffusion of these advantages in the host country's economy, it affects indirectly the structural competitiveness of domestic enterprises and their products (Lall, 1998). Moreover, the presence of foreign investors increases competition and forces domestic firms to modernize their production processes and products. These indirect effects are stronger in the case of investment in technologically advanced goods. FDI in these sectors causes an increase in productivity of capital and stimulates innovation activity. The upgrading of technology and the transfer of technical know-how may alter the pattern of competitiveness. Some econometric evidence, as well as case studies for some countries show that the technological externalities of FDI (like knowledge spillovers or demonstration effect), influence factor productivity of local firms and their propensity to export (Aitken, Hansen & Harrison, 1994; Markusen & Venables, 1997). More efficient production processes and introduction of new goods and services are expected to have an impact on export performance.

There are at least two methods, which can be used for measuring changes in export competitiveness. One is the unit value concept and the other is revealed comparative advantage (RCA) index.

A study by Nielsen (1999) based on the unit value proved that in case of Poland's export to the EU there is no significant catch up. In the 1990s Poland's competitiveness has been increasing slightly in price elastic product groups, and decreasing in the intermediate range with no improvement in quality competition (Nielsen, 1999).

A stability of Poland's export specialization is also proved by the analyses based on RCA index (Weresa, 2000).

The statistical data show that the commodity structure of Poland's trade with the EU has also been relatively stable since 1995 (table 3). The main export items during the whole period are machinery and plant, textiles, transportation equipment, and base metals and products.

Table 3. Commodity structure of Poland's foreign trade with the EU, 1995 and 2000 compared

Commodity Group	Poland's Export to the EU		Share in Total		Poland's Import from the EU		Share in Total	
	1995	2000	1995 (%)	2000 (%)	1995	2000	1995 (%)	2000 (%)
TOTAL	16036	22144	100.0	100.0	18781	29951	100.0	100.0
Livestock and animal products	533	402	3.3	1.8	255	200	1.4	0.7
Crop products	463	456	2.9	2.1	291	568	1.5	1.9
Fats and oils	160	5	1.0	0.0	139	111	0.7	0.4
Food products	355	423	2.2	1.9	773	743	4.1	2.5
Mineral products	1359	1240	8.5	5.6	653	719	3.5	2.4
Chemical products	780	788	4.9	3.6	2162	3575	11.5	11.9
Plastics and products	491	901	3.1	4.1	1488	2599	7.9	8.7
Leather and products	180	219	1.1	1.0	184	324	1.0	1.1
Wood and wood products	876	958	5.5	4.3	96	227	0.5	0.8
Pulp, paper, board and products	324	551	2.0	2.5	1096	1430	5.8	4.8
Textiles and products	2515	2374	15.7	10.7	2083	2235	11.1	7.5
Footwear and headgear	196	164	1.2	0.7	75	124	0.4	0.4
Stone and ceramic products, glass	292	429	1.8	1.9	469	756	2.5	2.5
Base metals and products	2684	2786	16.7	12.6	1550	2805	8.3	9.4
Machinery and plant, electrical and electronic equipment	1632	4911	10.2	22.2	5173	8810	27.5	29.4
Transportation equipment	1844	3241	11.5	14.6	1371	3451	7.3	11.5
Optical photographic. measuring and control instruments	75	129	0.5	0.6	490	573	2.6	1.9
Miscellaneous finished good, furniture, building elements, toys	1245	1959	7.8	8.8	377	615	2.0	2.1
Other goods	32	208	0.2	0.9	56	86	0.3	0.3

Source: Tabulated from GUS data.

The trade structure in 1995 is strongly correlated with the trade structure in 1999. The correlation coefficient for export is 0.81, while for import is 0.98. Despite acceleration of FDI inflow since 1995 there have been no crucial changes in the commodity structure of Poland's foreign trade with the EU.

The reasons for this stability are related to the role of technology in shaping country's international specialization pattern. In the short run country's technological capabilities, as well as the resource allocation are relatively stable (Amendola, Guerrieri & Padoan, 1998). They shape country's trade specialization and constitute a basis for FDI flows.

Inward investment and foreign trade patterns can be explained using Vernon's product cycle model (Vernon, 1966) or technological gap theory (Posner, 1961; Krugman, 1979). Both theories predict that countries, which are leaders in terms of technology, will maintain their leading position in the future. The crucial element of these theories is timing. Either time lag in technology diffusion decides about innovator's advantage (technological gap theory) or changes of product characteristic over time influences optimal location of production (product cycle concept).

These elements have been further developed in the concept of technological accumulation, where innovation is seen as a cumulative process. This cumulative nature of innovation explains the existence of technology gaps, which allow firms, sectors and countries to create specific competitive advantages. It is difficult however, to move from an established competitive advantage in one industry to another. Technological accumulation theory assumes that for each country technological accumulation is comparatively high in some sectors and low in others. The process of catching-up is faster in sectors where country has comparative advantage in innovative activity (Cantwell, 1989). It has been proved that countries hold technological advantages in particular industries for rather long period of time. This implies that the process of "catching up" would start as a revitalization of traditionally strong sectors, rather than the development of new industries (Cantwell, 1989). The technological accumulation has been often used as an argument for explaining the stabilization of a country's trade pattern. The innovation history and experience can "lock up" country's specialization pattern (Arthur, 1989). The alternative way predicts that a country moves along trajectories of technological accumulations (Pavitt, 1988), which means developing comparative advantage in fields strictly related to traditionally advantageous sectors.

The interdependence between technological and trade advantages has been tested empirically for some OECD countries (Soete, 1987; Amendola, Guerrieri & Padoan, 1998). The results confirm the links between the two patterns and their relative stability. The same conclusions were drawn earlier by Pavitt and Cantwell, who proved that the technological specialization (and thus trade specialization) was stable in the short and medium term, but in the long run (more than 50 years) these patterns tended to change. This change is connected with the development of new technologies and new industries, which can revolutionize established international specialization patterns. Thus, changes in trade pattern are significant only in the long run. They might result from break-through inventions, but they might also be an effect of gradual upgrading of local production. FDI might speed up the process of technology imitation and diffusion, but the significant impact can be noticed over the longer period.

This theoretical explanation seems to be appropriate for Poland, as the empirical results show the stable commodity structure of Poland's trade with the EU during the 1990s.

Moreover, Poland has been developing a comparative advantage in trade mainly in fields strictly related to traditionally advantageous sectors, such as textiles and wood processing (table 4).

Poland maintained a traditional comparative advantage in trade of livestock and animal products, crop products, minerals, wood, textiles, footwear and headgear, base metals and products, transportation equipment, and furniture. The commodity groups where Poland lost its comparative advantage in trade with the EU were fats & oils and leather products, which might be connected with FDI inflow to these sectors, as RCA indices were negative for companies with foreign capital.

Table 4. Poland's specialization in trade with the EU, 1995 and 2000 compared

Commodity Group	RCA in Poland's Trade with the EU		RCA in FIEs' Trade	
	1995	2000	1995	2000
Livestock and animal products	0.90	1.00	1.21	0.95
Crop products	0.62	0.08	-0.12	-0.23
Fats and oils	0.30	-2.80	-2.47	-1.34
Food products	-0.62	-0.26	-0.13	0.34
Mineral products	0.89	0.85	0.45	-1.04
Chemical products	-0.86	-1.21	-1.72	-1.39
Plastics and products	-0.95	-0.76	-0.42	-0.39
Leather and products	0.14	-0.09	0.23	-0.30
Wood and wood products	2.37	1.74	1.16	1.02
Pulp, paper, board and products	-1.06	-0.65	0.08	0.14
Textiles and products	0.35	0.36	0.57	0.31
Footwear and headgear	1.12	0.58	0.58	0.33
Stone and ceramic products, glass	-0.32	-0.26	0.07	0.14
Base metals and products	0.71	0.30	0.31	0.29
Machinery and plant, electrical and electronic equipment	-1.00	-0.28	-0.38	-0.21
Transportation equipment	0.45	0.24	0.26	0.40
Optical, photographic, measuring and control instruments	-1.72	-1.19	-1.11	-1.09
Miscellaneous finished goods, furniture, building elements, toys	1.35	1.46	1.37	1.34

RCA is calculated here using the following formula: $RCA_i = \ln [\, X_{ij}/ M_{ij} : X_j/ M_j\,]$, where X_{ij} is export of commodity i by country j, and M_{ij} is import of commodity i by country j. X_j and M_j are total country's j exports and imports. When RCA>0 a country is relatively specialized in this group of goods.

Furthermore, FDI is undertaken mainly in industries where Poland has a comparative advantage in total foreign trade, although these sectors are sometimes disadvantageous in trade with the EU. The food industry, for example, attracted the largest foreign capital flows (nearly 10% of the total FDI in Poland). The RCA index for food products is positive for all of both Poland's trade and the trade of FIEs, but it is negative for Poland's trade with the EU.

This means that FDI in the food sector was motivated by the potential export to non-EU countries.

Although there is no significant statistical evidence that the activity of FIEs caused restructuring of Polish exports to the EU, empirical findings confirmed the positive impact of FDI on the production processes, which over the longer period might result in upgrading the quality of manufacturing export. The results of the survey of a random sample of enterprises (foreign and Polish owned) showed that 46% of FIEs and 40% of domestic firms introduced crucial changes in production process during 1995-2000.

Table 5. Share of firms having introduced on the market any new or technologically improved product or process, 1995-2000

	FIEs	Domestic firms
Percentage of firms, where products or production process were improved in 1995-2000	46.0%	40.0%
Changes in the field of:		
-Technology	93.1%	60.6%
-Product characteristics	96.6%	74.2%
-Distribution channels	24.1%	33.3%
-Organization of work	32.8%	25.3%

Note: The percentages do not add up to 100 since some of the subjects indicated several replies.

The survey used a sample of 291 companies (126 FIEs and 165 domestic firms) and was carried out by the author in November 2000.

Source: Calculations based on the results of the author's survey.

In 1995-2000 over 90% of FIEs surveyed, improved quality of their products. Some changes in product characteristics were also reported by 74% of domestic firms. Technological upgrading of the production process was noted in 93.1% of FIEs and 60.6% of domestic enterprises. The results of the survey were better for domestic firms than for FIEs in the field of distribution channels, where improvements were introduced by 24.1% of FIEs and 33.3% of domestic firms.

Apart from technology, FDI might influence the competitiveness by improvements in organization of work, management and marketing. The survey confirmed that FIEs were more flexible in changing the organization of work: in 1995-2000 32.8% of FIEs compared with 25.3% of domestic firms implemented some changes in the organization of the production process.

As FDI is a method of transferring technology to the Polish market and improving the competitiveness of products, to what extent this has been reflected in the foreign trade of high-tech products with the EU?

During 1995-1999, Poland's export and import of high technological products were growing. The same tendency can be seen in Poland's high-tech trade with the EU. There is however, a strong asymmetry in high-tech trade with the EU as well as in Poland's total foreign trade of this group. In 1999 Poland's total import of high-tech goods was over 6-fold higher than total export, while its import of high-tech goods from the EU exceeded export to the EU 5-fold, and the gap has grown since 1995 (table 6).

**Table 6. Poland's foreign trade with the EU in
high-tech products, 1995-99 (US $ million)**

	1995	1996	1997	1998	1999
Poland's export of high-tech products	529.5	709.4	675.6	872.4	793.7
Poland's export of high-tech products to the EU	294.9	372.8	382.6	517.4	489.7
(million US$)	1.8%	2.3%	2.3%	2.7%	2.5%
As a percentage of total Poland's exports to the EU					
Poland's import of high-tech products	2551.4	3556.0	4384.3	4801.7	5071.4
Poland's import of high-tech products from the EU (million US$)	1523.4	1971.0	2338.4	2591.9	2784.9
As a percentage of total Poland's imports from the EU	8.1%	8.3%	8.7%	8.4%	9.3%

Source: Calculated from GUS data.

Although foreign trade in high-tech goods has been increasing in terms of value (except export in 1999), there have been upward and downward swings in the annual growth rate of high-tech export since 1995. Nevertheless, the growth rate was higher for export to the EU than for total Poland's high-tech export (figure 4). This result along with the growing share of high-tech goods in Poland's exports to the EU (1.8% in 1995 compared to 2.5% in 1999) indicates a slight improvement in Poland's position in high-tech export to the EU.

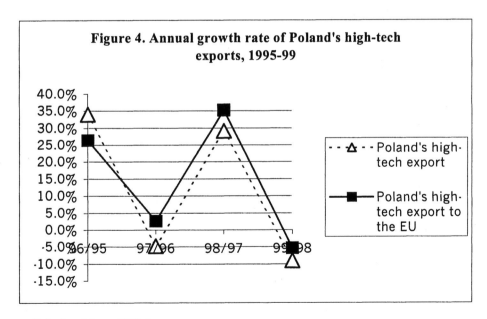

Source: Calculated from GUS data.

However, there were no significant changes in Poland's high-tech specialization in trade with the EU. In 1999 the products comparatively advantageous for Poland in trade with the EU were the same as in 1995. They included non-electrical machinery, aircraft, radio & TV components. In 1995 as well as in 1999 trade in computers, R&D equipment, drugs and chemicals was comparatively disadvantageous (table 7).

**Table 7. Poland's specialization in high-tech trade with the EU:
1995 and 1999 compared**

High-tech Product Groups	RCA Index	
	1995	1999
Non-electrical machinery	2.63	2.27
Electrical machinery	1.55	1.85
Aircraft	2.45	0.29
Radio, TV & communication equipment	0.26	0.19
R&D equipment	-0.40	-0.05
Computers	-1.22	-0.51
Drugs	-0.50	-1.53
Chemicals	-0.75	-1.65

Source: Own calculations based on GUS data.

As Poland's high-tech export specialization towards the EU was not changed in 1995-99, so there is no statistical evidence that FIEs activity improved the competitiveness of Poland's export of high-tech products.

POLICY IMPLICATIONS

Since the beginning of transition Poland has significantly increased its openness to FDI and foreign trade. As these two phenomena are interrelated policy measures addressed to one usually affect both of them.

Empirical evidence assessing FDI impact on trade competitiveness indicates the following:

- although the export propensity of FIEs is higher than that of domestic firms, there is no significant statistical evidence that the activity of FIEs caused restructuring of Polish exports to the EU;
- the quality level of Polish exports is still lagging substantially behind that of the EU countries;
- there are no significant shifts in Poland's export specialization towards the EU. Poland is increasingly specializing in traditional, price sensitive sectors, and this process is, to some extent, supported by inward FDI.;
- the changes in Poland's high-tech export to the EU are very slow, so FIEs have not yet contributed to the competitiveness of Poland's export of high-tech products.

These conclusions based on empirical results should be reflected in Poland's trade and FDI policy.

The main features of Poland's trade and FDI policy towards the EU in the 1990s are to a great extent a result of the Uruguay Round and WTO membership, the Europe Agreement (which provides for the adoption of the *acuis communautaire*).

The obligations tied with WTO membership include tariff bindings, the dismantling of quotas and other quantitative restrictions, the acceptance of disciplines in the field of export subsidies, agriculture, services, trade-related aspects of intellectual property rights (TRIPs), trade-related investment measures (TRIMs), health and safety regulations.

Apart form these general obligations connected with WTO membership Poland's policy towards the EU is shaped by the regulations of the Europe Agreement. Priority areas for the adaptation of laws include customs law (including elimination of tariffs and quantitative restrictions on imports), company law (and gradual facilitation of foreign investor's activity), intellectual property, financial services, competition policy, state aids, technical standards and environmental protection.

Within the framework of these international obligations Polish government has to identify priority objectives for the FDI and trade policy. From the trade competitiveness perspective they should include:

- more emphasis on attracting export-oriented investment;
- efforts not only to attract FDI, but also to divert it to selected sectors;
- targeted incentives promoting R&D related investment;
- wider promotion the development of linkages between foreign - owned and Polish firms.[3]

It is also increasingly important to ensure the coherence between foreign investment policy, trade policy and other domestic policies and regulatory regimes. This includes domestic capacity building and efforts to reduce of several structural barriers, which might distort markets, as for example state aids, taxation policy, telecommunication regimes or anti-competitive business practice.

REFERENCES

Aitken B., Hanson G., Harrison A., (1994), *Spillovers, Foreign Investment, and Export Behavior,* NBER Working Paper 4967.

Amendola, G., Guerrieri, P., Padoan, P.C., (1998), "International patterns of technological accumulation and trade" in: D.Archibugi and J.Michie (eds.) *Trade, Growth and Technical Change,* Cambridge University Press, Cambridge, pp.141-168.

Arthur, W.B.,(1989), "Competing technologies, increasing returns and lock-in by historical events", *Economic Journal,* 99, 1989, pp.116-31.

Bhagwati J.N., Brecher R.A., (1980),"National Welfare in an Open Economy in the Presence of Foreign-Owned Factors of Production", *Journal of International Economics,* Vol. 10, pp. 103-115.

Cantwell, J., (1989), *Technological Innovation and Multinational Corporations,* Basil Blackwell, Oxford.

---

[3] Here, for example, the Hungarian experience can be used. In 1997 Hungarian government developed "Targeted Programme for Subcontractors", which was aimed at creating a network of domestic suppliers enjoying improved credibility with foreign - owned firms (OECD, 1999).

Dunning J.H., (1993), *Multinational Enterprises and the Global Economy*, Addison-Wesley Publishing Company, Wokingham.

Kojima K., (1978), *Direct Foreign Investment,* Croom Helm, London.

Krugman P., (1979), "A Model of Innovation, Technology Transfer and the World Distribution of Income", *Journal of Political Economy,* 87.

Lall S., (1998), "Changing perception of Foreign Investment in Development", in: P.K.M. Tharakan and D Van Den Bulcke (eds), *International Trade, Foreign Direct Investment and Economic Environment,* London, MacMillan Press Ltd.

Markusen J.R., Venables A.J., (1997), *Foreign Direct Investment as a Catalyst for Industrial Development,* NBER Working Paper 6241.

Mundell R.A., (1968), *International Economics,* Macmillan.

Nielsen Uff-Møller J., (1999), "Foreign Direct Investment in Poland and Quality Catch-up of Polish Foreign Trade".

Olesiński Z., (ed.), (1998), *Bezpośrednie inwestycje zagraniczne w Polsce*, PWE, Warszawa.

OECD (1999), *Background Report on Enhancing Market Openness through Regulatory Reform*, OECD, Paris.

Pavitt, K., (1988), "International patterns of technological accumulation", in: N.Hood and J.E.Vahlne (eds) *Strategies in Global Competition,* Croom Helm, London.

Posner, M., (1961), "Technical change and international trade", *Oxford Economic Papers,* vol.13.

Purvis D.D., (1972), "Technology, Trade and Factor Mobility", *Economic Journal*, September, pp. 991-999.

Sadowski Z., (ed.), (2000), *Kapital zagraniczny w Polsce – warunki działania*, PTE, Warszawa.

Soete, L. (1987), "The impact of technological innovation on international trade patterns: the evidence reconsidered", *Research Policy,* 16(2-4), pp.101-30.

Stern R.E., (1997), "Foreign Direct Investment, Exports and East-West Integration: Theory and Practice" in: Cooper R.N. Gacs J. (eds), *Trade Growth in Transition Economies Export Impediments for Central and Eastern Europe",* Elgar , Chelternham, pp.329-357.

Weresa M.A., (ed.), (2000), *Foreign Direct Investment in a Transition Economy. The Polish Case*, SSEES UCL, London.

Weresa M.A. , (2001), "The Impact of FDI on Poland's Trade with the EU", *Post-Communist Economies,* Vol.13, No.1, 2001.

In: European Economic and Political Issues, Volume 5   ISBN 1-59033-322-5
Editor: Frank Columbus. pp. 105-121.   © Nova Science Publishers, Inc.

Chapter 6

INSTITUTIONS OF THE NEW REGIONALISM: THE CASE OF ENGLAND

Darren Webb

INTRODUCTION

Regional Development Agencies (RDAs) were formally established in eight of the nine regions of England in April 1999. The ninth region—London—received its own Agency, together with elected mayor and Greater London Authority, a year later. A great deal of hullabaloo accompanied the establishment of the RDAs, reflecting the fact that they are, as Bennett and Payne rightly indicate, 'a New Labour flagship. They are the most important aspect of Labour's changes to the institutional structures that influence local and regional economic development' (Bennett and Payne, 2000, p.71). This paper examines the RDA programme in light of the wider social and theoretical context provided by the 'New Regionalism', a body of thought which is quickly becoming an orthodoxy in the field of economic and political geography. In particular the paper analyses the way in which the 'New Regionalism' has been interpreted in policy discourses in England and assesses the extent to which the establishment of Regional Development Agencies can be said to demonstrate a general adherence to a 'New Regionalist' agenda on the part of the Labour government. The paper begins by asking what the 'New Regionalism' itself actually is—an important question often bypassed by those who deploy the phrase. This is followed by a consideration of whether RDAs represent a 'new-model' democratic form appropriate to the new phase of capitalist development that the 'New Regionalism' suggests we have entered. The arguments informing the establishment of RDAs in England are then examined and it is suggested that the Agencies can be seen as an integral part of the Labour government's 'New Regionalist' accumulation strategy. Finally, some of the criticisms that have been levelled at the 'New Regionalism' are considered and their implications for the RDA programme assessed.

WHAT EXACTLY IS THE 'NEW REGIONALISM'?

The 'New Regionalism' refers to a body of thought which highlights the resurgence of the region as the key economic space within capitalism and which also, following on from this, points to the emergence of the region as the most appropriate level for policy formation and co-ordination. In contrast to traditional regionalist arguments and movements, the calls for regional government (or rather governance) are underpinned by economic concerns over competitiveness rather than by political concerns over autonomy or autarky. In addition, 'the region' itself has been redefined in economic terms so that it no longer refers to a 'place' or territory bound by a shared culture, nor even to a geographical space defined by political or administrative boundaries, but rather to a nexus of economic clusters and networks. In this sense, the term 'New' designates less a rethinking of the *political* ideology of regionalism and more the transformation of this ideology into an essentially *economic* argument.

Emphasising its predominantly economic concerns, Lovering suggests that the New Regionalism is characterised by '(1) the historico-empirical claim that 'the region' is becoming the 'crucible' of economic development; and (2) the normative bias that 'the region' should be the prime focus of economic policy' (Lovering, 1999, p.380). This corresponds to two distinct meanings implied by the suffix *ism*, namely, a process or result on the one hand and a normative doctrine on the other. The New Regionalism as an historico-empirical claim works *down* (by means of a negative logic) from the demise of the nation-state and traditional regional planning to the level of the region which becomes, almost by default, the locus of economic activity and political governance. The New Regionalism as a normative doctrine works *up* (by means of a positive logic) from the micro-economic and even the psychological level and declares that the region, by virtue of its own institutional capacities, is the most dynamic and therefore appropriate level for economic activity and political governance.

The negative logic of the New Regionalism as a process is inextricably tied in with the supposed transition from Fordism to post-Fordism. Drawing on the insights provided by French regulation theory (Aglietta, 1979; Lipietz, 1986; Boyer, 1990), the Fordist 'regime of accumulation' is said to have collapsed under the weight of its own internal contradictions as the saturation of markets threw the system of mass production and mass consumption into a crisis from which it could not recover. In response to the prolonged accumulation crisis of the 1970s, many small firms began to adopt a system of flexible specialisation—quite simply flexibility plus specialisation—as a means of dealing with the uncertainty engendered by the fragmentation of formerly secure and stable mass markets (Piore and Sabel, 1984). This signalled the re-emergence of 'the region' as, conceptually, the system of flexible specialisation encouraged spatial clustering and integration at the regional level whilst, empirically, the most dynamic post-Fordist economies just so happened to be those *regions*— the Third Italy, Baden-Württemberg, Silicon Valley, Route 128—which had successfully responded to the crisis of Fordism by adopting the system of flexible specialisation (Sabel, 1994). Importantly, however, the term 'region' came to designate spaces typified by networks of inter-firm collaboration rather than neatly defined political or administrative units.

Compounding the economic resurgence of the region in the context of the transition to post-Fordism has been the political resurgence of the region in the context of what Ohmae (1997) terms 'The End of the Nation State'. Economic globalisation and the liberalisation of markets have greatly enhanced the mobility of capital and have reinforced the underlying power of market mechanisms in determining the trajectory of contemporary capitalism. There is widespread consensus that these developments have rendered the nation-state an inappropriate level at which to formulate and co-ordinate economic policy. Too small to deal with capitalism as a global system and too large to respond effectively to the rapid changes taking place at the local level, the nation-state has been forced to devolve more and more of its powers to surpra-national bodies above it and to sub-national bodies below (Amin and Tomaney, 1995; Mittleman, 1996; Keating, 1997, 1998). This so-called 'hollowing out of the state' (Jessop, 1990, 1994) has seen the region acquire more decision-making and regulatory functions in response to the crisis of legitimacy faced by the state at the national level.

The failure of traditional 'top-down' regional policy is emphasised by all those who work within the New Regionalist framework. It is deemed to have failed on its own terms, proving unable to generate self-sustained endogenous growth even during its heyday (Amin, 1999), and is regarded as completely impracticable now that the international mobility of capital has greatly diminished the ability of governments to steer investment (Keating, 1997). Fortunately, however, the economic developments associated with the transition to post-Fordism and the hollowing out of the state have prompted the emergence of a new kind of regional policy, more spontaneous and multipolar than its 'traditional' counterpart and emanating from 'below' rather than 'above' (Mittleman, 1996). The nature of this new policy regime is captured by the phrase 'governance', which is neatly counter-posed to the term govern*ment*. The central argument here is that a nascent mode of regulation and co-ordination based around inter-firm networks and public-private partnerships at the regional level has developed from below in response to the palpable failure of top-down policies to deal with the subtle complexities of local and regional development in a globalised world (Ohmae, 1997). The region thus comes to displace the nation-state as the locus for political governance by virtue of both processes directed from above (the hollowing out of the state) and by developments emerging from below (the grass-roots construction of an alternative to traditional regional policy).

These descriptive arguments are seldom advanced on their own but tend instead to be accompanied by the 'normative bias' referred to by Lovering. This normative bias suggests that the processes described above should be bolstered and developed further so that 'the region' is equipped with the 'devolved institutional capacity' required in order 'to design and deliver policies which are attuned to the nuances of their own regional economies' (Morgan, 1997, p.501). This is where the positive logic of the New Regionalism steps in, a logic framed by 'the institutional turn' in regional development studies (Morgan, 1997; Amin, 1999; Raco, 1999). The term 'institution' is used to refer to 'recurrent patterns of behaviour – habits, conventions and routines' (Morgan, 1997, p.493) and the 'institutional turn' describes the growing recognition of the importance played by these in the process of regional economic development. The essence of the argument is that institutional norms such as trust, co-operation and reciprocity form 'untraded interdependencies' (Storper, 1995, 1997) which impact greatly upon the behaviour of economic actors and have a positive effect upon the innovative capacity of those economies possessing 'institutional thickness', i.e., in which untraded interdependencies are thoroughly 'embedded in networks of interpersonal relations' (Amin, 1999, p.366). Because the region seems to be the level at which institutional thickness is best developed—it is small enough to allow for the regular face-to-face interactions upon which trust and co-operation are built and yet big enough to sustain a critical mass of interpersonal networks—'the region has central theoretical status in the process of capitalist development' (Storper, 1995, p.211) and becomes 'a fundamental basis of economic and social life' within post-Fordism (Storper, 1997, p.3).

The 'institutional turn' combines with neo-Schumpeterian endogenous growth theory to form the basis of a New Regionalist consensus (Amin, 1999). It is from endogenous growth theory that many of the ideas most commonly associated with the New Regionalism are drawn—the emphasis placed on entrepreneurship and competition as the source of innovation-led economic growth and the almost obsessive amount of attention paid to the agglomeration economies to be gained from spatial clustering (Porter, 1990, 1998). The essentially economic concerns of the New Regionalism become quite evident here. For the starting point for the New Regionalists is almost always the concept of 'regional competitiveness' and the combined might of endogenous growth theory, institutional economics and cognitive psychology is drawn upon so that insights might be gained into the nature of competitiveness. The basic insight gained from these bodies of thought is that 'the enduring competitive advantages in a global economy lie increasingly in local things— knowledge, relationships, motivation—that distant rivals cannot match' (Porter, 1998, p.78) and the policy prescriptions made on the basis of this insight suggest the need to broaden and deepen the regional 'institutional base' constituted by these local things. The concept of the 'learning region' becomes crucial here, as learning itself (firms learning from customers, suppliers or other firms in close proximity) is viewed as the principal factor sustaining a region's competitive advantage (Cooke, 1996; Morgan, 1997). Fundamental importance is therefore attached to the 'institutional capacity' of a region, i.e., to the way in which local knowledge, relationships and motivation interact to create a milieu conducive (or not) to learning, innovation and growth. The primary concern of policy-makers should therefore be the construction of a framework which nurtures the region's untraded interdependencies, which facilitates institutional learning, which strengthens networks of association and which generates clusters of innovation.

One returns here to the key notion of governance. Regional competitiveness in a globalised world, or so it is claimed, is best served through the further development of a 'Schumpeterian workfare regime' in which 'hetararchic' negotiation displaces the market and the state as the primary mechanism for economic co-ordination (Jessop, 1998). In terms derived from cognitive psychology, this translates as a move away from the suffocating (inflexible, responsive, procedural) rationalities associated with the state/market dichotomy and towards a problem-seeking/problem-solving 'reflexive' rationality based around group learning (Jessop, 1998; Amin, 1999). In more readily comprehensible terms, this means a move away from restrictive 'top-down' state management and towards a supply-side orientation which recognises that regional economies are socially/institutionally constituted entities rather than a collection of individual actors. The key to successful governance within a post-Fordist global economy lies, therefore, in strengthening the supply-side resources (primarily knowledge and skills but also mutual support mechanisms) required by the indigenous networks of the 'associational economy' (Cooke and Morgan, 1998). This in turn requires the devolution of political power so that regions can develop their own competitive advantages within their own institutional context.

Within the New Regionalism, then, arguments for regional devolution are really little more than a sub-category of the arguments for regional competitiveness. The concern with regional competitiveness developed in response to two closely related phenomena. The first was the failure of traditional regional policy to stimulate self-sustained regional growth, the devastating consequences of which were highlighted during the economic crisis of the 1970s. The second was the so-called 'Second Industrial Divide' (Piore and Sabel, 1984), which saw a small number of regions rejecting Fordist mass production and building economic success upon the new production paradigm of flexible specialisation. The model of economic development adopted within these 'New Industrial Districts' (Piore and Sabel, 1984) or 'New Industrial Spaces' (Scott, 1988; Storper and Scott, 1989) was held up as a shining example to all of how regional competitiveness could be wrought out of economic crisis. More sophisticated research followed, offering detailed analyses of the key to economic success within these new industrial spaces. Thus emerged a proliferating number of models, concepts and theories, each of which emphasised the important role played by interpersonal networks, untraded interdependencies, institutional learning and clusters of innovation in the stimulation of sustainable regional development. Accompanying the clarion calls for greater institutional thickness at the regional level came the calls for regional devolution, not as a means of fostering regional 'democracy' or 'autonomy' as a socio-political end in itself, but rather as a means of nurturing the structure of governance required in order to stimulate innovation, thus competitiveness, thus growth in the context of a globalised economy. In many ways, the 'Regional Development Agency' can be seen as a model form of the institutional structure of governance petitioned for by the New Regionalists.

RDAs AS A 'NEW MODEL' OF GOVERNANCE?

Whilst Regional Development Agencies are hardly 'new' (1909 saw the establishment of the Development Commission in Britain and a number of RDAs emerged throughout Europe during the 1950s), they really came to prominence as an institutional form during the mid-1970s and then began to 'mushroom' during the 1980s (Halkier and Danson, 1997). The modern RDA is described by Halkier and Danson as 'a particular form of new-model bottom-up policy' the popularity of which reflects 'the shift from top-down to bottom-up policies and the increasing role of bodies outside the mainstream government apparatus in policy implementation' (1997, pp.244-245). Roberts and Lloyd develop this line of argument and suggest that the emergence of the 'new model' RDAs 'reflects the transition from a Fordist to post-Fordist era of production' (1998, p.10). In order to illustrate their point, they place the new model policies in the context of 'the key changes that have taken place over the past two or three decades' (figure 1).

Figure 1. Regional Development Agencies: Policies and Styles

Feature or Characteristic	Traditional Model	New Model
Dominant Direction of Policy	Top-down	Bottom-up/Top down
Model of Government	Centralised	Devolved
Method of Approach	State-dominated	Partnership
Organisational Paradigm	Fordist	Post-Fordist
Key Strategic Objective	Maximum promotion of regional economic growth	Balanced regional development
Major Target of Policy	Large mobile manufacturing firms	Mix of size and types of firm
Policy Instruments	Bureaucratic regulation, financial inducements, advisory services and general public provision	Greater autonomy, some financial assistance, advice and support services, and mixed public/private/voluntary provision
Key Competitiveness Factors	Economies of scale	Innovation, networking and partnership
Economic Focus	Public sector investment	Balance of public and private investment
Social Context	Low and paternalistic	Higher, with emphasis on role of community
Environmental Approach	Greening in order to attract investment	Broader ideas of sustainable development and ecological modernisation

Source: Roberts and Lloyd, 1998, p.10.

This picture captures the spirit of radical change (and in particular the sense of optimism and hope) which pervades much contemporary thought. The old Fordist dragon—with its emphasis on top-down, bureaucratic, centralised planning—has been slain by its own internal contradictions, to be replaced by a post-Fordist regime based around flexibility, partnership and the democratisation of decision-making. The mushrooming of RDAs in Europe is seen as a function (or a 'reflection') of this radical change.

Much depends here, of course, on how one defines a Regional Development Agency. In their seminal study, Halkier and Danson (1997, p.245) define a 'model' or 'ideal-type' RDA as 'a development body' which complies with three specific criteria: 1) 'organizationally being in a semi-autonomous position vis-à-vis its supporting political authority'; 2) 'strategically supporting mainly indigenous firms by means of 'soft' policy instruments'; and 3) 'implementation being integrated, i.e., drawing upon a broad range of policy instruments'. On the basis of such a definition, Danson, Halkier and Damborg (1998, p.14) suggest that:

> RDAs can easily be construed as the 'manageable' bottom-up alternative [to traditional spatial policies], avoiding the bewildering maze of local initiatives but allowing for flexibility and receptiveness to the specific problems of indigenous industry within the region. At the same time, a position outside the mainstream government apparatus appears to make it possible to pursue public policies without evoking the ghosts of interventionism or state dirigisme, and so to make it easier to adopt a long-term perspective, while the distance from government frequently generates an operating environment more closely attuned to the needs of enterprise.

There seems to be a case, therefore, for suggesting that the Regional Development Agency represents a new 'post-Fordist' democratic form, or alternatively, a 'model' for the form of governance described and prescribed by those working within the framework of the New Regionalism.

With regards to the RDAs in England, it is not immediately clear that they satisfy the three criteria laid down by Halkier and Danson. It is the first criterion which raises problems here, as the semi-autonomous position of the RDAs vis-à-vis the government can be questioned (Lynch, 1999). Nonetheless, Halkier and Danson (1997, p.247) offer an extremely broad rendering of the term 'semi-autonomy' such that it covers bodies subject to political supervision, whose boards are appointed by government, whose resources are allocated by government and whose general policy framework is set by government. So long as the development body possesses strategic initiative and discretionary powers then it can be said to operate at 'arms length' from its political sponsors and can be said to possess semi-autonomy. In this sense, then, it would seem that the English RDAs can be incorporated into a more general discussion of RDAs as a new form of policy regime.

Danson, Halkier and Damborg argue, however, that the RDA programme in England 'is particular to its time and place' and should not be interpreted in terms of the concerns motivating the older RDAs in Europe (1998, p.15). They also add that: 'The current accompanying academic debate over the potential advantages of introducing this particular form of intervention are similarly specific to the concerns of the 1990s: globalisation and European integration, regulation theory, regional competitiveness under new regimes of flexible specialisation' (ibid.). Whilst this is undoubtedly true, it is precisely the concern of the New Regionalism (and particularly of regulation theory) to offer *ex post* analyses and explanations of the new forms of policy regime that emerged from the ashes of Fordism and came to displace 'traditional' regional policy. The analyses themselves, moreover, focus almost entirely on notions such as globalization and regional competitiveness under new regimes of flexible specialization. As such, the current academic debate over the RDAs in England can be tied in quite neatly with debates concerning the rise of RDAs in Europe during the 1970s and the widely noted change in ethos governing the pre-existing RDAs in the UK during the 1980s (Danson, Lloyd and Newlands, 1992).

In any case, contemporary commentators certainly view the establishment of RDAs in England as a belated move towards the adoption of more reflexive, bottom-up modes of governance based around localised decision-making and partnership (Nathan et al, 1999). This is also the way in which the establishment of RDAs in England has been presented by the government. It would seem fair, therefore, to suggest that the context in which the new RDAs are set is the context provided by the New Regionalism as a descriptive historico-empirical claim. The context is that of a rupture, a radical transformation in the way in which capitalism operates; a transformation demanding new forms of governance to regulate and co-ordinate economic policy at the regional level. It will be argued here that the RDAs in England take their place as such a new form of governance within the overall accumulation strategy followed by the New Labour government.

NEW LABOUR'S NEW REGIONALIST ACCUMULATION STRATEGY

The concept of 'an accumulation strategy' is quite straightforward. For Jessop 'an 'accumulation strategy' defines a specific economic 'growth model' complete with its various extra-economic preconditions and also outlines a general strategy appropriate to its realization' (1990, p.198). The economic growth model adopted by the New Labour government comprises a three-pronged strategy to enhance national competitiveness. The three prongs are to 'build UK capabilities', i.e., skills, entrepreneurship and innovation; to 'collaborate to compete'; and to strengthen competitive pressures (DTI, 1998a). It is suggested here that the RDAs form an integral part of the general strategy to realise this economic growth model. It is also suggested that the accumulation strategy as a whole can be viewed in terms of the agenda laid down by the New Regionalism.

In formulating its economic growth model, the government borrows heavily from the conceptual vocabulary of endogenous growth theory. In his foreword to the 1998 Competitiveness White Paper (DTI, 1998a), for example, Tony Blair proclaims the dawn of a 'new world' in which old-fashioned state intervention cannot work and in which 'commercial success and prosperity' depends upon 'knowledge, skills and creativity', 'enterprise, flexibility and innovation', 'the creation of a culture of enterprise' and 'a new entrepreneurial spirit'. The role of government in this new world is confined to promoting the new enterprise culture, investing in skills and forming public-private partnerships in order to 'collaborate for competitive advantage'. So much emphasis is placed by the government on the virtues of innovation, entrepreneurship and the free operation of competitive market pressures that these key phrases become a hypnotic mantra, saturating not only the pages of the White Paper but also the 'Analytical Report' which accompanies it (DTI, 1998b).

Within the overall framework supplied by the vague conceptual language of endogenous growth theory, the government emphasises the need for businesses to respond to the new needs of the 'knowledge-driven economy', which for all intents and purposes is synonymous with the economy of post-Fordism. Thus the emphasis is placed upon flexibility, both within the firm and within the workforce (DTI, 1998a, p.2), and on the combination of aggressive competition and collaboration. Here the insights provided by the New Regionalism as a prescriptive norm really take hold, as the government declares that 'networking and clusters play a critical role in sharing knowledge and upgrading skills' (ibid., para3.7); that 'businesses need to be willing to collaborate—to learn from others, including their competitors' (ibid., para3.1); and that networks of development need to be formed in order to help 'business collaborate sectorally, regionally and locally' (ibid., para3.3). The Analytical Report cites Porter's influential claim that 'clusters can be an important source of durable competitive advantage' (DTI, 1998b, para5.14) and it then proceeds to highlight how 'the need for proximity to other firms or a pool of skilled and complementary labour has led firms to cluster together in specific locations' (ibid., para1.17); how 'the development of a knowledge driven economy is changing the way firms organise themselves, promoting new partnerships between employers and employees and encouraging collaboration between firms in networks and clusters' (ibid., para5.1); how 'co-location and repeated contact helps build up a relationship of trust' (ibid., para5.17); and how networks reduce uncertainty and facilitate the process of collective inter-firm learning (ibid., para5.18).

It thus becomes clear that the historico-empirical claims and the normative bias of the New Regionalism have had at least some impact on government policy-makers. At the historico-empirical level, the formation of networks and clusters is seen as a function of the transition to a new form of capitalist development. At the normative level, the formation of networks and clusters is seen as a good in itself, facilitating collective learning, skills development and the formation of relations of trust. Clusters and networks are viewed as a source of competitive advantage, constituting a framework for innovation and creating a culture of enterprise. Whilst the formation of clusters is by no means viewed as the *sole* source of economic growth, it is certainly viewed as important. Indeed, it forms the cornerstone of one prong of the government's three-pronged strategy ('collaborate to compete'), it provides a foundation on which 'UK capabilities' are to be built and it is seen as a dynamic response to the strengthening of competitive pressures. The Commission on Social Justice (1994, pp.307-309) went so far as to report that 'networks, norms and trust that facilitate coordination and cooperation for mutual benefit', i.e., 'untraded interdependencies' *avant la letter*, had now become essential foundations for social cohesion and economic competitiveness.

So the economic growth model outlined by the New Labour government prioritises concepts such as competition, innovation and entrepreneurship and emphasises the need 'to exploit new sources of competitive advantage' (DTI, 1998a, p.2). Whilst it would be churlish to suggest that policy-makers in Whitehall have kept themselves fully abreast of theoretical developments in the field of economic geography, they have at least recognised that new sources of competitive advantage lie in such things as tacit knowledge, collaboration, knowledge sharing, inter-firm learning, the development of relations of trust and mutual reciprocity. With regards to the general strategy appropriate to the realisation of this growth model, it is clear that the RDAs are to play an important role. Each is instructed to 'take forward at the regional level' the priorities set in the Competitiveness White Paper (DETR, 1999a, p.1) in order 'to ensure that its region meets the challenges of the knowledge driven economy' (DETR, 1999b, ch.2, p.1). More importantly perhaps, in marketing the RDAs the government states that 'we recognise that the distinct economic and social regions of modern England demand new forms of governance to serve their needs for now and for the future' (DETR, 1997, ch.2, p.1). More specifically: 'In establishing the Regional Development Agencies, the Government have clearly in mind that the English regions are all different and need different approaches and strategies.' (DETR, 1997, ch.9, p.1). The RDAs thus herald 'a new approach to public policy' (DTI, 1998a, para1.11) in which central govern*ment* takes a step back so that regional govern*ance* can take centre stage. In this way the RDAs come into the world already swaddled in the clothes of the New Regionalism.

The retreat of the New Labour government from the realms of 'traditional' regional policy has, in fact, been total and complete. The role of central government is confined to ensuring 'that we have the right macro-economic and fiscal climate to help people to develop entrepreneurial skills, and to remove barriers to growth' (DTI, 1998a, para2.3). In real terms, of course, this means little more than price and exchange rate stability coupled with supply-side intervention to address market failures and develop the skills required by industry. Whilst at the regional level too, the RDAs are to act as little more than facilitators or catalysts, they are assigned the crucial responsibility of taking forward the government's New Regionalist agenda. An important part of their catalytic remit is therefore to 'develop and promote' public/private partnerships (DETR, 1999b, p.2), 'to promote creative collaboration between businesses and within regions' (DTI, 1998a, p.2) and to 'support the development of clusters and networks in their region . . . encouraging and facilitating the development of collaborative networks and co-ordinating support for clusters and networks across a wide range of regional partners' (DETR, 1999b, ch.2, p.13). Recognising that competitive advantages are increasingly becoming dependent on local assets, and recognising also that the development and promotion of these assets 'will need to be done at the regional or local level' (DTI,

1998b, para5.26), the government has created regional bodies the prime responsibility of which (aside from co-ordinating the extant programmes they have taken over) is to develop and promote, by means of 'soft' policy measures, a culture of innovation and entrepreneurship founded upon the assets specific to each region.

All of this ties in exactly with the concerns of the New Regionalists, and in particular with their claims regarding the need to displace the stale and inflexible rationalities of the market and the state with a reflexive rationality based around collective learning and partnership. The retreat of the state becomes paramount as the interests of regional competitiveness require that cognitive room be created for the bottom-up formation of a heterarchic associational economy. In terms of both form and function, then, the RDAs can be seen as an integral part of the general strategy deemed 'appropriate' for the realisation of an economic growth model based around endogenous development. In terms of form, the RDAs have been interpreted as a further 'hollowing out of the state', i.e., as a regional solution to the continuing existence of economic disparities forged in response to the nation-state's inability to steer investment in a globalised market place (Nathan et al, 1999). In terms of function, the government's accumulation strategy is to be delivered by RDAs equipped with the only functions appropriate to the new post-Fordist regime—the catalysing of networks of collaboration by means of advice and encouragement, strategic supply side intervention and the formation of public/private partnerships.

In broad terms, of course, the RDAs have been introduced 'in an attempt to resolve the problems associated with the long-standing absence of consistent and meaningful territorial management' in the English regions (Roberts and Lloyd, 2000, p.76). The fact that the region has *now* been deemed a meaningful scale for territorial management, however, reflects a shift in focus from the 'new localism' of the 1980s (based upon the assumption that regenerating cities and the 'pockets of deprivation' therein held the key to economic growth) to a 'new regionalism' based upon the assumption that strategic coordination at the regional scale holds the key to economic growth (Deas and Ward, 2000). In this context, the RDAs in England can readily be interpreted as 'new institutional spaces' (Jones, 1999) created in an attempt to develop regional 'action frameworks' capable of generating 'institutional thickness' whilst energising the appropriate 'supply architecture' required for endogenous innovation and growth (Jones and MacLeod, 1999).

It might also be added here that throughout all of this the government's 'regional agenda' has been motivated by primarily *economic* concerns. The RDA programme has not been constructed around arguments for regional 'autonomy' as an end in itself but rather from the simple observation that 'the English regions are underperforming compared to equivalent regions elsewhere in Europe' (DETR, 1997, p.2). As such, the RDAs signify something more than a mere 'staging post' (Harman, 1998, p.194) or 'the first strand of the Government's English devolution proposals' (Lynch, 1999, p.75). They signify an overriding concern with the issue of regional *competitiveness* and they represent an institutional form deemed appropriate to the realisation of an economic growth model aimed precisely at tackling the issue of regional competitiveness. The rationale behind the establishment of RDAs in England has thus been very much informed by the economic arguments and concerns of the 'new' regionalism as opposed to the social and political concerns of 'traditional' regionalist movements.

THE POLITICAL ECONOMY OF THE
NEW REGIONALISM — CRITICAL PERSPECTIVES

Complex theoretical arguments seldom translate easily into practical policy regimes and those responsible for devising policy regimes seldom pay due attention to the complexities of theoretical arguments. I do not for a second, therefore, wish to suggest that the establishment of RDAs in England represents a practical 'realisation' of the New Regionalism as a body of thought. My aim instead has merely been to highlight the ways in which the key normative *concerns* of the New Regionalism have become inscribed within the RDA programme— concerns for regional competitiveness, for processes of collective learning based around collaboration and partnership, for the move towards a reflexive rationality founded on networks of association and away from the procedural rationality of traditional regional policy, for the subsequent retreat of the state and the adoption of 'soft' supply-side policies which facilitate the formation of self-supporting clusters of activity. These concerns, it has been suggested, have had a significant impact upon the way in which the RDA programme has been developed.

In offering a critical perspective on these developments, there are many lines one could adopt. One could, for example, criticise the *way* in which the concerns of the New Regionalism have been incorporated into policy, focusing perhaps on the chronic lack of funding made available for the RDAs to follow the competitiveness policies they are supposed to be pursuing with vigour. One could point to the way in which the concept of the region as an economic space has failed to make its way into policy considerations, or, alternatively, one could suggest that the concept of an economic space defined by networks of association could not possibly translate into policy because of the very spatial dynamism implicit in the concept itself. On this basis, one might stress the impracticability of mobilising structures of governance around such a shifting and abstract category as an economic region. Further to this, one could criticise the concerns of the New Regionalism as a whole. John Lovering has made this his own personal task and in so doing has raised a number of significant issues—for example, the way in which the 'productivist bias' of the New Regionalism accords undue primacy to the high-tech knowledge-intensive manufacturing sector whilst ignoring the role played by services, public spending and finance capital in raising per capita output, and also the way in which its arguments tend to 'decontextualise' the concepts of innovation and competitiveness (Lovering, 1999). In what follows, however, focus is placed on two lines of criticism, the first of which has significant implications for the success of the RDA programme in England and the second of which highlights the ideological underpinnings of the entire New Regionalist project.

The first line of criticism is already well rehearsed. As Lovering puts it: 'The New Regionalism is a set of stories about how *parts* of a regional economy *might* work, placed next to a set of policy ideas which *might* just be useful in *some* cases' (1999, p.384). In other words, many of the prescriptive recommendations made by the New Regionalists are based on interpretations of how a few prosperous regions or 'islands of innovation' have in fact become prosperous. These interpretations have then been generalised in the form of an economic imperative—do as the Third Italy does—without any heed being paid to contextual specificities. Looked at in a slightly different way, one could say that a conflict emerges here between the concepts of time and space; between the notion that temporal changes (such as the transition from Fordism to post-Fordism) take form over space and the idea that spatial differences (in economic culture, industrial traditions, regulatory norms, etc.) take form over time. The New Regionalism is accused of prioritising time over space (or of assuming a temporal movement towards spatial homogeneity) whereas much contemporary research into regional development points to a growing differentiation between regional development paths (Krätke, 1999). This then raises serious doubts as to whether a single economic growth model is applicable to all regions alike.

In all fairness, not all the advocates of the New Regionalism herald their models as universally applicable. With regards to the less favoured regions (LFRs) in particular, it is now accepted that the 'associational economy' cannot simply be conjured by means of 'soft' supply-side policies. The LFRs are seen to lack the institutional, social and cultural traditions which characterize growth regions and this suggests that 'infrastructural improvement, skill upgrading and funding for small-firm development will be insufficient to achieve self-sustaining growth' (Amin and Tomaney, 1995, p.178). For Amin and Tomaney, in fact, the policy agenda put forward by the New Regionalism will only serve to exacerbate the core/periphery divide, as the unleashing of market forces favours the most innovative and growth-oriented regions whilst the accompanying reduction in welfare expenditure impacts greatly upon the LFRs in which low income groups are concentrated and thus threatens the process of knowledge and skill formation central to supply-side policies. They thus conclude by suggesting that: 'The hour of supply-side policies means little more than regions being left to their own devices, with obvious implications for weaker regions' (Amin and Tomaney, 1995, p.174).

There is thus a strong (compelling?) case for traditional top-down central state intervention to 'kick-start' the economies of the LFRs, a case recognised by a small number of New Regionalist writers (Amin and Tomaney, 1995; Morgan, 1997; Amin, 1999). This is quite clearly not recognised by the New Labour government, however, which nowhere questions the assumption that the same conditions for success prevail everywhere. Instead, what we are offered is a uniform supply-side endogenous growth model which is heralded as the key to economic success in each of the regions of England. Not only, therefore, does this ignore the issue of regional specificity, but it brings with it the danger that those regions which fail to achieve success on the basis of the New Regionalist supply-side growth model will be left to rely on (but be forced to compete for) the universal panacea for economic lagging—increased levels of inward investment. As Amin consequently remarks, 'in the absence of a conducive macro-economic framework, it seems irresponsible to ask the regions to embark upon a long-term and comprehensive overhaul in pursuit of an endogenous pathway to prosperity' (1999, p.376).

The second line of criticism builds upon this first. For the uniformity of the regional economic growth models prescribed by the government can be explained if one views the establishment of RDAs as an integral part of a *national* accumulation strategy. Nor does this require a great deal of insight given that we are frequently informed that the RDAs 'will need to work within the framework of national policies' (DETR, 1999b, p.2), will 'aim to support and enhance national policies' (DETR, 1999a, p.3) and will facilitate the 'effective delivery of Government programmes' (DETR, 1997, ch.1, p.1). We are also told that 'the overall aim of each RDA's Regional Strategy will be to improve the competitiveness of each region and in so doing contribute to the overall effectiveness of the UK' (DETR, 1999b, ch.2, p.3) and that 'the Government's vision is of twelve powerhouse economies, each contributing fully towards the United Kingdom's success within Europe' (DETR, 1997, ch.2, p.4). As the official 'overview' to the RDAs Bill states, the government's strategy is founded on 'a belief that *to improve the economic performance of the country as a whole* it is vital to look at problems in regional terms as well as nationally' (Dyson, Wood and Barclay, 1998, p.22). Of course, it hardly requires stating here that, as the experience of the EU has shown, strategies designed to improve overall competitiveness tend to do so at the expense of the LFRs, which, in the absence of any kind of redistributive policies, are left to wait for 'trickle-down' or 'trickle-across' effects to come their way. The main criticism here, however, concerns the way in which a clear project *of* the state *in* the regions has been disguised and presented in terms of regional liberation when it is clear that the new policy regime heralded by the RDAs establishes nothing more than the institutional forms required to strategically regulate the national goal of capital accumulation (Jones, 1999; Jones and MacLeoad, 1999; MacLeod and Goodwin, 1999a, 1999b).

The ideological verbiage used to support the establishment of RDAs can be used to illuminate the ideological verbiage underlying the New Regionalism itself. For it is somewhat ironic that, given its historical origins in French regulation theory and the fact that some of its key proponents present their ideas in terms consciously borrowed from regulation theory (Scott, 1988, for example), the core insights offered by regulation theory have conveniently been overlooked within New Regionalist thought. With the notable exception of Bob Jessop, those who argue for the necessity of new forms of 'governance' present their ideas as a radical new 'third way' that will lead the regions of the UK and Europe into a self-perpetuating cycle of virtuous growth (Morgan, 1997; Amin, 1999). Even those who recognise the problems associated with the LFRs believe that given time and an appropriate macroeconomic context within which to develop their innovative capacities the LFRs, like the famed islands of innovation, can enjoy a rosy future based upon self-sustained endogenous growth. This is quite clearly not the case, however, for it ignores the fundamental fact (taken as a basic premise within regulation theory) that crises and patterns of uneven development are endemic to capitalism and it also neglects to mention that the present reconfiguration of the state is, like all reconfigurations, a means of regulating (rather than eradicating) the processes which engender crisis and uneven patterns of development.

The work of Bob Jessop provides a useful corrective to the sense of euphoria which often accompanies the 'rediscovery' of the region. For whilst he continually expounds the idea that economic development is now best served through a Schumpeterian workfare state based around the principles of heterarchic governance (Jessop, 1994), he is also well aware that governance as a social mode of regulation will, like the market and the state, fail in its attempts to co-ordinate capitalism and resolve the crises resulting from its own internal contradictions (Jessop, 1998). He is also keen to emphasise that far from signalling the 'end' of the nation state, the attempt to co-ordinate economic activity around the concept of governance is an example of what he refers to as a 'state project', i.e., a project *of* the state designed to secure the unity *of* the state (Jessop, 1990). In words that could have been specifically written with the Labour government's RDA programme in mind, he argues that: 'The state reserves to itself the right to open, close, juggle and re-articulate governance not only in terms of particular functions but also from the viewpoint of partisan and global political advantage'(1998, p.39).

The point here, then, is that a programme presented in terms of 'region building' is in fact nothing more than a contemporary example of good old-fashioned state building. As regulation theorists often point out, no medium-term solution has yet been found to the crisis of 'Fordism'. The 'regional turn' in policy-making both within the UK and within the 'Europe of the Regions' can perhaps best be viewed, therefore, as an 'institutional fix' (Peck and Tickell, 1994)—a short-term stop-gap policy regime which emphasises the importance of the local, the psychological and the micro-economic, not because some great sea change has taken place in the way in which economies work, but rather because the governments of the First World have yet to find a national macro-economic solution to the instabilities and uneven patterns of development engendered by the economic crisis of the 1970s. Interestingly, attempts to find such an institutional fix have now become synonymous with attempts to legitimate many of the key tenets of New Right ideology—the significance attached to the entrepreneur and the need for an 'enterprise culture'; the belief that we need to roll back the frontiers of the state even further and rely on strategic supply-side intervention; the primacy accorded to the small firm (or clusters thereof); and the eulogistic praise heaped upon the concept of 'competition'.

Many of those working within the framework of the New Regionalism are consciously aware that their ideas could potentially serve as 'an ideological smokescreen behind which neo-liberal doctrine can claim legitimacy' (Amin, 1999, p.185). They thus seek to dissociate themselves from 'the neo-liberal paradigm of the Right' (Morgan, 1997, p.491). The trouble is, however, that it is difficult to find any *major* sources of disjunction between the New Regionalism and New Right ideology in much the same way as it is becoming increasingly difficult to differentiate between New Labour's 'supply side socialism' and the economics of the Manchester School (Thompson, 1996). In both cases, the differences are a matter of degree and, ultimately, of window dressing. Far from being a new and emancipatory 'third way', therefore, the New Regionalism as a theory and a policy regime can best be viewed as a further 'embedding' of the neo-liberal strategic response to the economic crisis of the 1970s. So understood, the New Regionalism becomes a state project designed to normalise economic activity around 'an 'imagined unit of competition' at the urban/regional level' (Lovering, 1999, p.392) and the policy regime signalled by the New Regionalism (of which the RDAs form an integral part) becomes nothing more than a mode of crisis management—a further example of the way in which the state reconfigures its activities in order to create 'the room for manoeuvre' which enables it to continue in its wider attempt to manage and regulate the crisis tendencies of capitalism (Jessop, 1998).

CONCLUSION

For some, Regional Development Agencies 'are part of a new wave in regional policy' and their establishment in England 'marks a major change in regional policy-making in the UK' (Nathan et al, 1999, pp.4-5). This major change in regional policy-making has been prompted, so the New Regionalists claim, by the transition to a new mode of capitalist development in which the region has become resurgent. Within this new mode of development, economic success comes to depend increasingly upon the institutional capacity of a region, a capacity that can only be raised by means of a new mode of governance which encourages collaboration and partnership and facilitates the process of collective learning by reigning back the frontiers of the state so that a new reflexive rationality can be given room to

the resources and capabilities of member states and to improve interoperability among allies. Despite multiple benefits, U.S. and European military officials noted that the deployment of multinational forces into areas of intense conflict also presents drawbacks and challenges. These include friction between coalition members with differing policies and strategies, interoperability problems arising from incompatible systems, and imbalances in equipment capabilities and inventories. Nevertheless, officials said that the benefits of multinational operations outweigh the drawbacks.

The European allies and the European Commission led donors in providing development assistance to the Balkans region. Of the almost $15 billion disbursed from 1993 through 1999, European allies and the European Commission provided $6.9 billion and $3.3 billion, respectively, while the United States provided $1.2 billion. The European countries and the European Commission focused their assistance on humanitarian and economic reconstruction programs, while the United States focused on humanitarian assistance, economic restructuring, and programs to strengthen democratic institutions—for example, independent media and judiciary systems. European officials also identified the absorption of Balkans refugees into their countries as another significant contribution to European security.

European allies provided a large number of civilian personnel to support multilateral organizations that promote stable institutions and security in the region. For example, as of January 2001, European countries provided more than 2,000 civilian police to the United Nations. As of April 2001, they had provided about 500 people to the Organization for Security and Cooperation in Europe to perform tasks such as election monitoring, human rights education, media training, and legal and judicial reform, and another 139 people to support the European Union's security-monitoring mission. The United States, on the other hand, provided the largest national contingency of personnel to the U.N. civilian police and to the Organization for Security and Cooperation in Europe—764 and 141 people, respectively.

European Militaries Addressing Shortfalls, but Decisions on Competing Budget Priorities Slow Implementation

Operational problems experienced in the Balkans peacekeeping operations in the 1990s highlighted numerous shortfalls in the military capabilities of European allies. On a national level, European countries are addressing some of these shortfalls by restructuring their military forces to become more deployable, by moving toward all-volunteer forces, and by modernizing their equipment, but progress has varied depending on each country's ability to make defense spending a budget priority. Improvements in these three areas will give allies greater flexibility and capability to respond to a range of threats within and outside of Europe. The European allies we visited have made the greatest progress in restructuring their forces, which has meant changing the size and organization of their forces. For example, France, Germany, Italy, and the United Kingdom reduced their forces between 1990 and 2001 by an average range of 31 to 36 percent, and they are converting large, armored units into smaller and lighter infantry units that can respond to a range of threats. These countries have also developed rapid reaction units that can be deployed on short notice to operations within and beyond NATO's borders. In addition, France, Germany, Italy, and the United Kingdom have established centralized operational commands to enhance cooperation among the branches of the military and thereby improve operational deployments and resource management. Large implementation costs and other budgetary considerations have slowed the European allies' transition to all-volunteer forces and their modernization of equipment. Although an all-volunteer force will be more cost effective in the long run, more funding is needed up front to establish the system. In addition, limited funds have delayed or postponed European allies' efforts to improve capabilities such as air- and sea lift; command, control, and communications; intelligence and reconnaissance; and precision-guided munitions systems.

Two recent NATO and European Union defense initiatives, launched after Operation Allied Force, provide additional focus and incentive for European nations to improve their defense capabilities. Although European NATO countries have made progress in meeting some of the goals, inadequate funding hampers the implementation of both initiatives. The first initiative, NATO's Defense Capabilities Initiative, is a mechanism to highlight and promote needed improvements in five functional areas, using 58 long- and short-term objectives. The initiative has been incorporated into NATO's defense-planning process. The second initiative, the European Union's European Security and Defense Policy, is a broader political and security strategy to strengthen the European Union's capacity for more effective crisis management, particularly when NATO as a whole chooses not to be involved. Both concepts aim to improve the European allies' response to post-Cold War security challenges. Progress to date for both initiatives varies among countries, but nations have generally focused on goals that are easier to accomplish and less expensive, such as establishing logistics capabilities that can support multiple nations. NATO officials stated, however, that other items relating to improving a military's deployability, mobility, and command-and-control capabilities are a long way from completion. Similarly, most U.S. and European government officials agree that the biggest challenge for the European Security and Defense Policy lies in equipping the 60,000 troops for sustained, high intensity military operations.

While European allies are committed to taking greater responsibility for regional security by planning to purchase critical aircraft and preparing to bring together a European Union rapid reaction force, most are hampered by relatively flat defense budgets. This limitation is brought about by decisions concerning competing domestic budgetary pressures, varying threat perceptions, and other national priorities. For example, Germany's annual average real growth rate is projected to be -1.6 percent from 2000 through 2004, while the United Kingdom's annual average real growth rate is expected to increase by slightly less than 1 percent from 2000 through 2003. Italy's defense plans indicate a 4-percent annual average real growth rate for defense spending from 2000 through 2004. European budgets for major defense equipment have been of particular concern because they constitute the primary reason for shortfalls in defense capabilities identified in Balkans operations. While some nations, such as France and the United Kingdom, spent at least 20 percent of their defense budgets on equipment in 2000, Germany, Italy, and many other NATO countries spent less than 15 percent. In comparison, the United States spent at least 20 percent of its defense budget on equipment in 2000. European allies have pledged to increase equipment spending over the decade; however, some nations are facing difficulty doing so. Germany's annual average real growth rate for defense equipment is projected to be -1.3 percent in the years 2000 through 2004. According to budget projections from the United Kingdom, its annual average real growth rate for equipment is expected to increase by about 1.4 percent from 2000 through 2003.

Budget challenges are attributable in part to structural problems inherent in the defense budgets of certain NATO countries. Chief among these problems is large personnel costs.

Seven of the 19 NATO nations spent 60 to 80 percent of their defense budgets on personnel in 2000. Fewer resources are thus available to buy new equipment. While European nations have devised interim measures to meet some of their defense requirements, such as leasing airlift aircraft, more funding will be needed to achieve the objectives of the Defense Capabilities Initiative and European Security and Defense Policy before the end of the decade. Some European NATO countries are pursuing multinational cooperation in procurement to share the financial burden of acquiring expensive systems and equipment, such as with the A400M military transport aircraft. However, funding availability is delaying this and other multinational projects.

Concluding Observations

The breakup of the Soviet Union has prompted the United States and its European allies to use a much broader range of military and nonmilitary tools to foster security in the European region now than during the Cold War. In this new security environment, military contributions are no longer the sole mechanism for providing security. Development assistance to new or emerging democracies in Central and Eastern Europe, as well as the eastward expansion of NATO and the European Union, provide the second and third major tools for a secure and stable Europe. New trends in the military and nonmilitary contributions made by the United States and its European allies have emerged. Militarily, the United States leads its allies in providing combat capabilities to restore peace, as it did in the Balkans European allies provide most of the peacekeeping forces and the preponderance of nonmilitary aid to the region. NATO's focus on a wider set of threats and on the expansion of its membership to integrate former Warsaw Pact nations complements the role of the European Union, the leading source of nonmilitary assistance in the region through the European Commission, whose responsibilities and membership are also expanding.

Despite these achievements and contributions, weaknesses in European defense capabilities—now and in the near future—mean that European allies will depend on the United States to provide key combat capabilities should a major conflict break out in the region. Given this situation, the United States will need to continue playing an important role in the European region, particularly in the area of military capabilities, at least until the end of the decade.

Agency Comments

In written comments in response to a draft of this report, the Department of State concurred with the report's contents. These comments are presented in appendix IV. The Department of Defense provided oral comments and also concurred with the report's contents. DOD and the Department of State also provided technical comments, which we incorporated where appropriate.

INTRODUCTION

During the Cold War, the United States and its North Atlantic Treaty Organization (NATO) allies invested heavily in warfighting and combat support assets to protect the alliance against the threat of Soviet aggression. In the mid-1980s, the number of U.S. forces stationed in Europe peaked at approximately 350,000 personnel. In addition, our European NATO allies had about 3.6 million military personnel deployed to repel a full-scale attack on NATO's European fronts by the Soviet Union. NATO and its members funded the development and maintenance of infrastructure to support the presence of large armored ground forces and air units to defend its borders.[10] With this presence came a heavy reliance on the civilian population for logistic support in the event that war were to break out. Although European NATO countries provided considerable financial and political support to the U.S. military presence, concerns over the relative magnitude of U.S. commitments to European security provoked recurrent debates about burdensharing among American policymakers throughout the Cold War. In 1981, Congress required that the Department of Defense (DOD) report annually on the Allies' contributions to NATO and to other regional defense and security institutions elsewhere in the world.[11]

The end of the Cold War produced dramatic changes in Europe's geopolitical order. Twelve Newly Independent States (NIS) emerged as autonomous nations, but many of these nations have maintained diplomatic and economic ties to Russia through membership in the Commonwealth of Independent States.[12] After Communist state institutions in Central and Eastern European (CEE) countries collapsed, members of NATO's principal adversary, the Warsaw Pact alliance, began to elect governments democratically and to establish market-oriented economies.[13] New national boundaries and the adoption of new political and economic systems have transformed the European security landscape. Former Cold War adversaries have cultivated commercial and economic relationships with the West, and three former Warsaw Pact states joined NATO in 1999.[14]

This rapid economic and political transformation has altered the security environment across Europe. Although NATO remains committed to its mission to defend the Alliance against external enemies, the dissolution of the Soviet Union dramatically reduced NATO's vulnerability to conventional attack. However, new threats have emerged over the past decade. The creation of new states and the dismantling of old institutions aggravated ethnic and economic tensions within and between nations. Former Communist nations have struggled to establish democratic institutions against pressure from the leaders and supporters of the old authoritarian order. Financial, administrative, and judicial institutions often lack competent personnel and sufficient resources to successfully combat public sector corruption and organized crime. In the face of dwindling resources in the NIS, the Soviet infrastructure

---

[10] Infrastructure includes aircraft shelters, prepositioned weapon depots, and fuel distribution networks.

[11] Subsequent revisions of burdensharing-reporting requirements occurred in the 1984 and 1997 National Defense Authorization Acts, as well as the 2000 Department of Defense Military Construction Appropriations Act.

[12] The Newly Independent States include the former Soviet Republics of Armenia, Azerbaijan, Belarus, Georgia, Kazakhstan, Kyrgyzstan, Moldova, Russia, Tajikistan, Turkmenistan, Ukraine, and Uzbekistan. The three Baltic republics—Estonia, Latvia, and Lithuania — declared independence prior to the Soviet Union's official dissolution on December 25, 1991.

[13] The CEE nations include Albania, Bulgaria, the Czech Republic, Estonia, Hungary, Latvia, Lithuania, Poland, Romania, and the Slovak Republic.

[14] They are the Czech Republic, Hungary, and Poland.

for maintaining its nuclear arsenals has degraded, increasing the risk of environmental damage, the opportunity for diversion of nuclear weapons technology to "rogue" states or terrorist groups, and the potential for accidental or unauthorized use of nuclear weapons.

Since the dissolution of the former Yugoslavia, the Balkans[15] region has exemplified a worst-case scenario in the new European security landscape. The secession of Croatia in 1991 and Bosnia in 1992 resulted in a protracted civil war, as armed factions fought to have ethnically pure states. Albania's 1997 financial crisis precipitated the government's collapse and sparked riots and armed revolts that reportedly caused more than 2,000 deaths. Early in 1998, conflict erupted in Kosovo between Kosovar Albanian insurgents, who were fighting for the independence of Kosovo, and Yugoslav forces, most of whom were Serbian, fighting to retain Yugoslavia's sovereignty over the province. In February 2001, ethnic fighting erupted in the Former Yugoslav Republic of Macedonia between ethnic Albanian rebel forces and Macedonian authorities over the issue of obtaining greater rights for minority ethnic Albanians. These crises exacted a heavy humanitarian toll and created hundreds of thousands of refugees and internally displaced persons. Although NATO and United Nations (U.N.) peacekeeping forces have been critical to containing and preventing further violence in the region, these nations' civic institutions remain weak, and many former combatants retain their wartime objectives. In Bosnia and Kosovo, the international community oversees local political and legal institutions and pays for extensive development projects to rehabilitate the region's infrastructure and economic institutions.

NATO allies and partners have responded to changing threats through a combination of military and nonmilitary strategies aimed at preventing and containing instability in the region. The 1991 NATO strategic concept, which was updated in 1999, called for the allied militaries to adopt light, mobile forces that can respond rapidly to a broad spectrum of contingencies. The 1999 Defense Capabilities Initiative (DCI) established new standards for NATO forces, better reflecting the new types of conflicts they may face in a dynamic threat environment. The United States has responded to the reduced threat in part by drawing down personnel levels on the European continent to approximately 100,000. Many European allies have likewise downsized their forces and cut defense expenditures, and a few have implemented defense-restructuring programs. Civil-military outreach initiatives such as the NATO Partnership for Peace (PfP) emphasize greater cooperation and engagement between the militaries of former adversaries. The NATO enlargement process encourages the institutional development of partner states by emphasizing respect for human rights, transparent public institutions, and civilian control of armed forces. NATO efforts to promote stability in former Warsaw Pact nations are complemented by U.S. and European bilateral economic aid and technical assistance for good governance, economic restructuring, and nonproliferation programs.

The European Union (EU) has developed a common foreign and security policy to complement its economic power and to raise its visibility in international and regional affairs. This policy represents a new effort by the EU to formulate foreign policy positions that best represent the interests of the EU and its member states. Under this policy, the EU has taken an active diplomatic role in successive Balkans crises and is working with NATO officials to

---

[15] For the purpose of this report, the Balkans region is defined as Albania, Bosnia, Croatia, the Federal Republic of Yugoslavia (Serbia, Montenegro, and the Serbian province of Kosovo, hereafter referred to as Yugoslavia), and the Former Yugoslav Republic of Macedonia. Bosnia's official name is Bosnia and Herzegovina. The Socialist Federal Republic of Yugoslavia, which dissolved in 1991, is referred to in this report as the "former Yugoslavia."

broker peace in the Former Yugoslav Republic of Macedonia. A central element of this policy is the European Union's development of a military component to respond to post-Cold War threats when NATO chooses not to be involved, thereby enhancing the credibility of EU diplomacy. Progress in building defense capabilities depends in large part on the ability of EU member states to provide adequate resources for military requirements.

European multilateral institutions have adapted to the post-Cold War environment by transforming their functions and developing connections with peer institutions. Initiated in 1973, the Conference on Security and Cooperation in Europe has since evolved from a forum for arms control negotiations into the Organization for Security and Cooperation in Europe (OSCE), an association that manages a range of programs throughout Europe and Central Asia relating to conflict prevention and early warning, crisis management, and post-conflict rehabilitation. Activities include, for example, election monitoring; developing democratic institutions, processes, and mechanisms; and police monitoring.[16] Given its expanded role in European security, the OSCE has coordinated its programs with other international organizations, such as the EU, the United Nations, and NATO. During the Cold War, the EU concentrated its efforts on the economic integration of Western European nations. However, the EU has recently played a more visible international role through its Common Foreign and Security Policy (CFSP) and is currently developing a European Security and Defense Policy (ESDP) to enhance its military and civilian crisis-response capabilities. EU enlargement, another significant foreign policy activity, offers substantial economic and technical assistance to accession candidates to support democratic and free-market reform.

Objectives, Scope, and Methodology

In response to the Floyd D. Spence National Defense Authorization Act for Fiscal Year 2001 mandate requirement, we identified and assessed (1) U.S. and European military and nonmilitary contributions to security and stability in the European region, (2) U.S. and European military and nonmilitary contributions to security and stability in the Balkans, and (3) the status of NATO and European defense initiatives to improve military capabilities for conflict management. In addition, we also summarized the results of a companion GAO report concerning the effects of forwarddeployed U.S. forces in Europe on mobility requirements in the event of a regional conflict in Europe or the Middle East.[17] The data used in this report reflect information collected before the Department of Defense completed the Quadrennial Defense Review and before the terrorist attacks of September 11, 2001. The way in which the United States and its European allies respond to these events will affect U.S. and European interests, military force postures, and budget priorities. However, it is too early to discern what the effects will be. DOD issued the Quadrennial Defense Review report on September 30, 2001, and we summarize pertinent information about overseas presence in our report. DOD is now engaged in the program and budget review and is conducting follow-on analysis regarding overseas presence and other related issues, particularly in light of the events of September 11, 2001.

---

[16] OSCE members include 55 countries across Europe, Central Asia, and North America.
[17] See GAO-02-99, Nov. 28, 2001.

To meet our objectives, we analyzed a range of documents and interviewed numerous military and civilian officials from the United States and five European allies.[18] We focused on France, Germany, Italy, and the United Kingdom because they accounted for nearly 70 percent of the total gross domestic product and defense spending by all European NATO members in 2000. We also focused on Turkey because of its unique security environment and the critical role it plays in an unstable region. We visited these countries in March 2001 and met with officials from the respective countries' embassies in Washington, D.C. In addition, we met with officials from NATO's Supreme Headquarters Allied Powers, Europe (including the Supreme Allied Commander); the EU; the OSCE; the Organization for Economic Cooperation and Development (OECD); and the United States European Command. We worked closely with officials at the Department of Defense and Department of State in Washington, D.C., and at the U.S. embassies in the countries we visited. We also reviewed documents and interviewed officials from the World Bank and the United Nations. Finally, we interviewed analysts at numerous think tanks in the United States and Europe, including the Brookings Institution, the Center for Strategic and International Studies, the Center for Strategic and Budgetary Assessments, and the CATO Institute, all in Washington, D.C.; the Institute for Security Studies of the Western European Union, in Paris; the Institute of International Affairs, in Rome; the Konrad Adenauer Institute, in Berlin; and the Centre for European Reform and Royal United Services Institute for Defense Studies, in London.

To address the first objective, we collected and analyzed DOD and NATO reports that identified U.S. and European troop strengths, the costs of permanently stationing U.S. military forces in Europe, and the costs of deploying and supporting U.S. forces in regional contingencies, such as in the Balkans. To identify financial and other contributions that our European allies provide to maintain the U.S. forces in Europe, we obtained and assessed reports on direct and indirect host country support, including the DOD *Allied Contributions* report.[19] We discussed these costs with U.S. and host country officials. These officials also identified other unquantifiable costs associated with hosting U.S. troops in European countries. We relied on NATO defense budget data to identify the historical defense-spending trends of NATO allies.

We identified and assessed the political, military, and economic benefits and drawbacks of maintaining a U.S. military presence in Europe by analyzing government and nongovernment studies and by discussing these issues with a wide range of U.S. and European civilian and military officials.

We identified key nonmilitary financial contributions to Central and Eastern Europe and the Newly Independent States by relying on development assistance and nonproliferation assistance data. Development assistance includes grants and concessional loans that have a grant element of at least 25 percent that are provided by national governments and multilateral organizations. We focused on contributions provided by the United States, European nations, and the European Commission—the leading multilateral donor of development assistance to Central and Eastern Europe and the Newly Independent States. We did not include nonconcessional loans, such as those provided by the World Bank and the International Monetary Fund, because these require repayment by the recipient country.

---

[18] For this report we define European allies to include European NATO and/or EuropeanUnion member nations, plus Switzerland.

[19] *Report on Allied Contributions to the Common Defense*, Department of Defense, March 2001.

Further, we did not include any private-sector flows to the region. For development assistance data from 1990 to 1999, we relied primarily on OECD's Development Assistance Committee statistical database, which we converted to constant 1999 dollars. We use constant 1999 dollars throughout the report, unless noted otherwise. We discussed the development assistance programs with the U.S. Department of State and with officials from the EU, the OECD, and the foreign affairs ministries of the countries we visited. We selected nonproliferation assistance as a way to quantify national and multinational efforts to address critical nonproliferation concerns in the Newly Independent States. To identify nonproliferation assistance to the NIS, we relied on reports provided by the EU and the Departments of Defense and Energy. We also met with European officials to discuss European objectives, priorities, trends, and future efforts, and relied on GAO reports for similar information on U.S. nonproliferation programs.[20] We analyzed data available from 1992 to 2001.

We identified and assessed the contributions of NATO and the EU to security and stability in Europe in the post-Cold War decade by focusing primarily on their enlargement programs. We relied on recent GAO work on the NATO Partnership for Peace program, and we obtained documents from France, Germany, Italy, Turkey, and the United Kingdom that identified their Partnership for Peace activities with prospective NATO member nations.[21] We obtained cost data from the EU and from economic databases to document the EU's current and projected financial contributions to countries seeking EU membership, and those contributions' effects on donor and recipient countries' economies. We discussed these issues with U.S. and European officials and obtained their perspectives concerning the contribution of these enlargement programs to security and stability in Europe.

To address the second objective, we obtained and analyzed NATO and U.N. peacekeeping reports from 1992 to 2001 concerning the number and type of military personnel deployed in direct support of the Balkans peacekeeping operations. We also interviewed senior U.S., NATO, and European military and policy officials, to discuss the roles and contributions of the respective forces since 1992. We relied on past GAO work and on DOD and European reports to identify the military contributions of U.S. and European allies to Operation Allied Force. In interviews with U.S. and European civilian and military officials, we discussed the benefits and drawbacks of participating with our allies in regional contingency operations, such as in the Balkans. These U.S. and European officials, including former commanders of Balkans operations, provided valuable perspectives based on their personal experiences in the Balkans and other contingency operations. We identified key nonmilitary financial contributions to the Balkans by relying on development assistance data from 1993 to 1999. We relied primarily on OECD's Development Assistance Committee statistical database. We discussed these development assistance programs with the U.S. Department of State and with officials from the EU, the OECD, and the foreign affairs ministries of the countries we visited. We focused on U.N. civilian police, OSCE, and EU Mission Monitoring programs to identify the number and type of nonmilitary personnel provided by donor countries that participated in the Balkans peacekeeping operations from 1992 to 2001. These three programs together represent the majority of civilian personnel temporarily provided by the United States and European countries to support the Balkans

---

[20] GAO-02-226T, Nov. 7, 2001.
[21] See NATO: *U.S. Assistance to the Partnership for Peace* (GAO-01-734, Jul. 20, 2001).

operations. We interviewed U.S., U.N., EU, and OSCE officials and reviewed agency documents to obtain the number of personnel assigned to the Balkans operations and their qualitative contributions. We obtained and analyzed data from the U.N. High Commission for Refugees (UNHCR) for statistics on numbers of refugees migrating from the Balkans to the U.S. and to European countries, and we discussed the numbers with various U.S. and European officials.

To address the third objective, we reviewed defense policy and budget documents from NATO, the EU, selected European countries, and the United States. We obtained reports addressing the status of defense reform and modernization efforts in France, Germany, Italy, Turkey, and the United Kingdom. We corroborated this information with European and U.S. officials. We reviewed NATO, EU, and U.S. documents on the status of NATO's Defense Capabilities Initiative and the EU's European Security and Defense Policy. We also interviewed a wide range of officials from NATO, the EU, selected European countries, the United States, and think tanks to obtain their perspectives on the progress of these security initiatives and their potential contribution to security and stability in Europe.

To compare defense expenditures of NATO members on a historical basis, we first converted the NATO inflation-adjusted local currency figures to their 1995 U.S. dollar equivalents, using the 1995 U.S. exchange rate for each NATO member. We then applied the change in the U.S. gross domestic product (GDP) deflator from 1995 to 2000 to obtain defense expenditures for all members in constant 2000 U.S. dollars.[22] We recognize that exchange rate fluctuations may have a significant effect on the reported levels of defense spending after these currencies are converted to a common currency, such as the U.S. dollar. This is particularly true in periods when there are significant changes in exchange rates, such as occurred between the U.S. dollar and many European currencies during the 1995 to 2000 period. The ratio of defense expenditures to GDP is a more consistent indicator of relative defense burdens or commitments, because it is not affected by exchange rate fluctuations. Therefore, we emphasize this ratio and the trend in defense expenditures in the domestic currencies in our discussion of defense burdens.

To present unclassified information on future defense spending, we obtained spending projections for key budget components, such as personnel and equipment, and for total defense spending from the respective governments of Germany, Italy, the United Kingdom, and the United States.[23] However, we found the data provided to us were not fully compatible with NATO data. To make our projections consistent with NATO's historical defense expenditures and components, we calculated the rates of growth implied by the data that NATO member countries supplied us, and we used NATO information for the year 2000 as a base for our projections. We also used forecasts of gross domestic product from DRIWEFA —an economic consulting firm—to compute projected ratios of defense spending to GDP.[24] To determine the future composition of defense expenditures for "personnel" and "equipment" categories, we applied the implied growth rate from the defense budget

---

[22] Our methodology is similar to the one NATO uses and to the one we used in our 1999 report. NATO uses 1995 local currency defense-spending deflators and 1995 exchange rates to convert to 1995 dollars. However, NATO does not further convert 1995 dollar defense expenditures into year 2000 dollars, as we have done in this report.

[23] NATO defense budget projections forecast for NATO members are classified.

[24] DRI-WEFA *World Outlook Comparison Tables, Forecast Data, 2001*, third quarter. The projected GDP figures may not reflect the economic shocks that have occurred since September 11, 2001.

projections that NATO members provided us to the respective data from NATO for the year 2000.

We discussed our methodology with DOD officials. DOD indicated that it preferred using year 2000 exchange rates and 2000 local currency defense spending deflators for converting the local currency defense expenditures into 2000 dollars. However, we did not use DOD's suggestion, because NATO uses a methodology similar to ours, which uses 1995 exchange rates. Because some European currencies have been subjected to significant depreciation between 1995 and 2000, using 2000 exchange rates substantially lowers defense expenditure figures expressed in dollars for these European NATO members.

POST-COLD WAR ENVIRONMENT DRIVES CONTRIBUTIONS TO EUROPEAN SECURITY IN NEW DIRECTIONS

The breakup of the former Soviet Union has prompted the United States and its European allies to use a much broader range of military and nonmilitary tools to foster security in the European region than were used in the past. The United States and its European allies have reduced their military forces and defense budgets since 1990, yet their forces have remained actively engaged in peacekeeping and other security-enhancing activities in the region during the post-Cold War period. The United States has reduced its military presence in Europe to a current level of about 100,000 military personnel, which cost $11.2 billion to support in fiscal year 2000. Increasingly, the United States and its European allies have used nonmilitary tools such as development and nonproliferation assistance to shape the regional security environment.[25] The type and level of assistance provided by each country reflects national interests, priorities, and threat perceptions. Since the end of the Cold War, multilateral organizations such as the European Union have also assumed wider responsibilities in shaping the security environment. In addition, NATO has begun to enlarge its alliance to include Central and Eastern European nations and has taken on important new missions, such as peacekeeping to help stabilize the Balkans. The European Union has developed a Common Foreign and Security Policy (CFSP), which uses a combination of political, military, and other measures to respond to regional crises. The enlargement of the European Union, whose accession programs are estimated to cost up to $60 billion from 2000 through 2006, is recognized by U.S. and European officials as a major investment in the region and as Europe's most significant contribution to regional security and stability.

---

[25] OECD defines official development assistance as financial flows to developing countries and multilateral institutions that are provided by official agencies and meet two conditions: (1) must promote economic development and welfare of developing countries as its main objective, and (2) must be concessional in character and convey a grant element of at least 25 percent.

Reduced U.S. and European Military Forces Provide Security Foundation in Post-Cold War Europe

Although the international security environment presents a diverse set of challenges very different from those of the Cold War, U.S. and European military forces still provide the foundation for security and stability in Europe. The number of U.S. and European military forces in Europe has declined since the end of the Cold War, as have the defense budgets that support these forces.

Size and Cost of U.S. and European Forces in Europe Have Decreased Since the End of the Cold War

Since the end of the Cold War, the United States and European NATO countries have reduced the size of their military forces and their corresponding defense budgets. The United States reduced its active military forces by 32 percent between 1990 and 2000, and its forces in European NATO countries by 65 percent. The United States reduced its defense expenditures by approximately 25 percent during the same period. Meanwhile, European NATO countries reduced their active duty forces by about 15 percent during the post-Cold War decade, and reduced their defense budgets by 14 percent.

Size of U.S. and European Forces Has Declined

The United States has reduced its military presence in European NATO countries from about 300,000 permanently stationed Army, Air Force, Navy, and Marine personnel in 1990 to about 100,000 personnel in 2000, as shown in figure 1.[26] The size of the U.S. presence in Europe has declined since 1990 in response to reduced threats in the region. U.S. personnel are stationed in NATO countries throughout Europe but are concentrated in five key countries, as shown in figure 2. In addition to the more than 100,000 permanently stationed personnel, forces that are rotationally and temporarily deployed also contribute to the U.S. military presence in Europe. For example, most of the 12,000 naval forces afloat rotate from the continental United States. In addition, the United States deployed about 11,400 troops in 2000 to support Balkans peace support operations. The Balkans forces came from units stationed either in Europe or in the United States.

---

[26] This reduction occurred in several steps. DOD initiated several studies in the early 1990s examining the scope of the U.S. military presence in Europe. The Congress also mandated in the National Defense Authorization Acts for fiscal years 1993 and 1995 that DOD maintain a presence of about 100,000 troops.

Figure 1: U.S. Troop Strength in European NATO Countries, 1990-2000

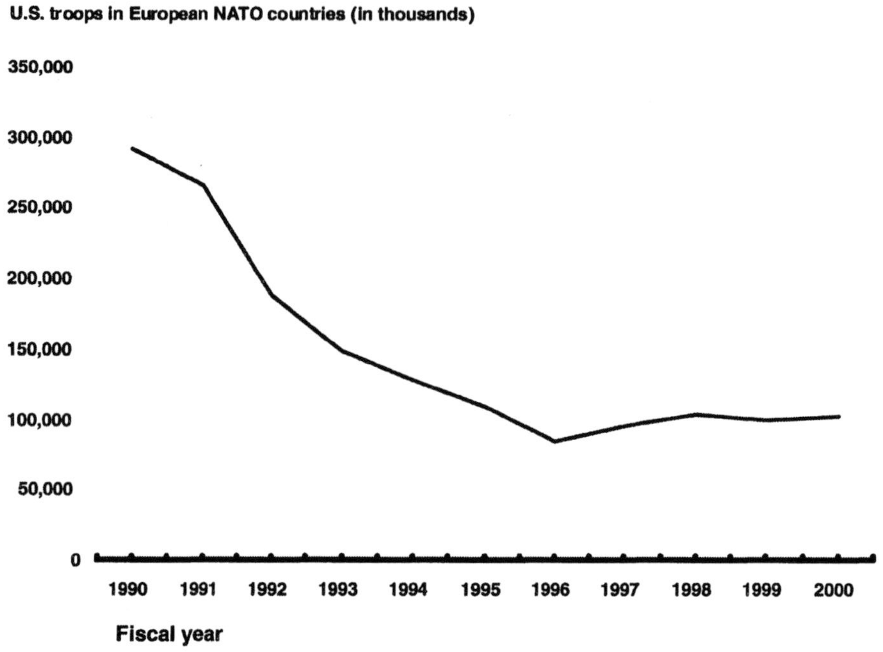

U.S. troops in European NATO countries (in thousands)

Source: NATO.

Infrastructure and prepositioned equipment are also part of the U.S. military presence in Europe.[27] As the United States has reduced the number of permanently stationed personnel in Europe, it has also returned bases and other facilities to European host nations. In 1991, the United States operated 858 European facilities; it now operates 241 facilities. Other facilities, such as communications centers, support a range of U.S. military activities in Europe and other regions. Prepositioned equipment facilitates the rapid reinforcement of personnel from the continental United States in the event of a crisis. Although the United States has reduced the scale of prepositioned equipment in Europe, it continues to maintain key prepositioned stocks, such as Army equipment for three heavy brigades and six Air Force airbase support sets. Finally, the U.S. en-route system of airbases supports its airlift aircraft in regional operations.

---

[27] Infrastructure includes the facilities that host or support U.S. military operations and activities, such as army bases, airbases, naval ports and naval air stations, training facilities, and communications facilities.

**Figure 2: Number of U.S. Military Personnel Permanently Stationed in
Five European Countries, September 30, 2000**

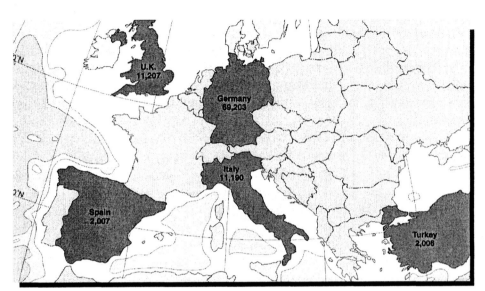

Source: DOD.

European NATO countries have also reduced their military force numbers and supporting infrastructure over the past decade, but not to the extent the United States has. As discussed in chapter 4, some European countries, such as Germany, have taken longer to reduce their personnel numbers because they maintain conscription.[28] As shown in figure 3, European NATO nations reduced their active military forces by approximately 15 percent between 1990 and 2000, from 3.5 million to about 3 million. Over the next 5 years these numbers could decline even further, as European nations look for savings that can be used to procure modernized weapon systems and equipment.

Costs in Support of European Security Have Declined

U.S. and European defense budgets have provided the resources for post- Cold War defense-related activities in Europe. As shown in figure 4, U.S. and European defense budgets declined and then generally leveled off after 1990. Similar trends exist with defense spending as a percentage of GDP, as shown in figure 5. While the United States still has a large defense budget—both in terms of total defense expenditures and as a percentage of GDP—the gap between U.S. and European defense budgets has narrowed during the post-Cold War decade.[29] European defense budgets primarily support European regional security, whereas only a portion of U.S. defense budgets supports U.S. security commitments in Europe. We were able to discover the cost of maintaining U.S. personnel and supporting infrastructure in Europe; however, identifying the total cost of U.S. security commitments in

---

[28] Conscription requires that citizens between certain ages serve in the armed forces for a period of time or provide alternative service to their country. In Germany's case, for example, nearly half of its armed forces are conscripts.

[29] Turkey and Greece spent more on defense as a percentage of GDP than did the United States—4.5 and 4.9 percent, respectively, in fiscal year 2000. U.S. defense spending as a percentage of GDP was 2.9 percent in fiscal year 2000.

Europe is more difficult, because some of this support comes from units and facilities located in the United States that have multiple mission responsibilities.

Figure 3: European Troop Strength in European NATO Countries, 1990-2000

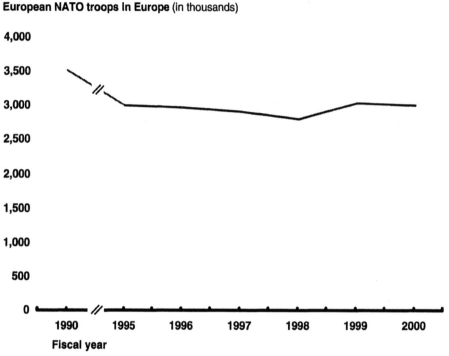

European NATO troops in Europe (in thousands)

Note 1: Years 1999 and 2000 include troops from the Czech Republic, Hungary, and Poland.
Note 2: NATO data were not available for 1991-1994.
Source: NATO.

The cost of supporting the U.S. military presence in Europe declined more sharply than did total U.S. defense expenditures between 1990 and 2000. DOD stated that for fiscal year 2000, the cost of supporting the U.S. military presence in European NATO countries, including permanent personnel and supporting infrastructure, was $11.2 billion. As shown in figure 6, this is a decline of about 50 percent from fiscal year 1990, when about $23 billion (in year-2000 dollars) supported about 300,000 troops.

Figure 4: Defense Spending by the United States and Selected European Countries, 1980-2000

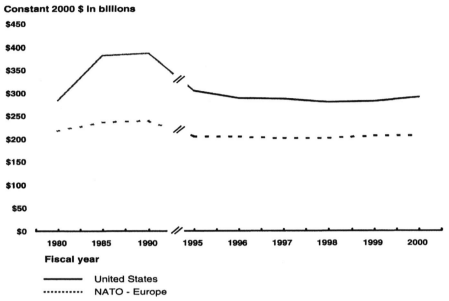

Note 1: Data from 1980 through 1995 were available only in 5-year increments.
Note 2: 2000 figures are NATO estimates. NATO will release actual figures in December 2001.
Source: NATO.

Figure 5: Defense Spending as a Percentage of GDP for the United States and Selected European Countries, 1980-2000

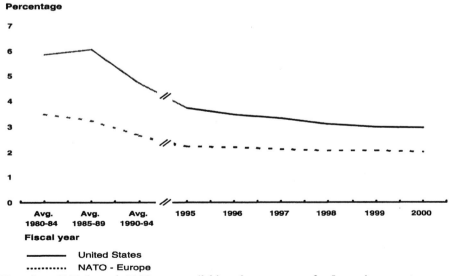

Note: Data from 1980 through 1995 were available only as averages for 5-year increments.
Source: NATO.

Figure 6: Costs to Support U.S. Permanently Stationed Forces in Europe,1990-2000

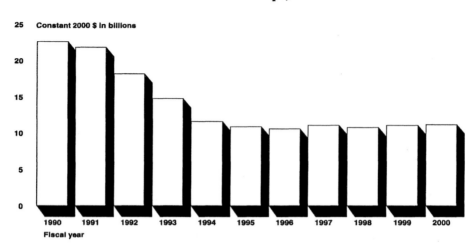

Source: DOD.

About $7.3 billion, or 65 percent, of the current cost of supporting the U.S. military presence in Europe is targeted in Germany, where the United States continues to station about 70,000 troops. DOD defines the cost of overseas presence as the costs that each of the armed services incurs for personnel, operations and maintenance, military construction, and familyhousing construction and operations in each country where active-duty personnel are permanently stationed.[30] This does not include other costs, such as commissary activities and some depot maintenance for equipment. DOD budget officials stated that the overseas costs are not incremental costs and do not represent the potential savings of returning any or all of these forces to the United States.

In addition to the cost of supporting permanently stationed forces, the United States also incurs the costs of participating in contingency operations in Europe. U.S. forces based in Europe, together with U.S. forces drawn from the continental United States and elsewhere, have participated in various regional contingency operations, particularly in the Balkans region. DOD identified the incremental costs incurred during these contingency operations as those costs that would not have been incurred if it were not for the operation.[31] DOD has reported that from 1991 through 2000, the United States spent $15.1 billion to support U.S. military involvement in the Balkans.[32] Together with the United Kingdom and Turkey, the United States has also participated in efforts to enforce the nofly zone in Northern Iraq from bases in Turkey under Operation Northern Watch. The incremental costs for U.S.

---

[30] Defining U.S. overseas military costs is difficult because DOD budgets by service rather than by overseas country. DOD began calculating overseas presence costs in response to a mandate in the 1989 National Defense Appropriations Act to better account for the costs that it incurs in supporting overseas presence. In response, DOD developed the OP-53 report, which identifies service-borne costs by country. The report also specifies the costs for DOD-wide functions such as health care, schools, and other activities not covered in the service budgets.

[31] The principal categories include incremental pay for military personnel participating in contingency operations; other personnel support costs; incremental operating support costs for additional training, facilities, and other supplies; and operations-related transportation costs.

[32] For DOD contingency operations costs, see *Defense Budget: Need for Continued Visibility Over Use of Contingency Funds* (GAO-01-829, July 6, 2001).

participation in Operation Northern Watch have been considerably less than for the Balkans operations. Contingency costs for U.S. participation in that operation totaled about $600,000 from fiscal years 1997 through 2001.

During the Cold War, European NATO allies began to offset the cost to the United States for its military presence in Europe through direct assistance, such as host-country expenditures to support U.S. forces, and indirect assistance, such as tax exemptions. DOD reported that in 1999, European NATO countries provided about $2.3 billion in host-nation support.[33] Germany, the largest contributor, provided about $1.4 billion of this total.

U.S. Military Presence in Europe Offers a Range of Benefits and Some Drawbacks

U.S. diplomatic and military officials stated that the U.S. military presence in Europe helps the United States achieve key political and operational objectives, including U.S. leadership and influence in the alliance, joint operations with European militaries, and response capability to crises in the region and elsewhere. These officials also identified certain strategic and operational drawbacks to maintaining the current U.S. military presence in Europe.

Political Benefits

The U.S. military presence allows the United States to exercise political leadership and influence in the alliance. The United States has traditionally contributed and continues to contribute the greatest number of military personnel to the alliance. This is largely attributable to the more than 100,000 permanently stationed U.S. forces in Europe and the dual-based forces stationed in the United States that are dedicated to NATO operations in the event of a crisis. According to a senior NATO official, NATO has traditionally acted under a principle of proportionality, in that the country contributing the greatest number of forces to the alliance receives the leadership position. Through these contributions, the United States has secured many top command positions, such as the Supreme Allied Commander, Europe. A U.S. military official said that the United States is thus able to guide the NATO defense planning process and to control a range of regional security operations and activities.

Senior European officials stated that the U.S. military presence demonstrates that the United States remains dedicated to European security and stability. They said that a reduction of U.S. forces stationed in Europe below a certain level—which they did not specify—would call into question the U.S. commitment. This commitment to European security is a critical factor as EU nations move to organize a more independent defense posture, according to U.S. NATO officials. They stated that continued U.S. presence in Europe will provide greater assurance that the United States has a voice in the process, even though it is not a member of the European Union. The Supreme Allied Commander, Europe, stated that the U.S. military presence has had a steadying effect in a changing security environment, as West and East Germany reunited and the Central and Eastern European countries began their transition from authoritarian to democratic governments. A senior German diplomatic official said that the U.S. military presence provides the anchor for European security and stability and that it reinforces the image of the United States as the primary security guarantor. A senior Italian

---

[33] For DOD's complete assessment of allied host-nation support and other responsibilitysharing issues, see DOD's *Report on Allied Contributions to the Common Defense*, March 2001.

military official noted that the U.S. military presence added influence, weight, and credibility to the structure of the alliance.

Maintaining a military presence in Europe also makes it easier for the United States to call on its allies in the event of a crisis. For example, U.S. military officials stated that it would have been more difficult to call on European allies to host the large numbers of forces deployed from the United States to Europe in support of Operation Allied Force in 1999 if the United States had not already had forces based in many of these countries.

Operational Benefits

U.S. European Command officials stated that U.S. forces stationed in Europe can generally respond to crises in Europe and adjoining regions more quickly than could forces deployed from the United States, since they are closer to areas of conflict. U.S. forces stationed in Europe were the first to be deployed in support of peacekeeping operations in Bosnia in 1995 and Kosovo in 1999.[34] In July 2001, U.S. Marine Fleet Anti-Terrorist Support Teams were deployed from Naples, Italy, to provide additional security during attacks against the U.S. Embassy in Skopje, the Former Yugoslav Republic of Macedonia. The U.S. European Command provided 25,000 personnel to support NATO's Operation Allied Force (and related humanitarian efforts in Albania and the Former Yugoslav Republic of Macedonia). U.S. participation in Operation Allied Force was greatly facilitated by the network of U.S. and allied airbases in Europe.

U.S. military presence also encourages improved interoperability between the United States and European NATO countries, and it enables the United States to influence the development of European military capabilities. Since the end of the Cold War, the United States has focused on cooperative activities with regional militaries.[35] U.S. military officials argued that engagement activities, such as training foreign militaries in U.S. operating methods, are important because U.S. forces increasingly operate with a variety of countries in peacekeeping operations. Military officials at U.S. Naval Forces, Europe, added that, through overseas presence and frequent interaction, U.S. forces help shape other military forces and encourage the development of greater expeditionary capabilities.[36] They also noted that another important benefit of having permanently stationed U.S. forces in Europe is to develop and foster relationships with foreign military units. Units deploying from the United States find that establishing these relationships is more difficult, given the relatively short time they spend in the European theater.

One of the most important operational benefits of the U.S. presence in Europe is that the United States is able to respond faster to crises in neighboring regions and elsewhere in the world. U.S. facilities in Europe allow the United States to project personnel and equipment

---

[34] DOD officials said the U.S. Army in Europe plans to activate a second airborne battalion in Vicenza, Italy, starting in December 2001. The second airborne battalion will double the Army's light infantry presence and forced entry capabilities in Europe, enhance U.S. forces in NATO's southern region, and allow for simultaneous execution of noncombatant evacuation operations and maintenance of a rapid reaction force for the Balkans. Officials estimate that the activation will be completed by October 2003.

[35] According to DOD officials, these activities include 30 budget categories, ranging from naval ship visits and humanitarian relief operations to exercises with allies and non-allies.

[36] DOD defines the term "expeditionary" as the capability of an armed force to accomplish a specific objective in a foreign country. The Commandant of the U.S. Marine Corps elaborated on this definition, stating that an expeditionary force needs to be agile, flexible, and rapidly deployable. It must be able to enter the objective area forcibly, sustain itself for extended periods, withdraw quickly, and reconstitute rapidly to execute follow-on missions.

rapidly from the United States to other regions of the world—a key element of U.S. military strategy. The United States maintains a global network of 13 enroute airbases that facilitates the rapid deployment of forces from the continental United States to areas of conflict overseas. Six of these enroute airbases are located in Europe. The U.S en-route system of airbases is critical to operations in Europe and Southwest Asia. Without these bases, which provide refueling and other logistical support to U.S. airlift aircraft, it would be impossible to meet wartime requirements in Europe, the Middle East, and Southwest Asia.[37]

Military officials at the U.S. Central Command (the command responsible for U.S. military operations in Southwest Asia) said that en-route facilities and associated support personnel in Europe are critical to deploying U.S. forces to that region in the event of a crisis.[38] They added that reducing the level of U.S. support in Europe would severely limit their ability to deploy forces in a crisis. U.S. prepositioned weapons and equipment in the European theater would allow the execution of military operations in nearby areas more quickly and at a lower cost than would using air-and sealift from the United States. According to officials at the U.S. Naval Forces, Europe, rotational naval forces in the Mediterranean can reach the Red Sea to conduct strike operations in Southwest Asia 9 days faster than forces deployed from the eastern United States. Air Force aircraft and personnel deployed in Europe allow forces to respond more quickly to address small-scale conflicts in the area and to reduce the burden on airlift and sealift, than if the units came from the United States. Likewise, Army combat and support units stationed in Europe allow forces to move to small-scale conflicts in the area more quickly and at lower cost. The Army can also move these units by land at a lower cost than that for transporting them from the United States. Similarly, U.S. military and diplomatic officials stated that U.S. participation in multinational efforts to enforce the no-fly zone in northern Iraq under Operation Northern Watch would be severely limited if the United States did not have access to Incirlik Airbase in Turkey.

Strategic Drawbacks

Representatives from major research organizations in the United States and Europe identified certain strategic drawbacks to maintaining the current U.S. military presence in Europe in the absence of a clear military threat, such as the Soviet Union. Some representatives and certain U.S. military officials also identified drawbacks from the current positioning of forces in Europe. Their comments focused primarily on U.S. ground forces.

Representatives from U.S. research institutes said that although stationing U.S. forces in Europe strengthens the U.S. strategic position in Europe, these forces reduce the overall strategic flexibility of the United States because the forces are committed to Europe. They also noted that the level of presence required to achieve U.S. objectives in the region is not clear, and that a force level of somewhat less than 100,000 would not likely affect U.S. ability to respond to regional conflicts. Representatives of research institutes in Europe concurred with this point and said that, for example, a 10-percent reduction in U.S. ground forces stationed in Europe would not affect the U.S.-European strategic relationship.

Research institute representatives also raised a related concern about the positioning of U.S. forces in Europe. The United States continues to station most of its forces at facilities

---

[37] For a more detailed discussion of these issues, see GAO report *Military Readiness: Effects of a U.S. Military Presence in Europe on Mobility Requirements* (GAO-02-99, Nov. 28, 2001).

[38] European Command officials noted that prepositioned equipment in Europe also supports the rapid reinforcement of personnel from the United States in the event of a crisis.

that were used in the Cold War, particularly those in Germany. These officials have argued that the United States should base more of its forces closer to areas of potential conflict, such as in the Mediterranean region or further east, in the Central and East European region.[39] U.S. officials stated that although bases in Germany are closer to the Balkans than are those in the United States, it has nevertheless been a challenge to support peacekeeping operations in southeastern Europe.

Representatives from major research institutes identified financial and other drawbacks to maintaining the current level of U.S. military presence in Europe. A RAND study estimated that the U.S. units stationed in Europe would cost about 10 to 15 percent less if they were based in the United States. However, other representatives disagreed, stating that savings would occur only if all or a portion of U.S. forces in Europe were removed from the force structure, rather than returned to the United States. In an environment of scarce resources, certain critics also argue that the military presence in Europe could be reduced so that the resulting savings could be used more advantageously in other parts of the world. Further, several representatives from major research institutes stated that a large U.S. military presence in Europe creates a disincentive for Europeans to improve their own defense capabilities and shoulder more of the defense burden in Europe. Maintaining the current presence may hamper or discourage the European allies from taking greater responsibility for regional security, they said, because allies view the United States as the principal security guarantor in Europe.

Quadrennial Defense Review

The new administration examined a range of strategic issues, including the scope of U.S. military presence and activities overseas, as part of the 2001 Quadrennial Defense Review. The Quadrennial Defense Review Report, issued in September 2001, states that the U.S. overseas presence, concentrated in Western Europe and Northeast Asia, is inadequate for the new strategic environment in which U.S. interests are global and potential threats are emerging in other areas of the world. The report further notes that a reorientation must take into account these new challenges. The report states that the United States will maintain its critical bases in Western Europe and Northeast Asia, and that these bases may also serve as hubs from which to address future conflicts in other parts of the world. The DOD report does not identify specific changes in the number of U.S. military personnel in Europe. DOD officials emphasized that it is still engaged in reviewing these and related issues, particularly in light of the attacks of September 11, 2001, and that the results of continuing studies and discussions will emerge at a later time.

---

[39] Nevertheless, several factors may militate against permanently shifting forces from current locations in Europe, according to DOD officials. In negotiating the Founding Act on Mutual Relations, Cooperation, and Security between NATO and the Russian Federation (May 27, 1997), NATO countries made a political pledge to Russia to refrain from developing new bases in former Warsaw Pact countries. Further, the cost of building new bases and facilities would be considerable, according to these officials.

Europeans Lead in Development Assistance to the Newly Independent States and Central and Eastern Europe, but the United States Spends More on Nonproliferation and Threat-Reduction Programs

Since the end of the Cold War, the United States and European allies have increasingly used nonmilitary tools such as development and nonproliferation assistance to shape the European security environment. Their use of these tools has been based on differing regional interests and priorities. The European Commission and European allies have led in contributions of development assistance to Central and Eastern Europe (CEE) and the Newly Independent States (NIS), together providing about $47 billion of the just over $71 billion of development assistance disbursed to these regions from 1990 to 1999.[40]

The European Commission and European allies led in contributions of development assistance to the NIS from 1990 to 1999, disbursing about $20 billion of the approximately $35 billion provided by all donors during this period, as shown in figure 7.[41] European country contributions to the NIS came mostly from Germany, which spent about $11 billion during this period. While this partly reflects the costs associated with repatriating ex-Soviet troops during the early 1990s, German officials stated that their government also regards Russia's economic stability as a foreign policy priority and has invested heavily in technical assistance for private sector development and public administration reform. Other donor assistance supports Russia in rehabilitating social welfare services, such as public health and education.

Figure 7: Development Assistance Totaling $34.7 Billion Disbursed to the Newly Independent States, 1990-1999

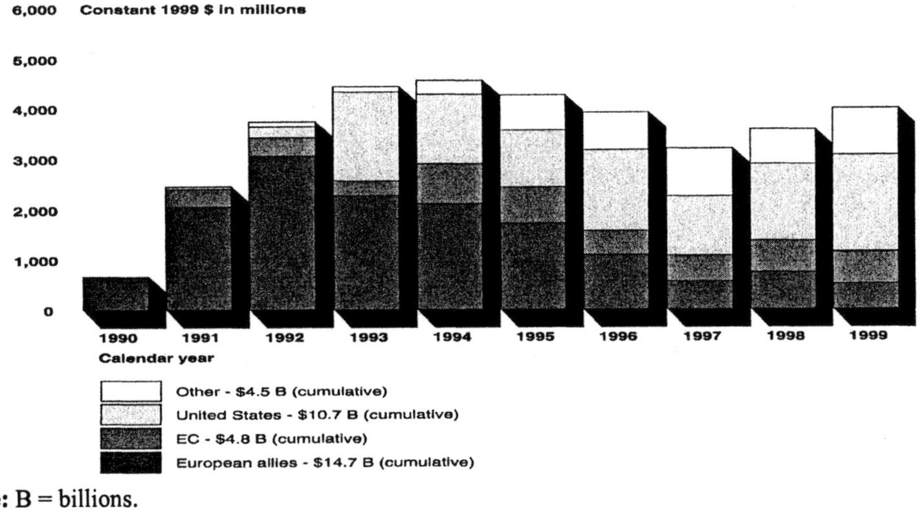

Note: B = billions.
Source: GAO analysis of OECD data.

---

[40] The European Commission, the executive agency of the European Union, manages EU multilateral development agencies and is responsible for EU external assistance programs.
[41] We did not include non-concessional loans.

The European Commission and European allies were collectively the leading donors of development assistance to Central and Eastern Europe from 1990 to 1999. This assistance supported economic and political reforms critical to the EU enlargement process, which will be discussed later in this chapter. Together, they disbursed over $27 billion of the more than $36 billion in development assistance provided to the region, as shown in figure 8. Although European country contributions have declined since 1995, this trend has been offset by increases in European Commission aid. European officials explained that national development assistance budgets have fallen in recent years because of fiscal constraints, and that governments have channeled development funding through multilateral institutions such as the European Commission. The rise in EC assistance to Central and Eastern Europe generally reflects this pattern, as does the expansion of EC programs to prepare Central and Eastern European countries for EU membership.

The United States regards stability among the Newly Independent States as vital to national security and has targeted a large portion of its development assistance funds to that region. As the second largest bilateral donor to the NIS, the United States spent about $10.7 billion from 1990 to 1999—nearly one-third of the development assistance provided to the NIS during this period. Supporting the former Soviet republics in their transition to democratic institutions and free-market economies is critical to U.S. national security interests, according to the Department of State. U.S. aid to national governments in the region consists of financial and technical assistance for reforms in the political, judicial, and economic sectors. Direct aid to civil society benefits private enterprises, educational institutions, nongovernmental organizations, and municipal authorities. The United States supports comparable reforms in Central and Eastern Europe, and it allocated about $6 billion to the region from 1990 to 1999. As figure 8 illustrates, U.S. aid to the region has declined since the early or mid-1990s, falling from a peak of more than $2 billion in 1991 to less than $150 million in 1999. Funding decreased as the recipient countries made the transition to democratic societies and free markets, and no longer required development assistance. By the end of fiscal year 2000, 8 of the 15 recipient countries no longer needed U.S. assistance, and the United States had shifted its focus to the countries of southeastern Europe.

**Figure 8: Development Assistance Totaling $36.4 Billion
Disbursed to Central and Eastern Europe, 1990-1999**

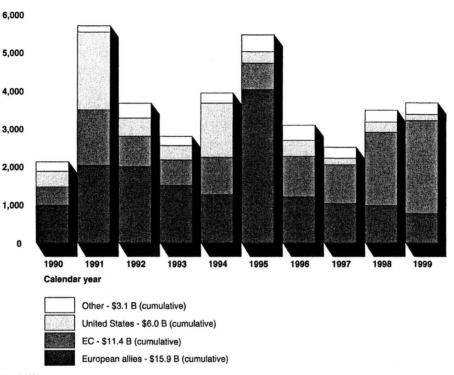

Note: B = billions.
Source: GAO analysis of OECD data.

The United States spent considerably more than the EU and its member states to control the spread of weapons of mass destruction.[42] The United States allocated more than $5.5 billion to nonproliferation and threat reduction programs in the Newly Independent States from 1991 to 2001, as compared with the approximately $540 million spent by the EU and its member states. According to U.S. and EU officials, the relatively low levels of European funding for nonproliferation and threat reduction reflect different perceptions of threat. As a senior EU diplomat explained, the Cold War conditioned Europeans to perceive weapons of mass destruction primarily as an "East-West" concern, whereby the United States, as the leader of the West, bore most of the burden in addressing the issue. Nevertheless, he stated that the establishment of a Nonproliferation and Disarmament, Weapons of Mass Destruction, group within the Commission indicates the EU's growing concern over the threats posed by weapons of mass destruction. The group is working to raise awareness among the European Union and its member states about the proliferation of nuclear, biological, radiological, and chemical weapons.

---

[42] 18Weapons of mass destruction include nuclear, biological, radiological, and chemical weapons.

NATO and the EU Adapt Objectives and Policies to a Changing Strategic Environment

NATO and the EU have responded to Europe's evolving post-Cold War order by redefining and expanding their roles and objectives. Despite institutional differences, the activities of NATO and the EU complement each other to strengthen the economic, political, and military dimensions of regional security and stability. Founded as a defensive alliance, NATO has revised its strategic concept to respond to the broader spectrum of the threats now facing greater Europe—those ranging from traditional cases of cross-border aggression to interethnic conflicts and acts of terrorism. Furthermore, NATO is facilitating the integration and eventual membership of Central and Eastern European nations in the transatlantic security community. The EU has likewise emphasized regional integration as being key to a safe and stable Europe, particularly through the deepening of political and economic ties among current members and through extending EU membership to CEE countries.

NATO and the EU Use Enlargement Programs to Enhance Regional Stability

According to U.S. and European officials, the largely complementary NATO and EU enlargement efforts will make important contributions to regional security and stability. As a military alliance, NATO contributes to regional security by offering new members an explicit collective defense guarantee in the event that they are attacked.[43] This guarantee discourages potential aggressors from attacking any member because it would prompt an alliance-wide response. Even though the European Union does not have a similar collective defense guarantee, both U.S. and EU officials pointed out that the political and economic integration of CEE nations into the European Union—and the development of common institutions and policies—also contributes to regional security and stability.

U.S. and European officials stated that the EU accession criteria and NATO expectations for aspirant members enhance stability because they require potential members to make important reforms in support of democracy, rule of law, and stable borders, as illustrated in figure 9. U.S. and European officials noted that the possibility of membership in either or both institutions serves as an important incentive for aspirant nations to undertake these reforms. For example, NATO and the EU require that countries seeking membership in either or both organizations must demonstrate that they have firm civilian control of the military and are not engaged in regional conflicts. Aspirant nations must also support democratic values and rule of law through transparent elections, autonomous judicial institutions, and protection of minority rights. Furthermore, the EU accession process fosters prosperity by supporting candidates' efforts to promote private enterprise, improve financial-sector transparency, and ensure macroeconomic stability. Outreach activities conducted in support of each institution's enlargement have reinforced relationships between current members and aspirant nations.

There are important differences between the two initiatives. U.S. and European analysts pointed out that EU accession processes are lengthy and detailed because potential members

---

[43] 19GAO has completed numerous studies examining the implications of NATO enlargement for the United States and the Alliance. See *NATO Enlargement: Requirements and Costs for Commonly Funded Budgets* (GAO/NSIAD-98-113, Mar. 6, 1998); *NATO Enlargement: Cost Estimates Developed to Date Are Notional* (GAO/NSIAD-97-209, Aug. 18, 1997); and *NATO Enlargement: U.S. and International Efforts to Assist Potential New Members* (GAO/NSIAD-97-164, June 27, 1997).

must be able to implement the body of EU laws and regulations known as the *acquis communautaire*.[44] By contrast, NATO does not have fixed accession criteria. Since NATO's inception, the decision to admit new members has been based on unanimous agreement of all members. Although NATO developed a set of guidelines for potential members in 1995 that encompasses alliance expectations in political, economic, and military matters, nevertheless, these criteria are less specific than those for the EU.

Figure 9: Security-Related Accession Criteria for the EU and NATO

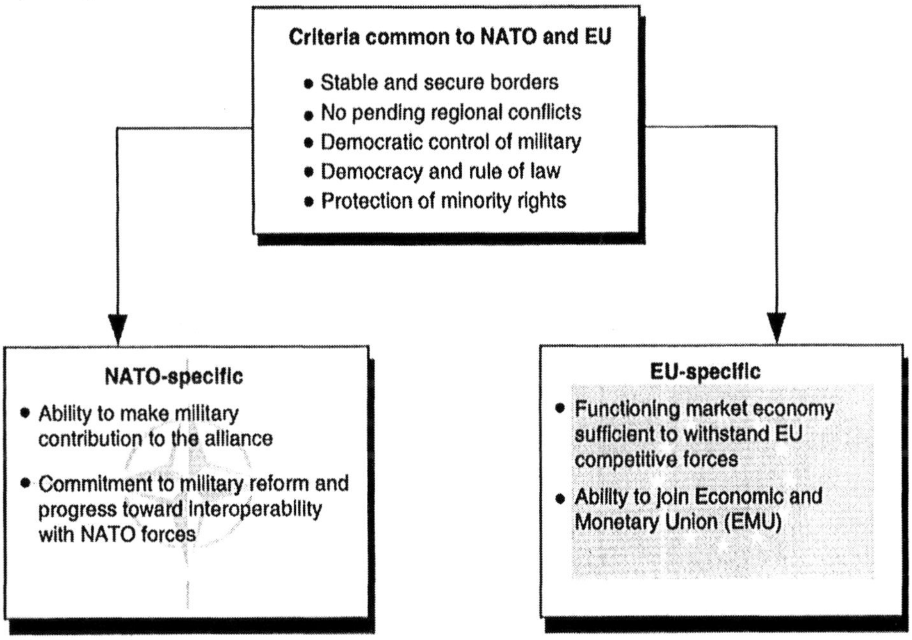

Criteria common to NATO and EU

- Stable and secure borders
- No pending regional conflicts
- Democratic control of military
- Democracy and rule of law
- Protection of minority rights

NATO-specific

- Ability to make military contribution to the alliance
- Commitment to military reform and progress toward interoperability with NATO forces

EU-specific

- Functioning market economy sufficient to withstand EU competitive forces
- Ability to join Economic and Monetary Union (EMU)

Sources: EU and NATO.

NATO and the EU Use Accession Programs to Prepare Aspirants for Membership

Both NATO and the EU use accession programs to prepare candidate nations for potential membership in their organizations. NATO uses the Partnership for Peace (PfP) initiative to help expand political and military cooperation throughout Europe, and the Membership Action Plan, launched in 1999, to help nations aspiring to NATO membership prepare to meet NATO goals and priorities. The EU has used a more centralized set of assistance programs that help aspirant nations reform their domestic institutions to meet EU accession requirements.

---

[44] Adopting the *acquis* requires candidate countries to implement more than 80,000 pages of EU regulations covering 31 categories or chapters. These chapters cover a range of issues, including the movement of people, capital, and goods within the EU; competition policy; the environment; and consumer protection. Some requirements can be satisfied by simple technical changes, while others require large investments. See *NATO: Implications of European Integration for Allies' Defense Spending* (GAO/NSIAD-99-185, June 30, 1999).

Contributions of NATO Members to Partnership for
Peace Reflect National Interests and Priorities

In 1994, NATO established the PfP initiative to increase defense cooperation with nonmember European countries, particularly former Warsaw Pact members and other former Communist countries in Central and Eastern Europe. U.S. and European defense officials said that PfP has been NATO's principal outreach initiative in the post-Cold War period. The initiative plays a key role in developing the military capabilities of participating partner states, increasing interoperability among NATO allies and partners, and reforming their defense establishments. PfP activities reinforce bilateral relationships between certain NATO members and aspirant nations.

As part of the PfP program, NATO members conduct activities, such as exercises or training, with aspirant nations' militaries to improve the capabilities of partner militaries and pursue common objectives such as interoperability. However, since NATO members decide how to target their PfP activities, their activities tend to reflect their national interests and regional priorities. As the program's largest donor, the United States has broadly engaged the aspirant nations through a combination of exercises, training, and nonlethal equipment transfer.[45] By contrast, European NATO countries have largely focused their more limited programs on specific nations or regions, especially those geographically close to them.

In addition to PfP activities, some countries run parallel or overlapping military outreach programs and activities with former Warsaw Pact nations. These programs and activities are part of a country's broader foreign and defense policies. For example, the United Kingdom conducts the majority of its military outreach programs, including PfP, under a component of its national security strategy known as "Defense Diplomacy."[46] Turkey has been very active in outreach activities targeting Central Asia and the Black Sea region. In addition to providing full funding for a PfP training center in Ankara, which trains military personnel principally from former Soviet republics in the Caucasus and Central Asia, Turkey has also taken part in organizing two multilateral security organizations that function independently of NATO. The Southeast European Brigade assembles militaries from throughout the Balkans and Black Sea region to train for peacekeeping operations, while the Black Sea Naval Cooperation Task Group brings together Turkish, Russian, Bulgarian, Romanian, Georgian, and Ukrainian naval assets for search and rescue operations, humanitarian assistance, and other tasks as agreed to by all parties.

EU Fosters Economic and Political Stability in Central and Eastern
Europe through Enlargement and Financial Assistance for Reform

The EU is making pre- and post-accession investments to strengthen democratic and economic sectors in Central and Eastern European countries seeking EU membership. U.S. and European diplomatic officials stated that enlargement represents the European Union's most significant contribution to regional security. The enlargement process stabilizes Central and Eastern Europe by integrating former Warsaw Pact nations into Western Europe's political and economic community and by facilitating their adoption of democratic, free-

---

[45] See *NATO: U.S. Assistance to the Partnership for Peace (GAO-01-734, July 20, 2001)*.

[46] The United Kingdom created the "Defense Diplomacy" mission to give greater priority and attention to conflict prevention and peacetime diplomacy activities. With regard to military outreach, it covers a variety of training and technical assistance programs in defense management, arms control and nonproliferation, demobilization and re-education of former Soviet troops, and English language training.

market principles. The membership process requires candidates to satisfy an extensive set of criteria requiring various reforms to restructure financial institutions, support democratic governance, and strengthen law enforcement institutions in return for EU financial and technical assistance—and eventual EU membership.

From 2000 through 2006, the EU estimates that the total cost for enlargement-related programs could be about $60 billion, roughly $20 billion during the pre-accession period and up to $40 billion once candidates join the EU. The European Union's primary pre-accession aid program helps accession candidates to adapt domestic policy to EU standards while training a range of civil servants and regulatory officials, including judges, environmental inspectors, customs officers, border guards, and financial analysts. The European Union's second-largest preaccession program focuses on improving environmental and transportation infrastructure. A third program devotes funding to agriculture and rural development.

European officials said that EU-supported reforms are having positive economic effects in Central and Eastern Europe and have facilitated that region's convergence with Western European markets. CEE exports to the EU grew by more than 40 percent from 1994 through 1999, and now the EU accounts for nearly two-thirds of CEE exports and imports. In addition to increased trade flows, the EU enlargement process also correlates with a sharp growth in foreign direct investment to Central and Eastern Europe, as shown in figure 10. International Monetary Fund and U.N. analyses attribute these in-flows, which spur growth of local private enterprises, to the favorable business climate created by EU-supported political and economic reforms.

Figure 10: Foreign Direct Investment to Selected Central and Eastern European Countries, 1990-1999

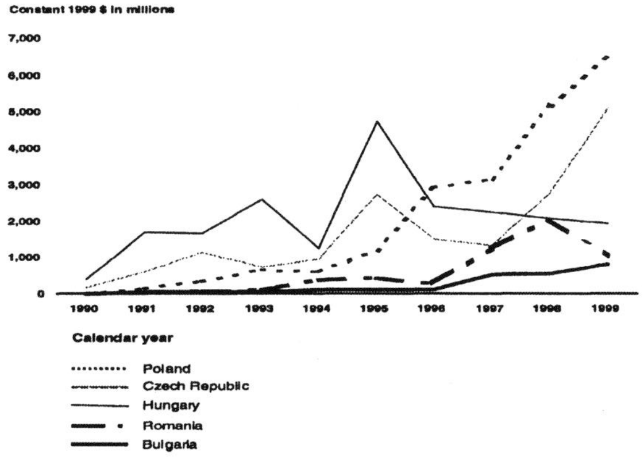

Source: OECD.

COMPLEX BALKANS SECURITY ENVIRONMENT ADDRESSED WITH A RANGE OF MILITARY I NTERVENTIONS AND NONMILITARY ASSISTANCE

Since 1992, the international community has used a combination of military and nonmilitary interventions to promote peace and stability in the Balkans. The United States has made key military contributions through its air combat capabilities and ground troops, whereas the European allies have contributed the largest contingent of ground troops and specialized support units to peacekeeping operations. In Kosovo, the United States provided 70 percent of the aircraft and flew more than 60 percent of the total sorties, which were essential to the defeat of the Yugoslav army. Meanwhile, European allies have consistently provided the majority of ground troops to support NATO operations and paramilitary specialists who are trained for post-conflict crisis interventions. European allies have also led efforts to support nonmilitary interventions, such as development assistance and personnel to support multilateral operations. Of the almost $15 billion, disbursed to the Balkans region from 1993 through 1999, the European Commission (EC) and European allies contributed about $10.2 billion, primarily to fund humanitarian and reconstruction programs such as rebuilding airports, bridges, and roads. During this same period, the U.S. distributed about $1.2 billion, primarily for emergency relief and institution building. European allies have consistently provided a large number of civilians to support multilateral institution-building programs in the Balkans, including more than 2,000 U.N. civilian police.

Military Interventions Included a Combination of Air Combat and Ground Troops That Resulted in Shared Benefits

The United States' most significant military contributions to regional security have been its tactical air combat capabilities and provision of ground troops. The European allies' key contributions have been their provision of the preponderance of ground troops and specialty units necessary to support peacekeeping operations, as well as their provision of military airbases and commercial airports to support the NATO air campaign. Although the United States and European allies have supported Balkans operations in different ways, U.S. and European military officials asserted that joint military operations are critical to future NATO operations, and that the benefits of such operations far outweigh the drawbacks.

United States Played a Dominant Role in the Balkans Air Campaigns

One of the most significant U.S. military contributions to regional security has been its tactical air combat capabilities in the Bosnia and Kosovo conflicts. In Operation Allied Force, for example, the United States contributed 70 percent of the more than 1,000 manned and unmanned aircraft used, and flew more than 60 percent of the 37,000 strike and support sorties from March through June 1999.[47] U.S. capabilities dominated in specific types of

---

[47] DOD and NATO define a "strike" sortie as an attack intended to inflict damage on, seize, or destroy an objective. "Support sorties" consist of both combat and noncombat missions. They include intelligence and reconnaissance,

strike sorties flown. For instance, the United States flew 87 percent of the sorties to disrupt or destroy Yugoslav air defenses. The United States also flew more than 70 percent of close air support missions, which provided protection for friendly forces on the ground. Furthermore, the United States led critical support sorties by providing intelligence and reconnaissance, intra-theater airlift, air refueling, and special operations. U.S. and European military officials stated that Operation Allied Force further highlighted the gaps in capabilities between the United States and its European allies, particularly in avionics, precision munitions, and tactical communications. These gaps limited the European countries' ability to conduct critical suppression of enemy air defense, as well as command-and-control missions. Appendix I shows the types of aircraft and capabilities provided by selected countries.

U.S. military officials stated, however, that the successful implementation of the U.S. air campaigns, particularly Operation Allied Force, was attributable in large part to military airbases and commercial airports provided by European NATO countries to support the air operations. They noted that in Operation Allied Force, U.S. forces depended heavily on Europe's provision of 22 land bases located in 8 countries, and particularly those in Italy and Turkey, to launch their sorties successfully (see figure 11). Officials also noted that the European bases provided critical logistical support, including air traffic control, to support the NATO campaigns.

Figure 11: European Bases Available to Operation Allied Force

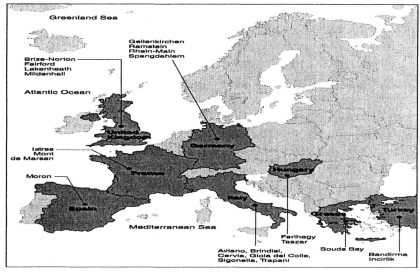

Source: DOD.

---

combat air patrols to protect strike missions, combat search and rescue, and aerial refueling. NATO categorizes combat sorties as battlefield air interdiction, combat air patrol, close air support, and suppression of enemy air defenses.

Europeans Contribute Majority of Ground Troops and
Provide Unique Peace Support Capabilities

European allies have made military contributions to security and stability in the Balkans by providing ground troops and specialty units trained in addressing post-conflict situations. As shown in figure 12, European allies collectively provided the largest number of ground troops to support U.N. peacekeeping operations in the Balkans from 1992 to 1995, and they provided the preponderance of ground troops to support NATO operations that began in December 1995.

Although the United States provided the largest single national contingency to NATO operations (for Bosnia since 1996, and for Kosovo since 1999), European allies have provided between 56 and 70 percent of NATO ground troops to the region since 1996. As of March 2001, European countries provided more than 60 percent of the 20,000 troops in Bosnia and 37,000 troops in Kosovo, with the United States providing about 20 and 15 percent, respectively.[48] Other countries, such as Russia and the United Arab Emirates, provided the remaining ground troops. In addition to ground troops, U.S. and European military officials cited the European countries' provision of specially trained personnel to serve in peace support operations as another significant contribution to regional security in the Balkans. These officials noted that Scandinavian countries contributed experts specially trained in controlling civilian affairs and responding to emergency crisis situations, particularly in war-torn areas that lack adequate health and public works services. Many European countries also provide uniquely trained constabulary forces, such as Italy's Carabinieri, to assist in post-conflict efforts to restore law and order. Several U.S. and European military officials considered these special constabulary forces to be the most critical link to restoring public order and maintaining stability in the Balkans. Constabulary forces perform a role between that of military ground troops and that of civilian police. They are trained to address counterterrorism issues, gather and analyze criminal intelligence, control riots, and provide military force protection.

---

[48] The U.S. military has instituted and follows the most stringent force protection measures among NATO allies, according to U.S. and European military officials. These measures have a significant effect on the number of troops needed for U.S. operations. In contrast, European nations generally devote a smaller percentage of their combat forces to force protection, which allows them to conduct operations with fewer troops on the ground.

Figure 12: Troops Supporting Peacekeeping Operations in the Balkans, 1992-2000

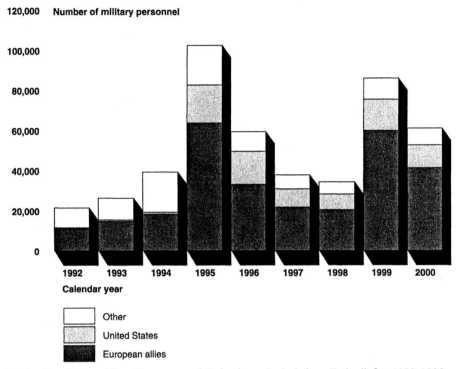

Note 1: The Czech Republic, Hungary, and Poland are included as "other" for 1992-1998, and as "European allies" for 1999 and 2000.
Note 2: Troop numbers reflect snapshots at various times during the stated year.
Sources: U.N. and NATO.

NATO has used constabulary forces to help maintain stability in Bosnia and Kosovo. Italy's Carabinieri represent the preponderance of NATO's constabulary forces in the Balkans. For example, Italy provides about 75 percent of the almost 500 special constabulary forces used in Bosnia and more than 80 percent of the 320 used in Kosovo. Although NATO's force goals for Kosovo have been met, as of April 2001, only 11 of the 19 platoons had been staffed in Bosnia. According to U.S. and European military officials, the shortfall of constabulary forces in Bosnia reflects the limited availability of such forces. Approximately 22 nations currently have special constabulary force capabilities that can be used in these operations and, according to U.S. and European officials, most have resource, funding, and training constraints. The United States does not possess these uniquely trained personnel.

Shared Operations Offer Benefits, but Pose Challenges

According to U.S. and European military and NATO officials, multinational operations have become more frequent during the post-Cold War era and have provided political and operational benefits that outweigh the drawbacks of such deployments. They also emphasized that effective crisis management depends upon joint U.S. and European participation in the full range of peace support operations and post-conflict reconstruction efforts. While U.S. and European contributions to security in the Balkans region reflect different military capabilities and approaches to conflict resolution, military officials at NATO and in the European countries we visited stressed the importance of shared responsibility and risk in current and future NATO operations—both on the ground and in the air. These officials noted that a joint U.S.-European ground presence is critical to maintaining stability in the Balkans, and that European countries need to play a greater role in future NATO air operations.

Senior U.S. and European political and military officials said that multinational operations in Bosnia and Kosovo provided political advantages of operating as a coalition because members and partner states established and reached NATO objectives together rather than unilaterally. French military officials said that maintaining consensus was a critical factor in Operation Allied Force's success. Coalitions are cited as beneficial also because no single country bears the entire burden, which lessens the staffing problems that some countries face when providing troops to multiple operations simultaneously. Staffing shortages were noted in the areas of medical personnel, linguists, and communications. European officials also noted that U.S. involvement provides considerable weight and credibility to an operation and greatly adds to NATO's cohesiveness.

Multinational operations also provide operational benefits that include the ability to combine the resources and capabilities of member states. During Operation Allied Force, for example, the United States provided significant air combat capabilities and equipment, while France provided specialty aircraft to assist in night-flight strike missions and search-and-rescue missions. Further, the United Kingdom played an important role in Bosnia to monitor checkpoints and cease-fire lines, and to lead nation-building activities involving joint civilian and military units. U.S. and European military officials also said that multinational operations improve interoperability and relationships among allies, particularly with the new NATO members—the Czech Republic, Hungary, Poland—and Partnership for Peace (PfP) countries. Military officials said that working together allows countries to train with and learn from other NATO members, which may have expertise in specific tasks. Training and the transfer of skills have helped the new allies adapt to NATO operations and have fostered relationships among partner countries and longstanding NATO members. U.S. and European officials said that enhanced interoperability, in addition to the pooling of assets and expertise, creates forces that are more flexible and thus better prepared for the diverse challenges of peace support operations.

Despite these benefits, U.S. and European military officials said that the deployment of multinational forces into intense conflicts such as Bosnia and Kosovo has faced challenges and drawbacks. These officials noted that as result of the Balkans campaign, interoperability problems and gaps in capabilities among member states were identified. For example, systems and equipment provided by member states.especially those used in command-and-control, communications, and targeting systems—were often different and incompatible. Another challenge was the imbalance in the warfighting equipment possessed by member states. Few NATO allies had the capacity to provide more sophisticated equipment, such as precision-guided munitions, in sufficient numbers or at all. Even France, one of the leading European contributors of precision munitions during Operation Allied Force, depleted its supply and spent about $100 million to purchase additional ones from the United States. European officials also noted political drawbacks to multinational operations: for instance, some coalition members had different policies and strategies. This issue was highlighted in decisions about using force or ground troops in Kosovo, where the United States was reluctant to commit ground troops.

U.S. and European Nonmilitary Intervention Includes Combination of Development Assistance and Nonmilitary Personnel

European countries and the United States led donor community efforts to restore stability and security to the Balkans by providing development assistance and the nonmilitary personnel needed to support multilateral operations. Of the almost $15 billion in development assistance disbursed to the Balkans between 1993 and 1999, the European Commission and European allies contributed about $10.2 billion primarily for humanitarian and economic reconstruction programs. The United States provided about $1.2 billion for humanitarian, economic, and democracy-building programs. The EC and European allies have led the donor community in pledging more than 80 percent of the $2.3 billion identified by the Stability Pact for Southeastern Europe program, and in supporting a new initiative allocating about $690 million in emergency winterization assistance to Serbia in 2000 and 2001. European officials identified the absorption of more than 1 million Balkans refugees into their countries as another significant contribution to stabilizing the region. European allies provided a large percentage of nonmilitary personnel to support multilateral organizations that promote social reconstruction and institution-building in the region.

Europeans Use Development Assistance to Foster Stability in the Balkans

European officials view the restoration of stability and security to the Balkans as a major priority and have used development assistance as a primary tool to foster change. Of the $15 billion in development assistance disbursed in the Balkans from 1993 to 1999, the European allies contributed about $6.9 billion, with top donors Germany, the Netherlands, and Austria accounting for more than 40 percent of the disbursements. As shown in figure 13, the European Commission was the single largest donor and disbursed more than $3.3 billion during this period.

According to EU officials, the priorities of the EC and many European development assistance programs during the 1990s have centered largely on stabilizing the region and integrating the countries of the former Yugoslavia into the European Union. To stabilize the region, the EC and the European allies focused resources on humanitarian assistance and economic reconstruction programs. Humanitarian assistance activities (1) provided emergency relief such as food and medicine to victims of war-torn areas, (2) reduced the suffering of refugees, displaced persons, and refugees returning to their homelands, and (3) carried out short-term rehabilitation and reconstruction work, such as repairing and equipping schools and hospitals. Reconstruction programs included the rebuilding of major physical assets in the Balkans such as airports, bridges, railways, and roads.

Many EU member countries have designed their assistance programs to foster economic and social reform and help bring the Balkans countries closer to European standards, with potential integration into the European Union as the ultimate incentive. The Stabilization and Association Process, established by the European Union in 1999, provides each Balkans country with a "list" of conditions and reforms designed specifically to enable that country to better meet EU accession criteria. Once the country meets the established conditions—such as political and economic reforms, and measures to strengthen democracy, human rights, and the rule of law—a Stabilization and Association Agreement is signed. As of November 2001, only the Former Yugoslav Republic of Macedonia and Croatia met the conditions. Each received an association agreement in April and May 2001, respectively.

U.S. Funding Focuses on Emergency Assistance and Institution-Building Programs

As the Balkans' second-largest bilateral donor, the United States has spent about $1.2 billion for development assistance activities from 1993 to 1999 (see figure 13). The primary goals of U.S. assistance programs in the Balkans are (1) to restore peace and reduce ethnic tensions, and (2) to promote democracy, economic prosperity, and security within the region. Accordingly, the U.S. assistance programs have centered largely on emergency assistance, economic restructuring, and institution-building programs. Emergency assistance has included food aid, medical supplies, and refugee relief efforts, particularly to Bosnia and Kosovo. The Support for East European Democracy Act has focused on economic restructuring and on the development of democratic institutions in the Balkans. Key economic restructuring efforts include the development of a functioning market economy through privatization, macroeconomic reforms, and the introduction of sound fiscal policies. The United States has promoted democratic institutions and multiethnic societies through independent media, free and fair elections, improved governance, and an independent judiciary. As of September 1999, more than half of U.S. assistance obligated to the Balkans has gone to Bosnia-Herzegovina, and it includes more than $500 million for reconstruction and infrastructure-building programs.

Stability Pact for Southeastern Europe Provides
Promise, but Problems Limit Disbursements

The Stability Pact for Southeastern Europe,[49] initiated by the European Union on June 10, 1999, is the primary regional framework to coordinate the development assistance needs of the countries of southeastern Europe and to accelerate the integration of a stable, reformed region into the Euro- Atlantic community. In March 2000, international donors, including multilateral institutions such as the European Investment Bank and the World Bank, pledged more than $2.3 billion to fund Stability Pact projects designed to develop infrastructure, promote private sector development, support policy and institutional reforms, and encourage democratization, reconciliation, and security. Of the $2.3 billion pledged, $1.7 billion was allocated for "Quick Start" projects that were to be completed within one year. As of December 31, 2000, the donor community had disbursed about $300 million through the Stability Pact program. The EC and European allies collectively accounted for about 75 percent of the disbursed funds. The Special Coordinator of the Stability Pact attributed the low disbursement rate at the 9-month mark to delays caused by both donors and recipients. The Special Coordinator noted that donors and investment banks often have bureaucratic procedures. Also, recipient countries often cannot absorb the considerable sums offered, and they do not have the legal framework or the administrative structures necessary to facilitate

---

[49] The Stability Pact's major participants include Albania, Bosnia, Bulgaria, Croatia, Hungary, Romania, Russia, Slovenia, the Former Yugoslav Republic of Macedonia, Turkey, the United States, Canada, Japan, and the European Union and other multilateral organizations and lending institutions, including NATO, the United Nations, the Organization for Security and Cooperation in Europe, the International Monetary Fund, and the World Bank.

the implementation of projects. U.S. and European development assistance officials noted that the implementation of complex infrastructure projects takes significantly more time than other types of programs and depends on the recipient country's capacities.

**Figure 13: Development Assistance Totaling $15
Billion Disbursed to the Balkans, 1993-1999**

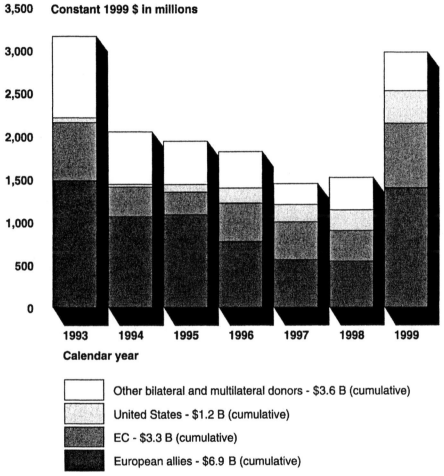

Other bilateral and multilateral donors - $3.6 B (cumulative)

United States - $1.2 B (cumulative)

EC - $3.3 B (cumulative)

European allies - $6.9 B (cumulative)

B = billions.
Source: GAO analysis based on OECD data.

Development officials also noted that other issues have hampered the progress of the Stability Pact program, including the lack of a strategy, the lack of prioritization of projects, and the recipients' unrealistic expectations. The original goal was to address a range of the most pressing problems of southeastern Europe, from security to post-conflict and reconstruction issues. The Quick Start Package was created as a "shotgun approach" to demonstrate donor support quickly. Other than categorizing projects into the three priority areas, however, the Stability Pact did not prioritize the needs of the countries or the 244 projects to be implemented. The May 2001 Coordinator's Report identified the need to develop a strategy, prioritize and focus on key areas, establish and deliver concrete and measurable results, and improve delays in project implementation.[50]

EC Leads Donor Community Efforts to Disburse Emergency Assistance to the Federal Republic of Yugoslavia

In fall 2000, the international donor community began providing assistance to the Federal Republic of Yugoslavia in direct response to and in support of Serbia's transition to democracy on October 5, 2000. By November, the EC had approved a $184 million emergency winter assistance package, of which about $90 million was disbursed by March 2001. The donor community met in December and pledged about $690 million to support winterization and other urgent program needs in the Federal Republic of Yugoslavia, particularly Serbia, that included fuel, electricity, food, and medical assistance. The United States was the single largest bilateral donor, pledging more than $87 million to Serbia and more than $70 million to neighboring Montenegro. The U.S. had disbursed about $36 million as of January 2001. While much of the emergency assistance commitments to Serbia still needs to be disbursed, the assistance provided to date has demonstrated the donor community's support and commitment to the new democratic government of Serbia.   In further support of the economic recovery and transition needs of the Federal Republic of Yugoslavia, the EC and World Bank sponsored a donor's conference in June 2001. The donor community, composed of bilateral and multilateral organizations, international financial institutions, and the Soros Foundation, pledged about $1.3 billion to restore macroeconomic stability, promote economic growth, improve social wellbeing, and build human capacity, including health and education. Although the pledges are still being finalized, EC and European allies have pledged 42 percent of the $1.3 billion, and the United States has pledged about 14 percent. Other countries, multilateral organizations, and the Soros Foundation pledged the remainder.

Absorption of Refugees Viewed as Significant European Contribution

European officials noted that absorbing Balkans refugees into their respective homelands and providing them with food, shelter, and living allowances for up to 1 year are significant contributions to European security. By the end of 1996, more than 70 percent of the 770,000 displaced persons or refugees from the Balkans had migrated to six European countries, according to U.N. High Commissioner for Refugees (UNHCR) statistics (see figure 14).

---

[50] *Report of the Special Coordinator on the Implementation of the Quick Start Package,* May 2001.

Figure 14: Balkans Refugee Migration to Europe and the United States, 1996

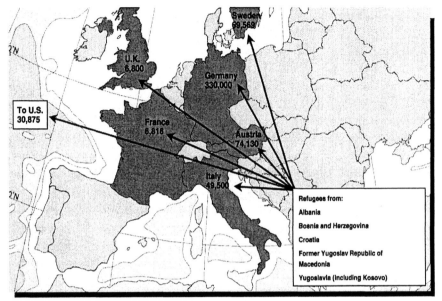

Sources: U.N. High Commissioner for Refugees and U.S. Department of State.

About 330,000 refugees from Bosnia-Herzegovina had emigrated to Germany by 1996, placing enormous burdens on Germany's social infrastructure. The May 2001 Stability Pact Special Coordinator's report notes that while many refugees from Bosnia and Croatia had returned home, more than 1.3 million persons from the Balkans region remain categorized as refugees or internally displaced persons and need some type of assistance.

European Allies Provide Majority of Nonmilitary Personnel to Multilateral Organizations in Region

The contribution of nonmilitary personnel to assist multilateral organizations is considered another critical contribution to regional security. Collectively, European allies provided more nonmilitary personnel to multilateral organizations that promote peacekeeping, conflict prevention, and post-conflict rehabilitation in the Balkans than did the United States. For example, as of April 2001, European allies provided about one-third of U.N. civilian police and almost 60 percent of the specialists to the Organization for Security and Cooperation in Europe. European allies also provided 139 persons to support the EU Monitoring Mission in the Balkans. The United States, however, was the single largest contributor of civilian police and personnel to support OSCE programs in the region, providing 12 percent of civilian police and 16 percent of personnel.

To support a critical element of peacekeeping operations and post-conflict interventions in the Balkans region, the United Nations has relied on civilian police provided by its member countries. Civilian police play a critical role in post-conflict interventions by helping war-torn societies restore the conditions necessary for social, economic, and political stability. The traditional role for U.N. civilian police through the mid-1990s was to advise, train, and monitor local police. In Kosovo, however, the United Nations refocused its role to restore and maintain law and order, and to help establish judicial reforms and rule of law.

As of January 2001, the international community provided more than 6,300 civilian police to support U.N. missions in Bosnia-Herzegovina and Kosovo. European allies provided more than 2,000 civilian police, while the United States provided about 764 civilian police. Other member countries, such as India, Jordan, and Pakistan, provided the remaining civilian police. See figures 15 and 16 for the contributions made by the European allies, the United States, and other donors to peacekeeping operations in Bosnia and Kosovo.

To address conflict prevention and post-conflict rehabilitation in the Balkans, the European allies provided the majority of personnel to support the Organization for Security and Cooperation in Europe's democratization, security-building, and political affairs programs. Of approximately 840 persons provided to OSCE missions in the Balkans in April 2001, the European allies provided about 500 persons. The United States, as the single-largest contributor, provided 141 persons. In addition, European allies provided 139 persons to support EU Monitoring Mission efforts to monitor and assess local security conditions. As shown in figure 17, the primary use of European and U.S. personnel in spring 2001 was in democratization and security-building programs.

Figure 15: Donor Contributions of Civilian Police to Bosnia

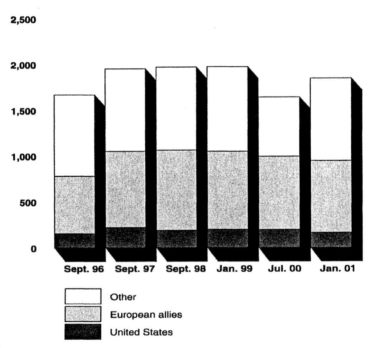

Bosnia: International Police Task Force

Source: U.N.

Figure 16: Donor Contributions of Civilian Police to Kosovo

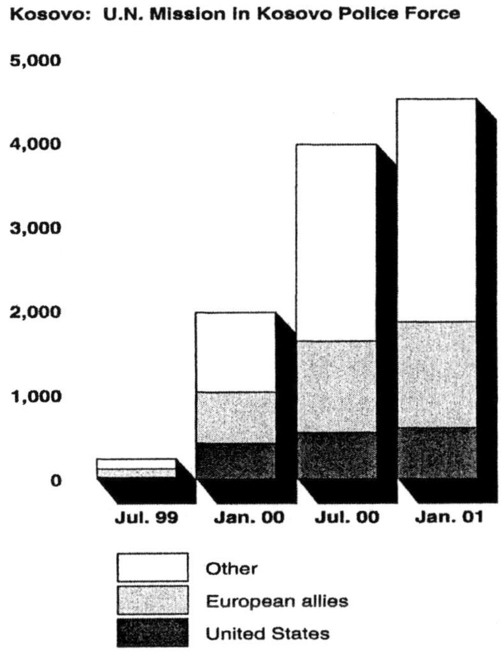

Kosovo: U.N. Mission in Kosovo Police Force

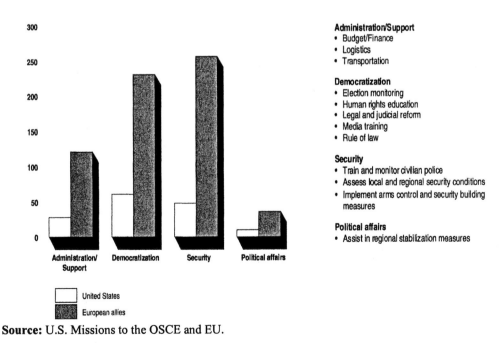

Source: U.N.

Figure 17: Personnel Provided to OSCE and EU Monitoring Mission

Administration/Support
- Budget/Finance
- Logistics
- Transportation

Democratization
- Election monitoring
- Human rights education
- Legal and judicial reform
- Media training
- Rule of law

Security
- Train and monitor civilian police
- Assess local and regional security conditions
- Implement arms control and security building measures

Political affairs
- Assist in regional stabilization measures

Source: U.S. Missions to the OSCE and EU.

EUROPEAN MILITARIES ADDRESSING SHORTFALLS, BUT COMPETING BUDGET PRIORITIES ARE SLOWING IMPLEMENTATION

Operational problems experienced in the Balkans peacekeeping operations in the 1990s highlighted numerous shortfalls in the military capabilities of the European allies. On the national level, they are addressing some of these shortfalls by restructuring their military forces, moving to allvolunteer forces, and modernizing military systems and equipment, but progress has varied according to each country's ability to make defense spending a priority.[51] On a multinational level, NATO and the European Union have recognized the need to improve defense capabilities and have launched initiatives that establish goals for addressing country shortfalls. NATO's Defense Capabilities Initiative (DCI) was designed to highlight the need for qualitative improvements in five areas of military capability. The European Union's European Security and Defense Policy (ESDP) is a broader political and security strategy to prepare EU member nations to conduct crisis management and contingency operations when NATO is not engaged. DCI and ESDP both recognize that the European allies need to acquire certain systems and equipment that will help them perform a range of military operations more effectively, particularly with combat forces. However, at a time when the European allies are taking on increased responsibilities for regional security, they are hampered by relatively flat defense budgets because of decisions about competing domestic and other national priorities. This likely will delay their ability to meet the goals and objectives of their defense initiatives until at least the end of this decade. It is too early to discern what effect, if any, the terrorist attacks of September 11, 2001, will have on future European defense priorities and spending.

Allies Restructure and Modernize Defense Capabilities

The European allies' participation in the Balkans operations in the mid- to late 1990s was constrained by the large and inflexible structure of their military forces and by a lack of key military assets, such as strategic airlift; command, control, communications, and intelligence systems; and systems for precision attack. Appendix I illustrates the capabilities provided by selected countries during Operation Allied Force. To address these shortfalls, most allies we visited conducted defense reviews or assessments in the late 1990s, with each country assessing its national needs. They have since begun to restructure their military forces, including reducing force numbers, creating more rapidly deployable units, and centralizing operational commands and support organizations. They are also moving toward all-volunteer forces, modernizing their military equipment, and implementing improved logistics and asset management.[52] Improvements in these three areas will give the allies greater flexibility and capability to respond to a range of threats within and outside of Europe. Overall, most

---

[51] The defense capabilities of U.S. military forces in Europe are also important to security and stability in the region. We have issued several reports that address the capabilities of U.S. forces in Europe and their ability to respond to a range of operations since the end of the Cold War. We do not address these issues in this report.

[52] We define logistics and asset management as the process by which European allies make their militaries more efficient and cost-effective through base reductions, closures, and consolidations; privatization initiatives; and the creation of separate agencies and initiatives to ensure efficiency within the armed forces.

European allies we visited have made the greatest progress in restructuring their forces. Efforts to move toward an all-volunteer force and modernize equipment have proceeded more slowly because of the cost of the initiatives. As a result, some programs have been scaled back, or dates for achieving goals have been delayed.

Allies Make Greatest Strides in Force Restructuring

The European allies we visited have made the greatest progress in force restructuring; that is, changing the size and structure of their forces. In the post-Cold War period, the European allies' large and cumbersome armies, still structured as heavily armored forces designed to resist a border attack by Soviet armored forces, hindered rapid deployment to the Balkans peacekeeping operations. Germany, Italy, and other European allies lacked smaller, all-volunteer forces that could be easily deployed, sustained, and integrated into multinational forces. Even British and French military forces, which have historically been more oriented toward expeditionary missions than have those of many other European nations, recognized that they were unable to meet some of the deployment demands of post-Cold War military operations. These demands included operating beyond NATO's borders and in areas with little or no supporting infrastructure.

Since the Balkans operations, the European allies we visited, with the exception of Turkey, have improved defense capabilities by developing smaller but more efficient forces, creating rapid reaction units, and moving toward centralized operational commands and support organizations.

Allies Reduce Force Numbers and Size of Units

Most European allies have reduced their force numbers and have restructured their militaries into smaller, more flexible units that can more effectively respond to post-Cold War contingencies. Between 1990 and 2001, the number of military forces in France, Germany, Italy, and the United Kingdom fell between 31 and 36 percent, as indicated in table 1. Countries such as Norway and Germany plan to reduce their force numbers even further between 2001 and 2006, with average cuts ranging from about 16 percent to 50 percent.[53] Force reductions have been necessary because of the high cost of maintaining personnel, especially with NATO allies facing static defense budgets. According to NATO officials, high personnel costs in Europe have left little money for research and development and for the acquisition of military equipment.

---

[53] Norway plans to reduce its total number of armed forces by about 50 percent between 2002 and 2005. Germany has indicated that it will reduce its force size by about 16 percent between 2001 and 2006.

Table 1: Changes in Number of Forces, 1990, 1995, and 2000

Country	Number of Forces (1990-1991)	Number of Forces (1995-1996)	Number of Forces (2000-2001)	Percentage Reduction (1990-2001)
France	461,250	409,000	294,430	36
Germany	469,000[a]	339,900	321,000	32
Italy	389,600	328,700	250,600	36
United Kingdom	306,000	236,900	212,450	31

[a] The number of forces was significantly larger in 1989, when East and West Germany had separate armies. At that time the combined number of forces was 521,000.
Source: The Military Balance, International Institute for Strategic Studies, London.

In addition to reducing force numbers, European allies are reorganizing their forces, eliminating many large division and armored units, and creating smaller, lighter infantry and other units to respond to a range of threats within and beyond NATO borders, such as in the Balkans. Force restructuring has been more difficult for some countries and has taken longer. German embassy officials stated that force restructuring has been slower than originally anticipated because financial resources have been devoted to drawing down significant numbers of personnel that were part of its large Cold War army, in addition to dissolving the structures and reincorporating the former East German forces. Also, German forces had to assume control over and in many cases destroy the equipment and weapons systems of the former East Germany, and to assist in moving Russian troops out of the country. Unlike other NATO allies, Turkey has maintained a large, combat-ready force of more than 600,000 personnel because of its strategic location and its need to defend its borders against potential threats in the region. According to Turkish defense officials, Turkey's large combat force has not been significantly restructured since the end of the Cold War. Officials stated that given the country's strategic location, it is unlikely that the Ministry of Defense will significantly restructure its forces in the near future.

Allies Form Rapid Reaction Units to Carry Out Missions

In an effort to quickly address regional instabilities, the countries we visited have focused on developing rapidly deployable units with varying levels of readiness, which would on short notice allow them to send units to missions within and beyond NATO borders, such as the Balkans. According to U.S. defense officials, countries such as France and the United Kingdom, which historically had some expeditionary forces, have made greater progress in this area. This has enabled the United Kingdom, for example, to take the lead in the current operations in the Former Yugoslav Republic of Macedonia. The French are implementing plans to transform their rapid reaction capacity from the 12,000 ground forces they had in the 1980s to 35,000-50,000 ground forces by 2002. According to NATO officials, France should be able to deploy 50,000 military personnel for alliance missions by 2002. The United Kingdom's joint rapid reaction force will provide force packages up to brigade size, and combat and support forces will be provided in two echelons, according to readiness. The highest readiness force is based on a light infantry battalion or commando group. Although the framework for the rapid reaction capabilities has been completed, British officials have indicated that full operation of the rapid reaction force, initially scheduled for 2001, will not take place until late 2002 or early 2003. This is because many of the people who would be involved in making these changes are currently serving in the Balkans and in other operations, such as in Sierra Leone.

U.S. and European officials have indicated that Italy and Germany have only recently developed rapid reaction capabilities and that they would need more time to fully staff and to acquire complete capabilities for their rapid reaction forces. Italy realized its need for rapid reaction capabilities after leading Operation Alba in 1997.[54] In 2001, Italy can deploy and sustain a contingent of 8,000 to 10,000 troops, and it is setting up a rapid deployment core within the next 2 years. In the future, the Italian Defense Ministry expects to deploy at least three times as many troops as it currently does. Germany has a crisis reaction force of 65,000 that it can deploy within time frames of up to 30 days. Country officials have stated that the size of Germany's rapid reaction force will increase to 150,000 by 2004, once it has transformed most of its armed forces.

Allies Shift Toward Cooperation Among Military Services

Four of the five European allies we visited have set up centralized national commands or headquarters to facilitate deployments to NATO and future EU operations. In addition, they have created cooperative organizations within their armed forces to manage their resources more effectively and to conduct operational deployments more efficiently. Prior to establishing these centralized commands, European nations found it difficult to deploy forces to contingency operations, such as those in the Balkans, because little coordination existed between the various military service branches and supporting organizations.

After experiencing deployment difficulties, Italy established a Joint Operations Headquarters in Rome, headed by the Chief of the Defense General Staff, to develop operational doctrine and to plan and conduct joint operations and exercises, and a "high readiness" headquarters in Milan, to meet the demands of deployments in the Balkans. France established a Joint Operational Command, with all military operations being executed under the Chief of Defense. In addition, France has developed a Joint Rapidly Deployable Force Headquarters and a Ground Action Force Command to manage the deployment of ground forces, including four rapidly deployable force headquarters. The United Kingdom established a Permanent Joint Forces Headquarters, a Joint Command Systems Initiative to unify operational communications systems, and a Joint Defense Center to handle doctrine. It is also establishing two deployable Joint Forces Headquarters. In addition, the United Kingdom established a number of joint forces and units, including a Joint Royal Navy/Royal Air Force Harrier force and a Joint Helicopter Command. In 2000, Germany set up a Joint Operations Command that will be operational by the end of 2001 and will be key in planning and executing military operations, according to German military officials. Germany also established a Joint Support Service and a Joint Medical Service to provide maintenance, logistics, intelligence, training, and medical support to all three branches of the military.

---

[54] Operation Alba's mission, led by Italy in the spring and summer of 1997, was to provide a secure environment so that emergency humanitarian relief and international assistance could be provided to Albania. This paved the way for Albania to begin restoring social peace and democracy. Seven thousand military personnel from various countries were involved at the height of the operation.

Allies Move to All-Volunteer Forces, but Efforts Are Slow and Expensive

Some European allies have found that the shift from conscript to allvolunteer forces has been more expensive than originally planned. This has slowed the European allies' transition to all-volunteer forces and has resulted in less savings to the armed forces than expected. Many European allies maintained militaries with large numbers of conscripts and stringent conscription policies throughout most of the 1990s. These policies constrained European allies' ability to engage fully in missions such as the Balkans peacekeeping operations. Germany's and Italy's conscription policies, for example, posed legal hurdles to deploying forces outside national boundaries. German and American officials noted that German army units could not deploy as one unit because they were composed of both volunteers and conscripts. To have a unit ready for deployment, military officials needed to pull volunteer forces from several units and train them for out-of-area operations. This process increased the amount of time needed for deployment.

The European allies we visited are taking different approaches to moving toward all-volunteer forces, which they expect will produce better trained, highly skilled, and longer-serving troops that are more suited to post-Cold War missions. Nearly 70 percent of NATO allies have moved to an allvolunteer force or have begun the process toward that end, as indicated in appendix II. France had pledged to end conscription by 2002 but was able to complete its efforts to move toward an all-volunteer force in 2001, more than 18 months ahead of schedule. Other allies, such as Italy, have faced more difficulties in moving to an all-volunteer force. In Italy, a 2000 parliamentary law sets out the framework for the gradual establishment of a professional force. Italy has pledged to end conscription by 2006, but it faces challenges in moving to a volunteer force and attracting personnel for missions. According to U.S. Department of State officials, Italy's slowness in moving to an all-volunteer force is a result of resistance from the public sector, such as charity organizations, which have relied on conscripts as a source of free or inexpensive labor.

Some nations we visited have decided to keep conscription or to reduce the amount of time conscripts must serve. Germany, for example, is moving toward a larger number of volunteer forces but has elected to keep a conscript base. It is reducing the number of conscripts from 135,000 in 2001 to 80,000 by 2006, and it has made efforts to reduce mandatory military service from 10 months to 9 months after 2002. According to German officials, conscription will remain because of the importance of national service in Germany's defense culture and because it acts as a safety measure in the event that a national crisis demands increased capabilities. Country officials stated that Turkey has retained a largely conscripted armed force because of the country's location, vast territory, and external threats. With 93 percent of its army composed of conscripts, Turkey has the largest percentage of conscripts among all the allies.

While acknowledging that an all-volunteer force will be more cost effective in the long run, European allies such as France, Germany, and Italy have found that the shift from a conscript to an all-volunteer force has been more expensive than originally planned and has resulted in less savings to the armed forces than expected. However, no cost data are yet available.

Allies Have Made Some Progress in Equipment Modernization

To remedy some of the operational shortfalls identified in post-Cold War operations, European allies have embarked on equipment modernization programs to improve their capabilities in the areas of air- and sealift; command, control, and communications; intelligence, surveillance, and reconnaissance; suppression of enemy air defenses; air-to-air refueling; and precision-guided munitions. As is the case with the previously discussed reform efforts, some allies have accomplished more than others because of the condition of their military forces at the end of the Cold War and because of the level of their defense budgets. Nevertheless, all five countries we examined in this report have had to stretch out, postpone, or cancel some modernization programs because of funding shortfalls.

Generally, the United Kingdom and France have made the most progress in equipment modernization. Italy has made some progress, and Turkey's recent financial difficulties have slowed its equipment modernization efforts. The United Kingdom and France initiated their defense reviews earlier than did Germany and Italy. They then proceeded to make the changes necessary to improve their defense capabilities. France initially focused its efforts on eliminating conscription, while the United Kingdom, with an all-volunteer force, was able to devote more of its resources to equipment modernization. Germany's progress has been slower because of its inability to concurrently fund many projects. Of the 28 priority equipment projects identified by German military officials, 17 currently receive funding. Six of the remaining 11 projects are not due to receive funding until 2006 or later. Turkey is experiencing particular challenges in funding defense modernization efforts because of its current economic condition. Turkey has 60 procurement programs in its current portfolio, but 32 acquisition projects have been postponed as part of an effort to relieve pressure on the country's economy. In addition to postponing projects, some have also been cut back. Appendix III identifies key equipment programs in France, Germany, Italy, Turkey, and the United Kingdom.

Some of the European allies we visited have implemented logistics and asset management programs that they believe will save them money over the long term and allow them to use the savings to modernize equipment. Some of these allies have focused on making their military support establishments more efficient and cost effective through base reductions, closures and consolidations, and privatization initiatives. Both Germany and the United Kingdom, for example, are implementing initiatives that they believe will result in savings and produce efficiencies for their Ministries of Defense. According to country officials, however, these countries have not been able to save as much as they originally intended because of the difficulty and expense in closing and consolidating bases, along with other factors.

NATO and EU Initiatives Provide New Frameworks for Improving Defense Capabilities

The European allies' performance in Operation Allied Force was an important factor in launching two recent NATO and EU initiatives that are providing additional focus and incentive for European nations to improve their defense capabilities. NATO's Defense Capabilities Initiative and the EU's European Security and Defense Policy are different concepts that share the objective of strengthening the capacity of European countries to act militarily. Countries have pledged to improve their capabilities for crisis management, including the availability, deployability, sustainability, and interoperability of their forces. European countries have made progress in various areas and are increasingly taking the lead in contingency operations such as those in the Former Yugoslav Republic of Macedonia. However, defense capability shortfalls, created by inadequate funding, may prevent them from conducting larger, more demanding operations until at least the end of the decade.

DCI and ESDP: Different Concepts, Similar Objectives

NATO designed DCI to help the alliance improve its defense capabilities and prepare for a broadened set of security obligations, as outlined in NATO's 1999 Strategic Concept. It is a mechanism to highlight and promote needed improvements in five areas and 58 long- and short-term objectives. The initiative has been incorporated into NATO's defense-planning process. The five areas are:

- mobility and deployability (moving forces quickly to crisis areas, using air- and sealift capabilities);
- sustainability (maintaining and supplying forces and logistics support for operations far from home bases);
- effective engagement (successfully engaging an adversary in all types of operations, from high to low intensity);
- survivability (protecting forces and infrastructure against current and future threats);
- interoperable communications (improving the compatibility of allied command, control, and information systems).

Progress to date varies among countries. According to NATO officials, nations have generally focused on goals that are easier to accomplish and less expensive, such as revising NATO's structures for improved interoperability and establishing logistics processes that support multiple nations. They stated that the more difficult objectives, such as those that require acquisition of expensive platforms or involve expensive research and development, are years from completion. High-cost items, such as electronic jamming for the suppression of enemy air defenses, fall into this category.

According to the DOD March 2001 Report on Allied Contributions to the Common Defense, while the NATO alliance has made modest progress in some DCI areas, in other respects progress toward DCI objectives has been disappointingly slow. The report notes that while the major European allies are set to acquire advanced fighters, long-range cruise missiles, medium-lift transport aircraft, and attack and transport helicopters, most of these systems will not be built or available in sufficient numbers until the latter part of the decade. In addition, the report notes the continued shortage in strategic and oversized cargo airlift capability. While some of the allies plan to acquire a new cargo aircraft—the A400M military transport—their level of financial commitment to the multibillion-dollar project is not clear, according to DOD. The report further states that the alliance's need for improved, secure, and deployable command, control, and communications capabilities remains unmet.

ESDP, a broader political and security strategy, was formally launched in 1999 as a tool to strengthen the European Union's ability to respond to crises and improve Europe's military contribution to regional security.[55] The EU's objective is to develop the capacity to make decisions and conduct EU-led military operations when NATO as a whole is not engaged as an alliance. Potential missions include humanitarian support and rescue missions, peacekeeping, and crisis management operations involving combat forces. To accomplish this goal, ESDP requires many of the same systems and equipment identified in DCI. However, the European Union will not have a separate or standing EU force. ESDP will allow European nations to provide an integrated response—with political, economic, and military means—to regional crises, according to EU officials. NATO will still be responsible for collective defense.

In 1999, EU member states established the Headline Goal—to be achieved by 2003—of deploying up to 60,000 persons for crisis management within 60 days and sustaining them in the field for at least 1 year. Their intention is that these forces should be self-sustaining, with the necessary command, control, and intelligence capabilities, logistics, and other combat support services. Air and naval elements would also be available, as necessary. To date, EU nations have pledged 100,000 soldiers, 400 aircraft, and 100 ships to meet the Headline Goal. To implement the ESDP missions and Headline Goal, EU member states have also established other defense capability goals, similar to those of DCI, in areas such as command and control, intelligence, and strategic transport. Most of these goals are medium- and long-term efforts that will likely be accomplished toward the end of the decade or later and will parallel certain DCI goals and objectives. Officials from the EU, NATO, and European member states confirmed that by 2003 the EU would be capable of responding to lower-level peacekeeping and humanitarian operations. Shortfalls in major defense systems and equipment would prevent them from leading sustained, higher-intensity military operations.

The EU has also established goals for providing civilian personnel, such as police forces and judicial specialists, to a regional conflict. According to the EU, these personnel are important components of post-Cold War crisismanagement operations. By 2003, the EU goal is to provide 5,000 police officers for international missions, 1,000 of whom could be deployed in fewer than 30 days. In addition, the EU has compiled a database of judicial and penal staff specialists that EU member states could make available when needed to enhance the effectiveness of police missions. According to DOD officials, the United States would find it difficult to provide this capability because these civilian personnel would not be readily available.

Although DCI and ESDP share many of the same objectives, the U.S. and European officials with whom we met pointed out that ESDP is providing enhanced motivation to European countries to strengthen their defense capabilities. The Dutch parliament, for example, earmarked funds specifically for ESDP. Several European officials pointed out that DCI's 58 objectives are too many for most nations to consider, and that the ESDP Headline Goal is a more realistic approach to European security. According to a senior U.S. NATO official, if ESDP is the motivation for European allies to improve their defense capabilities, then the United States firmly supports these efforts. He stated, however, that ESDP is not a

---

[55] Although ESDP was formally launched in 1999, the idea was generated many years earlier. A first attempt to create a European defense community occurred in the early 1950s, concurrent with the development of the European Coal and Steel Community. The EU's 1997 Treaty of Amsterdam formally identified ESDP, and the concept gained strength after the Franco-British Summit in St. Malo, France, when the United Kingdom overcame its reservations about an autonomous European defense capability in general and ESDP in particular.

"burdensharing panacea," and that differences between defense needs and financial resources will affect the EU's ability to implement its plans.

The September 2001 NATO operation to collect weapons from Albanian extremist forces in the Former Yugoslav Republic of Macedonia illustrates both European accomplishments and the challenges that lie ahead as European nations attempt to take greater responsibility for regional security and stability. Operation Essential Harvest relied primarily on European leadership, personnel, and military assets. The United Kingdom served as the lead nation, and as such it had to provide specialists not provided by other European nations, including bomb disposal experts, reconnaissance troops, engineers, logisticians, and medics. The United States provided logistical, surveillance, and medical support that was in short supply in theater. U.S. defense officials stated that this operation, while relatively small in size, demonstrates the European allies' willingness to assume responsibility for events in their region. However, officials also noted that certain EU nations still have capability shortfalls, and that the EU still has a way to go before it can carry out a sizeable operation on its own. A follow-on mission that began in late September 2001 under German leadership is tasked to protect international monitors who will oversee the implementation of the peace plan in the Former Yugoslav Republic of Macedonia.

European Allies Taking Steps to Address DCI and ESDP Shortfalls

U.S. and European defense officials highlighted the short- and long-term steps that European nations are taking to address DCI and ESDP shortfalls. In the short term, allies have sought solutions to provide airlift capability until the A400M military transport aircraft is deployed, toward the end of the decade. The United Kingdom currently is leasing four U.S. C-17 aircraft, and Germany is leasing six aircraft, when needed, from Ukraine. Italy has recently purchased C-130J aircraft from the United States, which will satisfy part of Italy's strategic lift requirement until the A400M aircraft is available. Italy is also leasing F-16 fighter aircraft from the United States, as it awaits delivery of the Eurofighter aircraft. European allies have made progress in upgrading combat aircraft and acquiring combat identification systems and deployable command-and-control capabilities. Operational cooperation has also improved allies' military capabilities.

In the long term, European allies are planning to procure major systems and equipment that require substantial amounts of financial resources. Increasingly, allies are participating in cooperative equipment-acquisition projects to share the financial burden of acquiring expensive systems and equipment. These cooperative projects enable nations to share the costs of developing major defense systems and also encourage interoperability between militaries. European allies are jointly acquiring and collaborating, primarily on large items such as strategic lift, fighter aircraft, and transport helicopters, as shown in table 2. Although this cooperation has produced advantages by pooling resources, the complexity of nations working together has also created problems for European allies because of differing national priorities and budgetary conditions. NATO officials identified cooperation at the bilateral level, where allies working together can help eliminate shortfalls. For example, the Netherlands recently offered to spend $38 million to upgrade four large German aircraft with air-to-air refueling sets. In return, Germany will provide the Netherlands with air transport, a capability they would not be able to finance alone.

Table 2: Major Multinational Equipment Projects Involving European Countries

Project	Participating nations	Anticipated delivery date[a]
Eurofighter – EF2000 (new fighter aircraft)	Germany, Italy, Spain, and the United Kingdom	2002
Airbus A400M (military transport aircraft)	Belgium, France, Germany, Italy, Luxembourg, Portugal, Spain, Turkey, and the United Kingdom	2008
Medium-range Extended Air Defense System (MEADS)	Germany, Italy, and the United States	2012
Tiger (support helicopter)	France and Germany	2003
NH90 (tactical transport helicopter)	France, Germany, Italy, and the Netherlands	varies by country[b]
Horizon Frigate	France and Italy	2005-2008
Meteor (long range air-to-air missile)	France, Germany, Italy, Spain, Sweden, and the United Kingdom	2012
Joint Strike Fighter (fighter aircraft)	Italy, the United Kingdom, and the United States	2010

[a] Official delivery date. Financial difficulties may delay the delivery date further.

[b] The anticipated delivery dates are 2003 for Germany, 2005 for France, 2004 for Italy, and 2007 for the Netherlands.

Source: National documents and country meetings.

European Defense Budgets Limit Short- and Mid-Term European Defense Objectives

At a time when European allies have agreed to take on increased responsibility for security in the European region, the level of their defense budgets limits their ability to make the necessary changes to their defense structures.[56] The relatively flat and in some cases declining defense equipment budgets are of particular concern because they constrain material improvements in defense capabilities. Structural problems, such as high personnel costs, combined with relatively low overall defense budgets affect the ability of the European allies to increase defense equipment spending significantly. Although the allies have identified interim measures to cope with capability shortfalls, the success of the DCI and ESDP initiatives continues to depend upon the provision of sufficient resources. Since European nations are unlikely to increase their defense budgets substantially in the near- and mid-term, according to U.S., NATO, and other officials, they are cooperating with joint equipment purchases to increase their defense capabilities and share costs. It is too early to discern what effect, if any, the terrorist attacks of September 11, 2001, will have on future European defense spending. U.S. and European officials have indicated, however, that some European allies are discussing changing their defense budgets and priorities as a result of these events.

---

[56] Our analysis in this section is based on the NATO definition of "defense expenditure." NATO uses a standard definition of defense expenditure to facilitate the comparison of defense budgets of NATO member countries. The NATO definition differs in some cases from definitions in national budgets. For example, some countries do

Defense Budget Projections Continue a Generally Flat Trend

Defense budget projections for 2001-2004 indicate that, of the countries we visited, France, Germany, and the United Kingdom are maintaining relatively flat defense budgets. Political decisions to balance competing needs will likely present challenges in the years ahead for defense budgets in the countries we visited, according to U.S. and European officials. As indicated in figure 18, Germany's defense budget is expected to decline from 2000 through 2004 at an annual average rate of -1.6 percent, in real terms. The United Kingdom plans to increase its defense spending at an annual average real growth rate of .7 percent from 2000 through 2003. We were not able to obtain formal defense budget projections from Turkey or beyond 2002 for France. However, French officials stated that, based on projected expenditures for defense equipment and personnel, France's total defense expenditures would likely increase at an annual average real growth rate of slightly more than 1 percent over the next 5 years. Italy's annual average real growth rate for defense spending is projected to be about 4 percent from 2000 through 2004.[57]

Defense spending as a percentage of GDP in NATO European countries has generally been lower over time than in the United States. These differences, which were particularly significant in the 1980s, will continue through 2004. In Turkey, defense spending as a percentage of GDP has been higher than in the United States since the mid-1990s. The average defense share of GDP in 2000 was 2.4 percent for all NATO members, 2 percent for European NATO members, and 2.9 percent for the United States. The average defense share of GDP is expected to continue to decline slightly from 2001 to 2004 for France, Germany, and the United Kingdom, as shown in figure 19, given relatively constant defense spending levels and GDP that is projected to grow at an annual average rate of 2.5 percent. If this economic trend continues, defense spending as a percentage of GDP for most NATO countries will continue to decline.

---

not include payments toward retirement pensions in their defense budgets. The NATO definition includes contributions to military pensions but not payments to current retirees.

[57] Defense budget projections provided by NATO member countries may be more definitive for some countries than for others, depending on their budgeting process. DOD and Department of State officials do not believe Italy's defense budget projections will change much as a result of the September 11, 2001, terrorist attacks, given the level of the projections.

Figure 18. Projected Defense Spending in Selected European Countries, 1995-2004

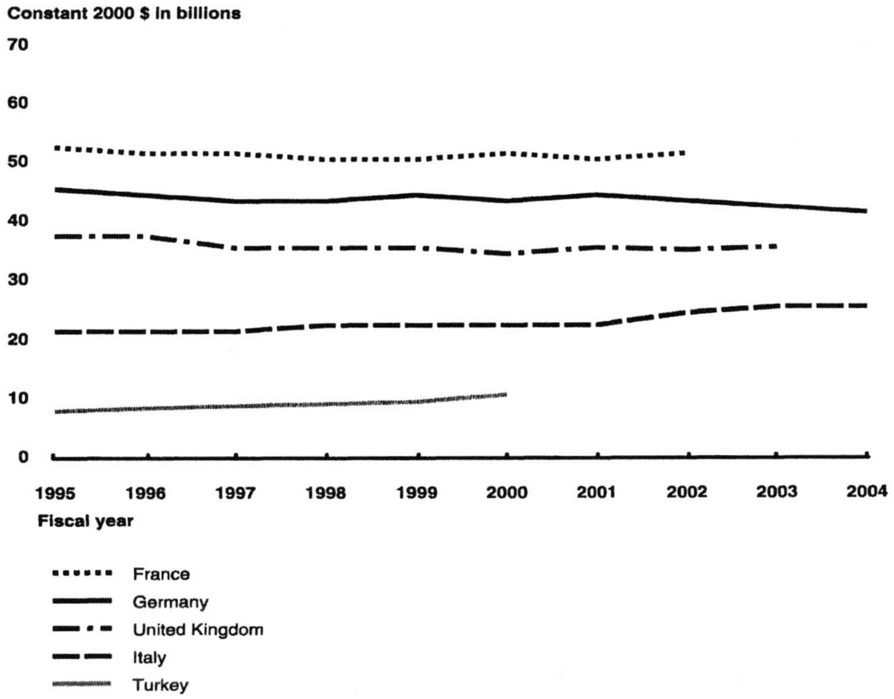

Note1: These levels (but not the trend lines) are dependent on the exchange rates used to convert national currencies into dollars. 1995 exchange rates were used for these calculations. Because of substantial exchange-rate depreciation in some countries, using a later base year would yield significantly lower spending levels. For a description of our methodology for these calculations, see chapter 1.

Note 2: 2000 figures are NATO estimates. NATO will release actual figures in December 2001.

Note 3: Turkey did not provide defense budget projections and France did not provide projections beyond 2002.

Source: GAO analysis of data from NATO and National Ministries of Defense.

Variety of Factors Drive European Defense Spending

Differences in defense spending levels between the United States and its European allies are attributable to a number of factors, such as competing domestic budgetary pressures, varying threat perceptions, and other national priorities. In addition, many EU nations face European Economic and Monetary Union fiscal constraints and other national requirements that have affected their ability to contribute to defense, as highlighted in figure 20. Recent budgetary debates in European countries have highlighted the trade-offs facing decisionmakers as they try to satisfy demands for social spending within a budgetary environment characterized by lower economic growth and fiscal constraint. U.S. officials stated that the U.S. global role and worldwide interests are important factors driving U.S. defense spending.

Most U.S. and European officials with whom we met stated that different threat perceptions are the driving force behind defense spending differences in the United States and Europe. Increasingly, European nations see their security affected by factors such as organized crime, illegal immigration, and economic instability, none of which can be resolved through defense spending. European officials we interviewed do not see the need for increased defense spending, given the demise of the Soviet threat and given rising domestic priorities. Nevertheless, Turkey's defense spending is influenced by the potential external threats surrounding it—Iraq, Syria, Russia, and Greece, according to Turkish officials.

Figure 19: Projected Defense Spending as a Percentage of GDP for Selected European Countries and the United States, 1995-2004

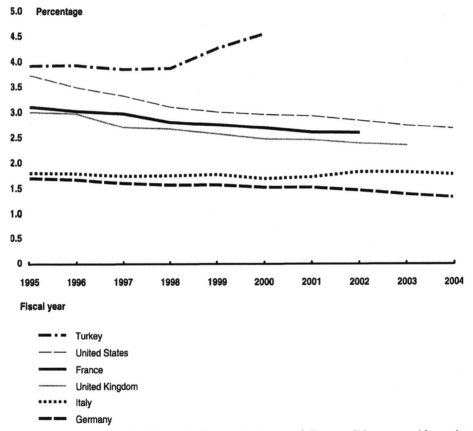

Note: Turkey did not provide defense budget projections and France did not provide projections beyond 2002.
Source: GAO analysis of data from NATO, National Ministries of Defense, and DRI-WEFA, a subsidiary of Global Insights, Inc. (Waltham, MA).

Domestic budgetary priorities are a key factor affecting European defense spending. Defense budgets face strong and increasing pressure from domestic spending in European countries. Historically, the countries we reviewed have spent a large portion of their GDP and government budgets on social programs such as pensions, health, and welfare. For example, according to the Organization for Security and Cooperation in Europe, in 1997—the latest year for which comparable data are available—France, Germany, Italy, and the United Kingdom spent an average of 26 percent of GDP on social programs, compared with 16 percent in the United States. Many officials we met with in France, Italy, Germany, and the

United Kingdom identified domestic budget priorities as the main reason why defense spending would not likely increase substantially in the near- and mid-term. Further, officials noted that, given upcoming elections in some European countries, domestic programs likely would be at the top of government priorities.

Figure 20: Factors Driving European Defense Spending

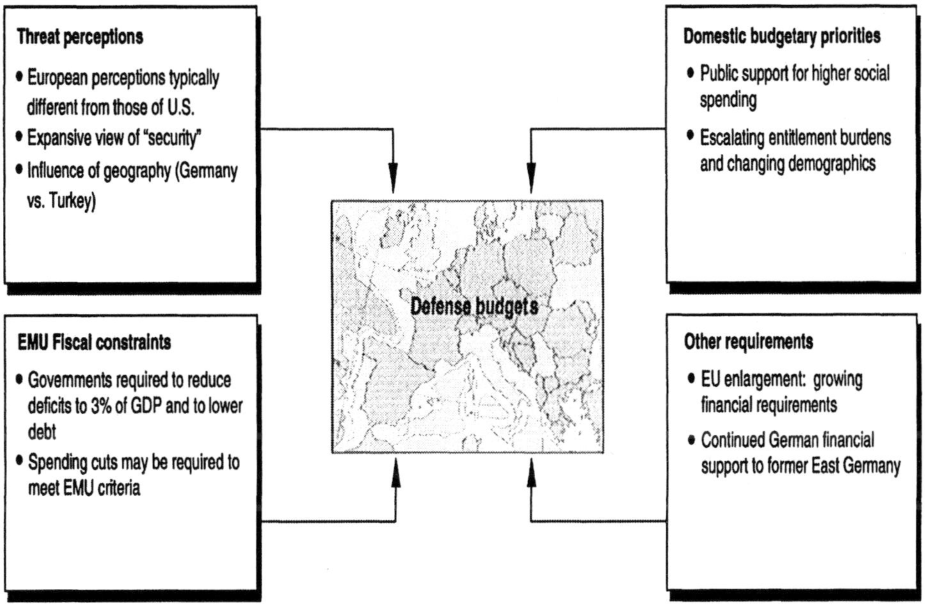

Threat perceptions

- European perceptions typically different from those of U.S.
- Expansive view of "security"
- Influence of geography (Germany vs. Turkey)

Domestic budgetary priorities

- Public support for higher social spending
- Escalating entitlement burdens and changing demographics

EMU Fiscal constraints

- Governments required to reduce deficits to 3% of GDP and to lower debt
- Spending cuts may be required to meet EMU criteria

Other requirements

- EU enlargement: growing financial requirements
- Continued German financial support to former East Germany

Defense budgets

Source: EU, NATO, and member countries.

We reported in 1999 that the costs associated with the financial requirements for membership in the European Monetary Union could also affect the flexibility of governments to allocate resources to various needs, including defense.[58] We noted that the European Monetary Union's requirement for countries to limit deficits and debt will constrain government spending options in the near- and mid-term.[59] For example, U.S. embassy officials in Rome said that EMU fiscal requirements are an important factor that would likely influence future defense spending levels in Italy.

Other factors unique to each country can also affect available resources for defense. For example, Germany continues to provide substantial financial support to the former East Germany. After the Cold War ended, Germany spent billions of dollars in reconstruction and investment in this new region.[60] German officials emphasized that Germany's funding and

---

[58] *NATO: Implications of European Integration for Allies' Defense Spending* (GAO-NsSIAD- 99-185, June 1999).

[59] The Maastricht Treaty on European Union, signed in 1992, set forth several economic conditions for countries to join the euro area. These included, in part, reducing general government deficits to 3 percent of GDP and showing progress toward lowering government debt to 60 percent of GDP.

[60] According to German officials, costs vary widely and are complex because they include, in the area of defense, destruction of weapons, environmental clean-up and decontamination of training sites, demolition and

support to the former East Germany contributes to security in the region. They said that the economic development of the former the East Germany is a priority that Germany will continue to support. According to the German government, the federal budget for the year 2000 allocated approximately $19 billion in funding for rebuilding the eastern part of Germany. Infrastructure investment projects alone, including transportation, housing and urban development, and environmental clean-up, totaled about $10 billion for 2000.

Funding for Defense Equipment Is Key to Improving Defense Capabilities, but Challenges Remain

The amount of funding that the European allies devote to defense equipment is critical to improving European defense capabilities and addressing capability shortfalls, such as those identified in the Balkans, according to U.S. and European officials.[61] However, as a percentage of the defense budget, funding for equipment has generally been relatively low for most NATO European nations. Between 1985 and 1989, Canada, Germany, Italy, Norway, the United Kingdom, and the United States spent an average of 20 percent or more of their defense budgets on equipment. In 2000, the Czech Republic, Norway, Turkey, the United Kingdom, and the United States devoted at least 20 percent of defense spending to equipment. Germany, Italy, and many others spent less than 15 percent during the same year.[62]

European allies have pledged to increase equipment spending over the decade; however, some nations are facing difficulties in doing so. Germany's annual average real growth rate for defense equipment is projected to be -1.3 percent for the years 2000 through 2004, while Italy's growth rate for equipment is expected to increase by about 4 percent over the same period. According to budget projections from the United Kingdom, its annual average real growth rate for equipment is expected to increase by 1.4 percent from 2000 through 2003. France's defense plans include a .8 percent increase for equipment from 2003 through 2008. Turkey could not provide equipment budget projections at this time.

European allies' defense budget challenges arise in part from the structural challenges inherent in many of their defense budgets. Chief among these is large personnel costs. Combined with generally low defense budgets, a relatively small percentage of the budget is left for equipment. This has affected the ability of some European nations, such as Germany and Italy, to carry out restructuring and modernization efforts, according to U.S. and European officials. In contrast, the United Kingdom, which has lower personnel costs, has greater flexibility and as a result has been able to spend a higher percentage of its defense budget on equipment.

Personnel expenses for many NATO countries constitute a large portion of their defense budgets—60 to 80 percent, for 7 of the 19 NATO nations in 2000. This has affected the ability of these countries to allocate additional funding for defense modernization.[63] In Germany and Italy, personnel expenses as a share of overall expenses rose to 59 and 74

---

reconstruction of new bases, deployments from eastern to western Germany, and personnel costs resulting from early retirement payments.

[61] Equipment expenditures refer to the costs for major equipment and associated research and development.

[62] NATO does not maintain official budget figures for France because it is not part of NATO's integrated military command and therefore does not participate in the defense planning process. However, France's defense budget data indicates that it spent more than 20 percent of its defense budget on equipment in 2000.

[63] In 2000, Belgium, Greece, Italy, Luxembourg, Poland, Portugal, and Spain spent more than 60 percent of their defense budgets on personnel costs, according to NATO.

percent, respectively, in 2000. These figures are expected to remain about the same through 2004, in part because of the initial expenses of moving toward an all-volunteer force. Officials stated that in the longer term, personnel expenses should decrease. In the United Kingdom, which has an allvolunteer force, personnel expenses have decreased relative to other expenses since the end of the Cold War and represent 39 percent of its defense budget in 2000. This has allowed the United Kingdom greater flexibility to spend more than other European countries do on equipment. Plans indicate that U.K. personnel costs will likely remain at this level through 2003. As a matter of comparison, personnel costs constitute 38 percent of the U.S. defense budget and will increase slightly through 2004. Figure 21 highlights projected trends in personnel and equipment spending for Italy, Germany, the United Kingdom, and the United States.

Given that equipment spending constitutes a relatively small portion of the defense budgets of most NATO European allies, one or more costly defense equipment projects can reduce the flexibility that countries have to buy other types of needed equipment. This is the case, for example, with the EF2000 Eurofighter aircraft, Europe's largest defense project, which involves four nations—Italy, Germany, Spain, and the United Kingdom. Aircraft deliveries are expected to continue for about 15 years. We reported in 1999 that Eurofighter acquisition alone accounted for a growing portion of equipment budgets in Germany, Italy, and the United Kingdom. In Germany, the Eurofighter represented 24 percent of the equipment budget in 1998 and 28 percent in 1999. It remained at about this level in 2001, according to U.S. embassy officials in Germany. Further, Germany's funding problems contributed to delays in the start of the program. In Italy, to fund such a large program, the government relied in part on financing sources outside the defense budget, such as from the Ministry for Production Activities.

Figure 21: Projected Trends in Defense Spending for Germany, Italy, the United Kingdom, and the United States, 2000-2004

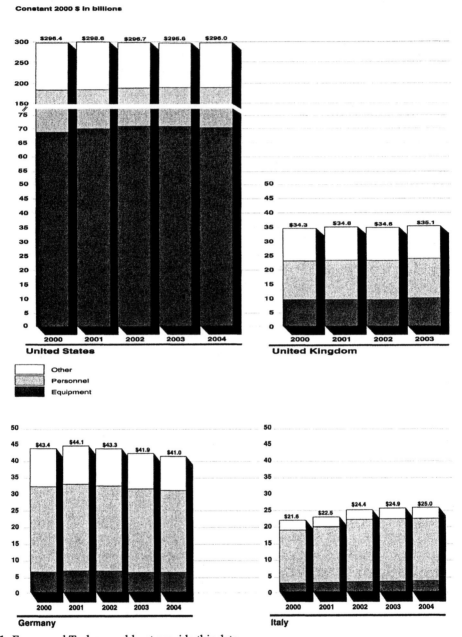

Note1: France and Turkey could not provide this data.
Note 2: 2000 figures are NATO estimates. NATO will release actual figures in December 2001.
Source: GAO analysis of data from NATO and National Ministries of Defense.

The challenges associated with the acquisition of the Eurofighter aircraft provide valuable lessons for planned European equipment programs, particularly the Airbus A400M military transport aircraft, a nearly $18 billion project that is considered to be the EU nations' "flagship" project. In 2008, nine European nations plan to begin deploying the first of an expected 212 aircraft. The aircraft are considered critical in resolving shortfalls in European strategic lift capabilities and will help European allies meet DCI and ESDP objectives. Although no contract had been signed as of October 2001, U.S. and European defense officials had raised several budgetary concerns. Chief among these was whether Germany can afford to fund its share of the program—the largest share of any participating country. As of October 2001, Germany had not yet decided whether to contribute to the developmental phase of the project. Germany will pay a larger unit cost once the aircraft are delivered if it does not contribute to the developmental phase. German embassy officials stated that if the German equipment budget remains relatively level, the combined cost of the Eurofighter aircraft and the A400M military transport aircraft could account for 40 to 50 percent of the German equipment budget in 2008. Although other nations do not face the same level of problems, they are pursuing other funding solutions. Italy, for example, will likely pursue some funding for the A400M costs outside of its defense budget, as it is doing with the Eurofighter. U.S. officials questioned the ability of European nations to fund two major aircraft programs concurrently, and stated that the A400M program is likely to be extended or postponed until sufficient resources become available. The number of aircraft planned for production may also be reduced, they said.

APPENDIX I: AIRCRAFT AND CAPABILITIES PROVIDED BY SELECTED COUNTRIES IN OPERATION ALLIED FORCE

Type of Mission	France	Germany	Italy	United Kingdom	United States
Combat air patrol.	M-200G		Tornado ADV; F-104	Sea Harrier	F-15; F-18; F/A-18
Suppression of enemy air defenses.		Tornado	Tornado		EA-6B; F-16; EC-130H
Close air support	M-2000C; M-2000D; Super Etendard; Jaguar-A-		AMX; AV-8B; Tornado	GR-7	A-10; AV-8B; B-1B; B-52; F-14; F-15; F-16; F/A-18
Reconnaissance	Etendard4P; Jaguar-A; Horizon (HELO); CL-289 (UAV); Crecerelle (UAV)	Tornado; CL-289 (UAV)	AMX; Tornado		F-14; F-18; F/A-18D; P-3C; SH-60B; U-2; Hunter (UAV); Pioneer (UAV); Predator (UAV)
Airborne early warning	E-3F			E-3D; MK-6	E-2C; E-3B/C
Airborne battlefield command and control center					EC-130E; E-2C
Air-to-air refueling	C-135F		B-707	VC-10	KC-135; KC-10; KC-130; S-3
Battlefield air interdiction	M-2000D; Mirage; Tornado F-1GT; Jaguar-A; Super Etendard		AMX; Tornado	GR-1; GR-7	AV-8B; F-14; F-15; F-16; F/A-18; F-117; B-2
Joint surveillance and target attack radar					E-8C

Note: The number of specific aircraft deployed is classified information.
Source: NATO's Supreme Headquarters Allied Powers, Europe.

APPENDIX II: PROGRESS OF NATO ALLIES' EFFORTS IN MOVING TOWARD AN ALL-VOLUNTEER FORCE

Country	Status	% of Conscripts in Total Forces (2000)	% of Conscripts in Army (2000)
Belgium	No conscription.	N/A	N/A
Canada	No conscription.	N/A	N/A
Czech Republic	Czech government announced a move toward ending conscription.	43%	62%
Denmark	Armed forces rely on conscription	23	34
France	Conscription ended in July 2001, more than 18 months ahead of schedule.	20	28
Germany	Move toward a more volunteer armed force began in 2000. A combination of conscript and professional armed force will remain, with mandatory service reduced from 10 months to 9 months after 2002.	40	46
Greece	Armed forces rely on conscription.	62	74
Hungary	Armed forces rely on conscription. Length of service will be reduced from 9 months to 6 months.	52	76
Iceland	No conscription.	N/A	N/A
Italy	Conscription is projected to end by 2006. Conscription already ended for citizens born after 1985.	45	54
Luxembourg	No conscription.	N/A	N/A
Netherlands	No conscription.	N/A	N/A
Norway	Armed forces rely on conscription.	57	59
Poland	Armed forces rely on conscription.	52	62
Portugal	Conscription is projected to end in 2003.	13	21
Spain	Conscription is projected to end by 2002.	31	30
Turkey	No plans by Ministry of Defense to eliminate conscription.	87	93
United Kingdom	No conscription.	N/A	N/A
United States	No conscription.	N/A	N/A

Source: Official country documents, the United Nations, and The Military Balance.

APPENDIX III: KEY EQUIPMENT PROGRAMS FOR FRANCE, GERMANY, ITALY, TURKEY, AND THE UNITED KINGDOM

Country	Equipment Priorities	Key Acquisition Projects
France	Power projection Command, communications Intelligence	Rafale fighter aircraft Tiger support helicopter NH90 transport helicopter Horizon frigate LeClerc main battle tank Helios II satellite
Germany	Strategic transport Command, control, communications Intelligence Reconnaissance Precision-guided munitions	SAR-Lupe satellite Medium-range air-to-air missile Strategic reconnaissance Tiger support helicopter Frigate F124/F125 Eurofighter Medium-range extended air defense system
Italy	Strategic transport Command, control, communications Intelligence Logistic support Upgrading missiles	C130-J Meteor long-range air-to-air missile Storm Shadow medium/long range missile Eurofighter Joint Strike Fighter NH-90 tactical transport helicopter New aircraft-carrier
Turkey	Attack helicopter Airborne early warning and control aircraft Battle tanks	AH-IZ King Cobra attack helicopter M60 tank Leopard main battle tank
United Kingdom	Strategic lift Command, control, communications Intelligence Force projection Precision-guided munitions	Roll-on roll-off vessel C-17 strategic lift aircraft Bowman battlefield communications system Meteor long-range air-to-air missile Joint Strike Fighter Eurofighter Astor airborne stand-off radar

Note: Equipment priorities are not listed in order of priority.
Source: National documents.

United States Department of State

Chief Financial Officer

Washington, D.C. 20520-7427

NOV I 5 2001

Dear Ms. Westin:

We appreciate the opportunity to review your draft report, "EUROPEAN SECURITY: U.S. and European Allies Contributions to Foster Stability and Security in Europe," GAO-02-174, GAO Job Code 711543.

The Department of State believes the report findings are essentially factual and correct. Technical comments were provided to your staff separately.

If you have any questions concerning this response, please contact Kim Savit, Director of Security Programs,, at 202-647-4584.

Sincerely,

Larry J. Eisenhart
Acting

Enclosure:

As stated.

cc: GAO/IAT - Mr. Joseph A. Christoff
     State/OIG - Mr. Atkins
     State/EUR/ACE - Ambassador William Taylor

Ms. Susan S. Westin,
     Managing Director,
          International Affairs and Trade,
               U.S. General Accounting Office.

ABBREVIATIONS

CEE	Central and Eastern Europe
CFSP	Common Foreign and Security Policy
DCI	Defense Capabilities Initiative
DOD	Department of Defense
EC	European Commission
ESDP	European Security and Defense Policy
EU	European Union
GDP	Gross Domestic Product
NATO	North Atlantic Treaty Organization
NIS	Newly Independent States
OSCE	Organization for Security and Cooperation in Europe
OECD	Organization for Economic Cooperation and Development
PfP	Partnership for Peace
U.N.	United Nations
UNHCR	U.N. High Commissioner for Refugees

INDEX